The Fury of the Northmen

John Marsden is the author of a number of books on the
early history of Scotland and Northumbria, most recently
Sea-Road of the Saints: Celtic Holy Men in the Hebrides.
He is married and now makes his home in the Western Isles.

'Ann. 793   In this year dire forewarnings came over the land of the Northumbrians, and miserably terrified the people: these were extraordinary whirlwinds and lightnings, and fiery dragons were seen flying in the air. A great famine soon followed these omens; and soon after that, in the same year, the havoc of heathen men miserably destroyed God's church on Lindisfarne ...'

Anglo-Saxon Chronicle

'D' MS: BL, Cotton MS Tiberius B. iv, f26ᵛ.

THE FURY
OF THE
NORTHMEN

saints, shrines and sea-raiders
in the viking age

AD 793–878

JOHN MARSDEN

KYLE CATHIE LIMITED

This edition published in 1996 by
Kyle Cathie Limited
20 Vauxhall Bridge Road
London SW1V 2SA

First published in Great Britain in 1994

Copyright © 1993 by John Marsden
Maps copyright © 1993 by Leslie Robinson

ISBN 1 85626 236 7

A CIP catalogue record for this book is available from the
British Library

Typeset by DP Photosetting Ltd, Aylesbury, Bucks.
Printed and bound in Great Britian by
WBC Book Manufacturers, Bridgend, Mid Glam.

contents

Maps

Illustrations

Between pages 82–83

acknowledgements

The author is grateful to John Gregory for his translations from Bede, Reginald of Durham, and the anonymous *Historia de Sancto Cuthberto* and to Methuen London (incorporating Eyre & Spottiswoode) for kind permission to use translations of Alcuin's letters from *English Historical Documents I*, edited by Dorothy Whitelock.

The author and publisher also wish to thank the following for their kind permission to reproduce the illustrations:

The British Library (*Anglo-Saxon Chronicle* MS); The Dean and Chapter, Durham Cathedral (Saint Cuthbert's coffin and portrait mural); English Heritage (Lindisfarne grave marker); Geoff Green (Iona, Bay of the Martyrs, Lindisfarne causeway); Historic Scotland (Maes Howe runes); Irish Tourist Board (Newgrange); Northumbria Airfotos (Lindisfarne); Stiftsbibliotek, St Gallen (Walafrid Strabo MS); Trinity College Library, Dublin (Book of Kells).

the sea-roads of the northern world
AD 793–877

ICELAND

NORTH ATLANTIC OCEAN

FAROES

SHETLAND

HEBRIDES

ORKNEY

IONA

PICTLAND

DALRIADA

North Sea

LINDISFARNE

NORTHUMBRIA

Dublin

York

MERCIA

EAST ANGLIA

WESSEX

Dorestad

ISLES OF SCILLY

ILE DE NOIRMOUTIER

Nantes

Tours

Mainz

Reichenau

Loire

Garonne

Rhône

Seine

Rhine

Elbe

Danube

Lérins

Rome

Cordoba

Mediterranean Sea

VESTFOLD

Birka

Baltic Sea

JUTLAND

Hedeby

Novgorod

Dvina

Kiev

Dneiper

the northumbrian context
AD 793–877

LINDISFARNE
Green Shiel
Priory
Heugh
- - - - MONASTIC SITE

Firth of Forth
Coldingham
Norham
Tweed
Tillmouth
Carham
Melrose
Bamburgh
LINDISFARNE
FARNE
ISLANDS
INNER FARNE
Warkworth
Whittingham
DERE ST
Corbridge
Tynemouth
Jarrow
Wearmouth
Carlisle
Tyne
Hexham
Chester-le-Street
Whithorn
Solway Firth
Wear
Durham
Hartlepool
Workington
Tees
Billingham
Wycliffe
Cliffe
Whitby
STAINMORE
Ouse
Crayke
Ripon
Stamford
Bridge
York
Brough
Humber

NORTH SEA

IRISH SEA

FOSSE WAY
WATLING STREET
ERMINE STREET
FEN ROAD
Tettenhall
Peterborough
Ely
Bury
St Edmunds

- - - - ROMAN ROADS ⊓⊓⊓⊓ HADRIAN'S WALL

the scottish context
AD 795–877

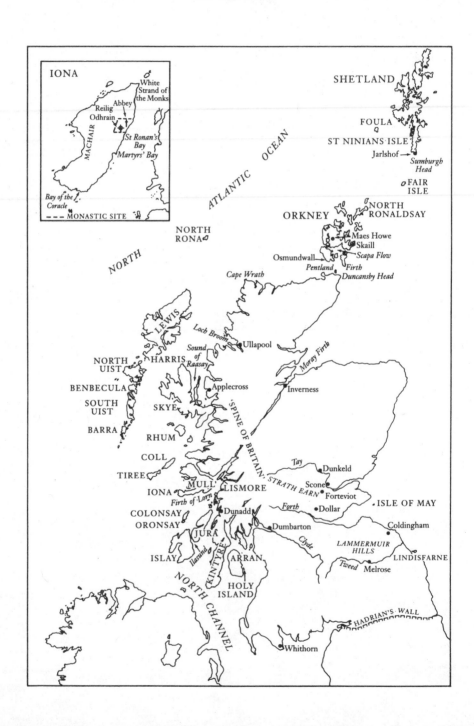

IONA

White Strand of the Monks

Abbey

Reilig Odhrain

MACHAIR

St Ronan's Bay

Martyrs' Bay

Bay of the Coracle

- - - MONASTIC SITE

SHETLAND

FOULA

ST NINIANS ISLE

Jarlshof

Sumburgh Head

FAIR ISLE

ATLANTIC OCEAN

ORKNEY

NORTH RONALDSAY

Maes Howe

Skaill

Osmundwall

Scapa Flow

Pentland Firth

Duncansby Head

NORTH RONA

NORTH

Cape Wrath

LEWIS

Loch Broom

Ullapool

Sound of Raasay

Moray Firth

NORTH UIST

HARRIS

BENBECULA

Applecross

Inverness

SOUTH UIST

SKYE

BARRA

RHUM

COLL

'SPINE OF BRITAIN'

Tay

Dunkeld

TIREE

Scone

STRATH EARN

Forteviot

IONA

MULL

LISMORE

ISLE OF MAY

Firth of Lorn

Forth

Dollar

COLONSAY

Dunadd

ORONSAY

Dumbarton

Coldingham

JURA

LAMMERMUIR HILLS

LINDISFARNE

Clyde

ISLAY

ARRAN

Tweed

Melrose

KINTYRE

NORTH CHANNEL

HOLY ISLAND

HADRIAN'S WALL

Whithorn

the irish context
AD 795–871

IONA

Dunadd

ISLAY

KINTYRE

NORTH CHANNEL

Malin Head RATHLIN ISLAND

Belfast Lough

Whithorn

Lough Neagh Bangor
Moville
Strangford Lough

INISHMURRAY

Lough Erne

Armagh Downpatrick

PEEL ISLAND

ISLE OF MAN

Dundalk Carlingford Lough
Louth
Anagassan
Monasterboice

INISHBOFIN

Lough Owel
Blackwater-Mattock
Kells
Lough Ree
Boyne
Tara

IRISH SEA

LAMBAY ISLAND

Clonard
Dublin Howth Peninsula

ANGLESEY

Clonmacnois
Clonfert
Lorrha
Durrow
Kildare
Liffey

Lough Derg
Terryglass
Shannon
Glendalough
Vartry Estuary

Clonmore

Limerick
Ferns

Cashel

Wexford

Waterford

Lismore

Ballinskelligs
Cork

SKELLIG MICHAEL

⊓ PREHISTORIC TOMBS OF THE BOYNE VALLEY

preface

A furore nordmannorum, libera nos, domine.

'From the fury of the northmen, O Lord, deliver us'
was a litany without need of vellum.
It was graven on the hearts of men whenever
and for as long as that fury fell.

Gwyn Jones, A History of the Vikings

T WELVE CENTURIES ago sea-raiders out of the north fell upon the holy island of Lindisfarne chosen by Saint Aidan as his 'Iona in the east' and hallowed as the shrine of its hermit-bishop Cuthbert, the great patron saint of the northern English.

By reason of that 'inroad from the sea', the year AD 793 is accepted by historians as marking the onset of almost three centuries of Scandinavian expansion into these islands still known – for reasons of convenience rather than precision – as 'The Viking Age'. Consequently the raid on Lindisfarne is noted by almost every modern study of the viking phenomenon for its principal, even sole, significance as a chronological benchmark.

For Alcuin of York, the most distinguished Englishman of his time writing home from the court of Charlemagne in response to news of 'the terrible fate which has befallen the church of Cuthbert', it was nothing less than a cataclysm.

It would seem that those who suffered the initial onslaught of the viking age were possessed of values and visions little less at variance from those of our own secular culture than they must have been from those of the northmen themselves. In that light, any full appreciation of 'the fury of the northmen' must demand some survey of the spirituality as well as the substance of the world on which the longships made their landfall.

What follows, then, is intended as a pilgrimage – framed within a sketch-map of its historical and cultural context – through a time anciently foretold as 'the last days of the world'.

JM

'the sixth age of the world'

An Introduction

The first age of the world is from Adam to Noah.
The second is from Noah to Abraham.
The third is from Abraham to David.
The fourth is from David to Daniel.
The fifth is from Daniel to John the Baptist.
The sixth is from John to the Judgement,
in which our Lord Jesus Christ
will come to judge the living and the dead
and the world through fire ...

Nennius: *Historia Brittonum*, c. 830

IN THE museum of antiquities beside the ruins of the Norman priory on Lindisfarne is displayed a fragment of carved stone which has survived from the Anglo-Saxon monastery in that place.

It is believed to be a grave-marker and to date from no later than the end of the ninth century. On one face of this stone are carved seven figures – evidently of fighting-men – advancing in line, clad in mail-shirts and brandishing swords and war-axes. Their arms, armour and aspect are in every respect those of a Scandinavian warband prompting the interpretation of the carving as a vivid and closely contemporary portrayal of viking onslaught.

On its other face a great cross appears in the heavens between two huge hands and beneath the circle of the sun and the crescent of the waning moon, and at its foot two figures kneel in prayer. It is this face which has prompted another interpretation to the effect that both of these ominous images in stone refer less – if at all – to sea-raiding northmen than to the apocalypse foretold in the Gospels and the *Revelation* of Saint John the Divine. It may well have been the verses from the Gospel according to Saint Mark which inspired the monastic artist-craftsman in ninth-century Northumbria.

> The sun shall be darkened, and the moon shall not give her light.
> And the stars of heaven shall fall, and the powers
> that are in heaven shall be shaken.
> And then shall they see the Son of man coming in the
> clouds with great power and glory.

Whether the carvings were intended to illustrate the onrushing fury of the northmen or to depict the dawn of Doomsday can be consigned to the speculation of the archaeological art historians. From the perspective of these pages both of those interpretations are synonymous, because the sudden and inexplicable onslaught from the sea on the most holy place of the northern English can only have first appeared to those on whom it fell as the onset of armageddon, the last days of the world revealed to John on Patmos made real on the sands of the Northumberland shore.

> And I stood upon the sand of the sea,
> and saw a beast rise up out of the sea,
> having seven heads and ten horns...
> and upon his heads the name of blasphemy.*

* *Revelation* 13:1

The monks on Lindisfarne in 793 – like the Venerable Bede writing his second thesis on chronology, *De Temporibus Ratione*, in the monastery at Jarrow seventy years before – believed themselves to be living through 'the sixth age of the world'.

> The sixth age is now in progress.
> The number of its generations and years is uncertain,
> but as the age of decrepitude it will end even in the
> death of the whole world.

This sixth age, which had begun with the Incarnation, would end with the Judgement of the sins of the world and in its wake the advent of the Kingdom of Heaven in the full splendour promised in visions and illustrated on the vellum of the gospel books.

While the inevitability of these cataclysmic events was nowhere in doubt, their precise chronology had been the subject of great debate for the church of the seventh and eighth centuries. The science of measurement of time and fixing of dates was of central significance for the historical and theological writings of Bede, already recognised by the time of his death in 735 as the most learned man in Europe. Bede shared the consensus of his time in believing God to have ordered the history of humankind into the sequence of 'ages of the world' and his historical masterwork, the celebrated *Historia Ecclesiastica*, was structured in five books as a symbolic correspondence with the five ages already past. Of the two Old English homilies on Judgement Day, one is a translation of Bede's Latin original and the second may even be his own work in the vernacular. Yet the scholar–monk of Jarrow had long disputed the entrenched orthodoxy that each of these ages spanned a thousand years and that the sixth age was predictably due to end with the millenium. He could call on the authority of the gospels to support him, not least the Gospel according to Saint Matthew.

> Watch therefore, for ye know neither the day
> nor the hour wherein the Son of man cometh.

Doomsday, argued Bede in *De Temporibus Ratione*, was not to be expected around the year AD 1000 but would come – in the words of Saint Peter himself – 'as a thief in the night'.

> And because none of the past five ages is found to have lasted a thousand
> years, but some contained more years and others fewer, and none had

4

the same sum of years as another, it must be that this present age similarly has a length indeterminate for mortal men, and known only to Him alone who bade his servants keep watch with girded loins and lighted lamps.

If the date of Doomsday lay beyond the competence of human foretelling, those keeping watch for its approach could look only to the omens of the heavens and tides of the affairs of men. So it was that the sixty-year-old Bede, at work on the closing chapters of the *Historia Ecclesiastica* in 731, expressed his own anxious concern over a new spirit of the age which he discerned throughout the once-mighty kingdom of Northumbria.

In these favourable times of peace and prosperity, many of the Northumbrian race, both nobles and commoners, are laying down their arms and preferring that they and their children should receive the tonsure and take monastic vows, rather than train themselves in the art of war. What the result of this will be, a later age will discover.

Bede's anxiety reflected the tradition of earlier writers on history whose books he had studied in the course of a lifetime in the great library at Jarrow.

The barbarian invasions which swept over the decline of the Roman imperium had been interpreted by continental classical historians as the instruments of divine retribution on a decadent empire. The Welsh–Briton Gildas, writing in the early sixth century, blamed the 'ruin and conquest of Britain' – ironically at the hands of the Germanic mercenaries who were the forbears of Bede's own English people – on the sins of the Romano–British warlords who had inherited the defence of a *Britannia* abandoned by the Empire. Two hundred years after Gildas, Bede was to take much the same view of the Islamic assault on Europe in the first decades of his own eighth century.

The first Berber raids had been launched across the Straits of Gibraltar against Visigothic Spain in 711 and by 720 the greater part of the Iberian peninsula had fallen to Islam. Within a decade the peoples Bede described as 'a grievous plague of Saracens' were breaking through the southern frontiers of Frankish Gaul and striking for the shrine of Saint Martin at Tours. The omens of dark portent seen in the heavens and heralding the northern surge of Islamic expansion are entered in the fifth and final book of the *Historia Ecclesiastica*.

5

In the year of our Lord 729, two comets appeared around the sun, striking great terror into those who beheld them. One of them preceded the sun as it rose in the morning and the other followed it as it set in the evening, as if they portended dire disaster to East and West alike; and certainly one was forerunner of the day, and the other of the night, to indicate that mankind was threatened by calamities both by day and by night. Their tails were like fiery torches, facing to the north, as if poised to start a fire, and they appeared in the month of January and remained for almost a fortnight.

At this time a grievous plague of Saracens ravaged Gaul with pitiable slaughter, and not long afterwards they paid the penalty that their treachery deserved in the same country.

When he heard the news that Charles Martel, king of Franks, had thrown back the Arab onslaught at Poitiers, Bede must have had good cause to ponder how poorly the defences of the Northumbrian kingdom would compare with those of the empire which was soon to produce the mighty Charlemagne should they be similarly tested by the scimitars of Islam. Yet, if he recognised the Saracens from the south as the 'beast out of the sea' described in the *Revelation*, the Venerable Bede was looking to the wrong direction.

When the cataclysm fell on Northumbria in the sixth age of the world it was to come as might have been foretold by the Old Testament prophet Jeremiah.

> Out of the north an evil shall break forth
> upon all the inhabitants of the land . . .

There has been a fashionable trend in historical circles in recent decades towards the reappraisal of the phenomenon of 'The Vikings'. This vogue had so greatly influenced both lay and learned opinion by 1980 as to prompt the eminent historian Patrick Wormald to observe – and not without a note of satire – that 'the Vikings used to be thought, in the immortal terminology of *1066 and All That*, a "bad thing"; they are now considered a "good thing"'.

The saga translator, writer and broadcaster Magnus Magnusson, writing just two years before Wormald addressed his remarks to a symposium at Cornell University, illustrates how much of this 'rehabilitation' has hinged on the conflation and confusion of very different phases of three centuries of Scandinavian expansion.

Today there is less emphasis on the raiding, more on the trading, less on the pillage, more on the poetry and artistry, less on the terror, more on the technology, of these determined and dynamic people.

It is a matter of undisputed historical record that the northmen first entered the history of western Europe as raiders. There is no reason why the raider should not also and on other occasions have been a trader – or a fisherman or a fell-farmer. Trading in amber, furs and walrus ivory was a prominent feature of Scandinavian expansion, but the great weight of evidence from these islands – largely ignored by the 'Viking' reappraisal – insists that their predominant mercantile activity was slave-trading. Plunder, whether of slaves or silver, was the principal object of the raiding from its outset, while the poetry of the saga literature was entirely the product of the literary culture of Iceland in the twelfth and thirteenth centuries. The 'technology' and the 'terror' are inextricably entangled when their war-axe and longship are recognised as the technology of terror, the very vehicles by which the fury of the northmen was first delivered.

Such disparities as these have been facilitated by the historical orthodoxy which defines the period bounded by the sea-raid on Lindisfarne in 793 and the defeat of the Norse king Harald Sigurdsson called *Hardradi*, 'the hard ruler', at Stamford Bridge in 1066 as 'The Viking Age'. The etymology of the Old Norse *vikingr* has never been conclusively resolved, but its meaning has always been quite clear. The masculine noun *vikingr* translates as 'a sea raider' and the associated feminine noun *viking* as 'a raid from the sea'. Set against those definitions, 'The Viking Age' would describe three centuries encompassing a complex sequence of sea-raiding, invading armies, land-taking and dynastic contest as 'the age of the pirate'. It is a notorious misnomer and the majority of recent historians of the period admit as much, yet retain its application to what is more accurately called the Scandinavian Migration Age on grounds of convenience. A viking, then, was no more and no less than a pirate and, in consequence, the viking age is most accurately applied to the onslaught of northern sea-raiders which represented the cutting-edge of Scandinavian expansion into these islands. Those are the meanings of the terms employed in these pages and, for that reason, the words are not dignified here with capital initials.

The Scandinavian origin and usage of 'viking' is confirmed by the German church historian Adam of Bremen who wrote in the later eleventh century of northern pirates 'who called *themselves* vikings'. The word is used only rarely and late in the primary sources, while its most frequent and widespread appearance is found in the Icelandic sagas informed by Scandinavian, and specifically Norse, tradition. It is even more significant that the word 'viking' occurs nowhere in the early English and Irish documentary record of the first raids just as the very earliest sources reveal the most meagre recognition of the lands from which the raiders came. While the *Anglo-Saxon Chronicle* reflects the predominantly Danish origin of the later onslaught on southern England in its general use of 'Danes' for all Scandinavian raiders and invaders whether of Danish origin or not, the *Chronicle* cannot be counted among the earliest sources for the period. It was first set down in Wessex in the last decade of the ninth century and the most ancient of its seven surviving manuscripts includes no reference to the raid on Lindisfarne. This original *Parker Chronicle* – referred to as the 'A' manuscript – was distributed to centres outside Wessex where it was transcribed and supplemented with additional material of regional interest. In this manner, material from an earlier lost northern history was incorporated into the 'D', 'E' and 'F' manuscripts collectively known as the 'northern recension'. It is this northern recension of the *Anglo-Saxon Chronicle* which preserves an earlier account of the Lindisfarne raid and also its earlier form of words describing the raiders only as 'heathen men'.

Such a description is entirely characteristic of the earliest English and Irish sources, all of which recognised the vikings principally in terms of the sacrilegious nature of their assault. Like all the Irish annals, the *Annals of Ulster* are a medieval compilation, but they are faithfully transcribed from sources of great antiquity – amongst them a lost chronicle first set down on Iona. They represent the most reliable source for the Scottish and Irish experience of the viking onslaught and preserve the earliest identification of the raiders as 'gentiles' – which is best rendered as 'heathens' – and 'pagans'. As the northmen advanced from the islands of the western sea to the Irish mainland, they are more often called by the Gaelic word *gaill*, which is usually translated as 'foreigners' but would be more emphatically rendered as 'aliens'.

It is in the continental sources, by reason of their authors' closer geographical proximity to the Scandinavian frontier on the Baltic, that the northmen are actually so-called in the Latin forms of *nordmanni* and *normanni*, while the Arabic sources of Islamic Spain follow the monks of the west in their colourful epithet of *majus*, or 'heathen fire-warlocks'.

Even from this brief survey of the nomenclature, it becomes clear that the documentary record of the viking age was set down exclusively by those who fell victim to its onslaught and the early medieval monastic scribe was not a military historian. What is known, for example, of the sword which was the viking's principal weapon and the longship which carried him on his sea-raiding has been learned from archaeological excavation confirming contemporary evidence carved on stone and not from any account set down by Alcuin or his contemporaries. The central importance of their writings for these pages lies in what they reveal of the impact of a dragon-carved longship and its pagan warband on holy men who believed themselves to be living through the last days of the world.

To all of which must be added the fact that there are no contemporary Scandinavian sources because the northmen themselves were creatures of a culture which had barely achieved any approximation of literacy by the end of the eighth century. While there is evidence of a form of the *futhark* – the runic alphabet of the northern world – from the viking age, recognisable runic inscriptions are barely evident in the Scandinavian homelands before the later tenth century.

At the time when Bede was writing the first history of the English people the runes represented nothing more sophisticated than magical symbols carved by shamans on swordblades and standing stones. While the Icelandic sagas have been shown to preserve fragments of Scandinavian oral history and tradition from viking times – and also a casual brutality remarkable if not unique in medieval literature – they are flawed as an historical record, if indeed they were ever intended as such. Even the later and most historically informative sagas were cast in a mould which served principally to support the aristocratic Norse lineage of the Icelandic settlement. To that end, the saga-makers portrayed the first settlers voyaging west-over-sea in the last decades of the ninth century as free-spirited *jarls* or warrior nobility who refused to bow to the overlordship of Harald Halfdansson called 'the fine-haired'. Other evidence which can be set against the revised chronology of the Norse kings shows land-seeking in the north Atlantic to have been pioneered long before Harald's reign by vikings seeking out forward bases for longer range sea-raiding.

The initial impact of the viking onslaught can be fully appreciated only in terms of the cultural chasm which lay between the northmen and those on whom they fell. A salutary index of that divide is the date of birth of the first Scandinavian vernacular historian, the Icelander Ari Thorgilsson, who was born in 1067, the year after the battle at Stamford Bridge, two hundred years after his viking forbears had burned the great library at York, and very nearly four hundred years after the birth of Bede.

Such was the great distance by which Scandinavia lagged behind the advancing civilisation of its southern neighbours in western Europe and it is best explained as a reflection of the enduring influence of the Roman empire on the known world for centuries after its decline and fall. The Scandinavian northmen, like the Irish Celts, had never suffered the imperial ambitions of Rome. Despite Agricola's looking across the Irish Sea from Kintyre contemplating conquest, no Roman force ever attempted to realise his contemplations and, likewise, no Roman invasion ever attempted to push the northern imperial frontier across the Baltic in the direction of the Arctic Circle.

Archaeological evidence has confirmed that there was some trading contact between the empire and the northlands, although most probably conducted through the agency of the merchant tribes settled in Bohemia and serving as mercantile 'middle men' between the Scandinavians, Celts and Romans. The classical world evidently knew something of the extent and economy of Scandinavia if only from the geographer Pytheas who wrote in the third century BC of a land he called *Thule* and described in terms which suggest some tentative exploration of the Norwegian coast. While the belief in the existence of Thule persisted among the classical geographers who came after Pytheas, its precise location remained uncertain for centuries. Agricola's fleet, off the north of Scotland in the waters around Orkney, reported their sighting of *ultima Thule* which must have been the misty prospect of Sumburgh Head on Shetland or even the island of Foula away to the west rather than the coastline of Scandinavia. An earlier Roman naval expedition had rounded the north of Jutland in AD 5 and, over ninety years later, Agricola's biographer Tacitus was able to name one Scandinavian tribe as the *Suiones* and describe them as a people more concerned with wealth than warfare. The territory of Tacitus' Suiones was the Uppland region of what is now Sweden and his description of their riches foreshadows the splendour of the 'golden age' of the Vendel culture which emerged in the mid-sixth century from the proceeds of their lucrative Baltic trading enterprise.

Tacitus' inclusion of the Suiones among the tribes listed in his

10

Germania underlines the fact that the peoples of the northlands sprang from the same primal Germanic stock as those who had flooded into the European vacuum produced by the collapse of the Roman imperium. The Franks and Burgundians in Gaul, Ostrogoths in Italy and Visigoths in Spain, like the Angles and Saxons in Britain, had been influenced by their long experience of Rome whether as allies or enemies, auxiliary troops or mercenary warriors. Consequently their successor states were cast largely in the Roman mould even to the extent of the grand imperial ambitions of Charlemagne, the king of Franks crowned Holy Roman Emperor at St Peter's in Rome on Christmas Day in the year 800.

The momentum which had transformed migrant Germanic warbands into the kingdoms of early medieval Europe was the influence of Christianity, the great civilising impetus of the middle ages, which had spread to the west along the arterial network of the Roman empire throughout the first centuries AD. Whatever the historical content of the Glastonbury traditions of Joseph of Arimathea, it is the execution of the Christian protomartyr at *Verulamium*, later called St Albans in his honour, which confirms an early Christian presence in Roman Britain by the first years of the third century. A hundred years after Alban, Constantine the Great was declared the first Christian Roman emperor at *Eboracum* – the military capital of Roman Britain and later the *Jorvik* of the northmen – in AD 306 and three bishops of the Britons are recorded in attendance at the first council of churches called by him at Arles eight years later in AD 314.

The fifth-century Christian Briton of Strathclyde who called himself *Patricius* was recast by later hagiographers into Saint Patrick the 'Apostle of Ireland', but there is no doubt that Christianity had reached the Celts of *Hibernia* long before Patrick came to Armagh. Whether it had first arrived by way of the Roman province of *Britannia*, aboard the wineships from Gaul, or even – on the enigmatic evidence of Egyptian holy men in the west of Ireland – directly from the Holy Land itself, is unknown, but the Irish church is certainly of the greatest antiquity, reflecting the older spirituality of the pagan Celts no less than the influence of the earliest Christian fathers. Island 'hermitages in the ocean' served the monks of the west as their counterpart to the remote 'desert places' of the monks of the east as clearly as the intricate artistry of the Celtic cross emerged out of the prehistoric tomb carving of the Newgrange megalith. The priests of the Celtic church who succeeded the druids and bards as keepers of the flame of knowledge and, in their turn, reworked the Latin alphabet to accommodate the Irish Gaelic laid the bedrock of the earliest vernacular literature in Europe. Similarly, the saints supplanted ancestral heroes as the patrons of the *tuath*, the dynastic clan at the core of the social structure of Celtic Ireland.

It was in the second half of the sixth century that the holy man Columcille came from Ireland to the Irish settlement of Scotic Dalriada in Argyll where he was to enter history as 'Saint Columba of Iona'. By virtue of his blood-kinship to the ruling dynasties of Dalriada and the Ui-Neill high-kings of Ireland, his holy island of *I-Columcille* became the royal church and sacred shrine of the Gael on both shores of the Irish Sea. Pre-eminent as the spiritual centre and intellectual powerhouse of the Celtic church, Iona was to succeed – and succeed where Rome had failed – in the conversion of the northern English.

The 'English' settlement of post-Roman Britain was a part of the great Germanic Migration Age of the fifth century. Angles, Saxons, Jutes and Frisians crossed the North Sea from their Baltic homelands in the wake of their compatriots who had been recruited, first by the Roman military and later by their Romano–British successors, as mercenary warbands for the defence of *Britannia*. Legitimate land grants in return for military service had been followed by mutinous revolt and the arrival of larger tribal groups of land-seekers. Within two hundred years they were to become the people Bede called his own *gens Anglorum*, but they arrived as Germanic pagans whose warrior kings claimed descent from Woden the 'All-Father' of the primeval northern world. In the course of the fifth and sixth centuries these warrior farmers had won control of the greater expanse of eastern England from the Wall in the north to the Kentish Channel coast and pushed the Christianity of the Romano–British Celts west into Cornwall and Wales and north into Cumbria and Lothian.

By the end of the sixth century the tribal settlements had emerged as the seven kingdoms of the Anglo-Saxon heptarchy, when Augustine arrived in Kent as Pope Gregory the Great's missionary to the English in the same year of 597 when Columcille was laid in earth on Iona. By the first decade of the seventh century, Northumbria – from the Old English *Northanhymbre* meaning 'the lands north of the Humber' – had achieved supremacy among the English kingdoms. Ten years later its king Edwin, son of Aelle, was called *rex Anglorum*, holding the authority of *bretwalda* as overlord of all the English kingdoms, and on Easter Day in 627 he was baptised at York by the bishop Paulinus, Augustine's missionary to the northern English. The new power recognised by the Germanic pagan as the 'White Christ' had successfully challenged the old gods' patronage of the warrior king and Edwin's overlordship affirmed the new faith as the proven path to greater glory, offering enhanced political power in this life as a foretaste of the heavenly kingdom in the next.

If the conversion of the *bretwalda* represented the great achievement of the Roman mission it was to be only short-lived. Five years after his baptism Edwin was slain in battle by the pagan king Penda of Mercia in alliance with the Welsh Britons of Gwynedd. His kingdom was ravaged by the invader and reclaimed for the pagan counter-reformation. It was Oswald, the royal saint of the northern English, who won back Northumbria for the dynasty of Ida its founder – and for the Christian faith – by his victory called 'Heaven's Field' in 633. He had found sanctuary on Iona when his father Aethelfrith, the last pagan king of Northumbria, had been killed in battle by his rival Edwin and it was from I-Columcille that Oswald summoned a holy man for the northern English.

When the Irish bishop Aidan arrived in response to that summons he came as Iona's missionary to a kingdom extending from the Humber to the Forth and representing the great power in the land of the Anglo-Saxon world. His church was founded as an 'Iona in the east' and located in full accordance with the instruction of the Rule of Columcille to 'be alone in a separate place near a chief city'. Just as Iona lay off the coast of Argyll to the north of the hillfort of the kings of Dalriada at Dunadd on Kintyre, so Lindisfarne lay within sight of the capital fortress at Bamburgh and became the royal church of the Northumbrian dynasty whose political supremacy sponsored its vast influence throughout the early English church. At least five bishops were to be numbered among its alumni as its offspring foundations appeared in great numbers throughout the Northumbrian kingdom and beyond its southern frontier on the Humber into Mercia. Within a hundred years of Aidan's death, his holy island was not only the wellspring of the entire achievement of Northumbria's 'golden age' but also the inspiration – second only to Iona – for the advance of Christian civilisation across western Europe even to the Baltic frontiers of Charlemagne's Frankish empire.

The northlands lay far beyond those frontiers of Christian civilisation until the Northumbrian Wilbrord, the Yorkshire-born bishop of Utrecht, made the first attempt to achieve the conversion of Scandinavia. His mission into Jutland met with very little success in the early eighth century and even Anskar, the bishop of Hamburg and Bremen accredited as the 'Apostle of Scandinavia', made only modest progress a hundred years later. The submission of the northmen to the White Christ eventually came about in the late ninth century, largely through the cultural influences encountered in the course of their first century of expansion. The gods of the northmen of the viking age were still the gods of the warband out of the ancient mythos of the primeval north.

Such evidence as survives for the world of the viking homelands is, in the absence of contemporary documentary record, almost exclusively archaeological but it clearly indicates a society centred on the warband and akin to those from which Anglo-Saxon England and Celtic Ireland had emerged some two centuries before. The pivots of such a 'warband culture' were gold and glory and its social structure was forever poised on the sword's edge. The warlord rose and fell by the sword, gathering the most courageous and celebrated fighting-men to his warband by the fame of his battle-prowess, and rewarding their loyalty in the blood-fray with plundered gold in the feasting-hall. Such had been the way of the warrior for Ida, the dynast of Anglo-Saxon Northumbria, in the sixth century as it had been for the high-kings at Tara who were his Celtic contemporaries across the Irish Sea. It was a world which would have been as familiar to the Germanic warbands described by Tacitus in the first century as it remained for the sea-raiding northmen in the last decade of the eighth century.

All the archaeological evidence for Scandinavia in the sixth, seventh and eighth centuries – from the splendid Vendel helmets to the traces of burnt farmsteads – confirms such a warrior-based society beset by internecine conflict and largely secluded by its topography from the wider world, yet fast developing the bold confidence which was to characterise the viking phenomenon and, indeed, the full spectrum of the centuries of Scandinavian expansion. The gods who stood guard over that way of the warrior are recognisable as kindred forms of those of the pagan Germanic peoples. The northmen's *Odin* was the Scandinavian incarnation of the Anglo-Saxon *Woden*. While his aspect changed to accommodate the changing world and time of the peoples who honoured him, he

14

endured as the All-Father of the northern mythos. The warrior–
farmer in Anglo-Saxon England would have recognised the hooded
one-eyed man bearing a spear-shaft as he passed by a gallows at dusk
as Woden-wanderer, just as the sea-raiding northman would have
known ravens flying over sea-cliffs to be Odin's birds waiting to bear
tidings of battle and bloodspill to the 'High One', their lord of the
slain.

It must not be forgotten that the colourful canon of what are
popularly called the 'Norse' myths derives, in the same way as do the
sagas, from medieval Iceland. The myths and legends compiled by
the thirteenth-century *skald* and saga-maker Snorri Sturlusson are no
less an elaborately-imagined fiction than are the nineteenth-century
music-dramas of Richard Wagner. Both draw their *dramatis personae*
and plotlines from earlier sources out of ancient oral tradition, but
there is little probability that the complex mythology of Snorri's
Eddas provides any more historically reliable evidence for the gods of
the viking age than does Wagner's *Ring* for the paganism of
Germanic prehistory. The awesome combat of gods and monsters
which brings about the world's end at *Ragnarok* in the grand finale of
Snorri's epic was the recycling of tradition by a late medieval
Christian author and has even been proposed as a reconstruction of
the *Revelation* in terms of northern mythic stereotypes. There are
clear echoes of Saint John the Divine in Snorri's transcription of
lines he attributes to 'the jarl's poet Arnor'.

> The bright sun will become a black one, the earth will sink into
> the dark sea, the sky will split, all the sea will crash on the fells.

Whatever the true antiquity of the sources of such Icelandic literary tradition, there is enough early evidence to indicate the principal
elements of the pagan beliefs of the northmen. Odin with his spear,
Thor with his hammer and Frey with his mighty phallus survive from
a date sufficiently early to confirm them as the gods revered through
the first century of the Scandinavian Migration Age. Thor, lord of
the thunder and patron of the land-seeker, must have guided the
voyagers west-over-sea just as Frey, lord of the harvest and patron of
fertility, would have been invoked when the seafarer returned home
to his farmstead and marriage bed. Behind and before both of those
stands Odin, lord of the slain and patron of the viking onslaught.

Saga tradition claims it was Odin battle-bringer who first devised
the stratagem called *svynfylking* or 'swine array', a 'flying wedge'

variation of the shield-wall phalanx of other Dark Age armies. The northmen with their fondness for riddle and ruse were never so successful in war as when they could use battle-trickery inspired by Odin the god of guile. Similarly, the hallmark of Odin shape-changer can be discerned in their warrior cult of the *berserkr* or 'bear-shirts' and its alternative form of *ulfhednar* or 'wolf-coats', as is vividly attested by fragments of a *Raven Song* attributed to the *skald* Hornklofi in the time of the Norse king Harald Finehair.

> I will ask thee, thou blood-drinker, of the mead of the Bearserks, what is given to them, men daring in war that plunge into the battle?
> Said the Raven:
>   Wolfcoats they call them, that carry bloody shields in battle, that redden their spearheads when they come to fight, when they are at work together.

These berserks were the 'special forces' of the Scandinavian war-machine and were identified in that role – on the evidence of *King Harald's Saga* – even as late as 1066. The prominence of berserks as the warrior élite of an eleventh-century Norse army must reflect their even greater importance in the earlier sea-raiding warbands. Frenzied fighting-men driven by blood-lust and battle-hysteria are the traditional viking stereotypes, but the saga evidence insists that such warriors did feature in Scandinavian warfaring and they would be most convincingly accommodated in the earliest accounts of the sea-raiding.

None of which should suggest that the viking onslaught was in any way akin to a 'holy war' in the Islamic mould. Blood-lust and gold-lust to the point of religious hysteria is far from unknown to humankind and certainly not confined to early medieval Scandinavia, yet it is the only form of spiritual impetus which might be discerned in the viking age. The northmen raided monasteries not because they represented the White Christ, but because they offered exposed and undefended repositories of plunder. It has been tentatively suggested that later ninth-century Danish armies may have intended some measure of vengeance for the militant Frankish 'crusading' around the Baltic, but the first sea-raiders betrayed no initial recognition of any spiritual significance of the holy places they devastated. For the pagan sea-raider the value of a gospel book lay no deeper than the precious metals of its binding and fruit of the vine blessed for the eucharist served just as well for the plunder-feast. For the viking, it was quite simply wine.

The 'causes' of the viking phenomenon as the prelude to the Scandinavian Migration Age have been the subject of even more speculation than the etymology of the word viking. There have been climatological theories to explain the eruption of the northmen into world history and they have been authoritatively countered, just as there have been politico-historical theories proposing the pressure of Frankish expansion on the Baltic frontier of the northlands which have proved no less unsatisfactory. While these pages intend no contribution of substance to that specialist debate, the suggestions offered by the Icelandic authority Krístjan Eldjárn to the Cornell symposium of 1980 throw the light of such excellent sense on both questions as to serve a useful introductory purpose here.

Eldjárn accepts that the viking was by definition a sea-raider, adding the proviso that the same man was to be called a viking only when undertaking that specific activity, and goes on to propose the noun *vikingr* as deriving from the verb *vikja* meaning 'going away' or 'leaving home'. The viking, then, was the man who left his northern homeland in the company of a warband in search of whatever might be sought across the sea. He would have been most probably young, necessarily sturdy, and no less keen for glory than for gold, the same venturesome warrior kind found throughout the most ancient literature, legend and history of the northern peoples. Odin/Woden had himself been such a wanderer in the world, as had been the *Beowulf* hero and the historical Edwin of Northumbria who travelled through Wales and the English Midlands as a journeyman warrior before winning his kingdom in the blood-fray.

Barbara Crawford, the historian of Scandinavian Scotland, has succinctly described the viking phenomenon as 'the last ripple of the Germanic barbarians' search for *lebensraum*'. Taken from that historical perspective, the Scandinavian Migration Age is revealed as a late phase of the long centuries of the *Volkwanderung*, the Germanic 'folk-wandering' which dominated the early medieval history of Europe. While the southern Baltic tribes had moved into the realms abandoned by Rome in the fifth century and there established not only the embryonic nation states of Europe but some semblance of empire, their northern neighbours remained largely isolated in their prehistoric tribal world of Scandinavia.

It must be explained here that these northern tribes, later to emerge in the national identities of Norse, Dane, and Swede, are best considered as a single people bound together by a common language and culture at the outset of the viking age. For that reason,

I have followed here the continental sources in their use of the term 'northmen' until such times as they need to be separately identified by regional origin as 'Norse' and 'Dane'.

In the wake of the fifth-century Germanic migrations, the tribal group who were to become the Danes had already been on the move southward into the Baltic islands and the Jutland peninsula left vacant by the Angles, Jutes and Saxons of the English settlement. This southernmost dominion of the northmen – representing a region rather greater than modern Denmark – brought the northern tribes into sufficient contact with continental Europe to produce the first semblance of an early medieval Scandinavian kingdom in the reign of Godfred, 'king of the Danes' and Charlemagne's contemporary, who was bold enough to consider himself Charlemagne's equal. It was this Godfred who raised the earthen rampart of the *Danevirke* along the base of the Jutland peninsula to form the southern frontier of Scandinavia and who occupied and enlarged the former Frisian trading centre at Hedeby in the Baltic into the great marketplace of the northern world.

There is firm evidence in Gregory of Tours' sixth-century *History of the Franks* for at least one incursion launched from northern Jutland or southern Sweden against the Frisian settlement between the lower Rhine and the Zuyder Zee.

> They landed, devastated one region of Theudoric's kingdom [of Franks], and took the people prisoner, after which they loaded their vessels with captives and plunder, and were ready to return to their own country. News was brought to Theudoric that his land had been ravaged by foreigners, whereupon he sent his son Theudobert into those parts with a strong force and great armament. The Danish king was killed and the enemy severely defeated in a sea battle.

Gregory identifies these raiders who 'crossed the seas with their fleets' in 521 as 'Danes and their king Chlochilaicus' and he was evidently describing the same raid referred to by the *Beowulf* poet 'in which Hygelac was slain, when the Geats' king, Hrethel's son, died of the sword-drink in Friesland'. Gregory's 'Danish' *Chlochilaicus* and the Geat *Hygelac* are without doubt the same warlord, but whether he came from Danish Jutland or Geatish Sweden remains unclear. While his foray must be accounted a 'warband' hostility typical of its time, it nonetheless bore characteristics foreshadowing the later viking raiding.

It has been suggested that the overlordship of Godfred and his dynasty restrained the independent activities of such tribal warlords as Hygelac, just as the sovereignty of Harald Finehair later sought to restrain the Norse vikings. If that were the case, then the sudden westward surge of Danish vikings in the mid-ninth century must have erupted out of the collapse of the royal dynasty which followed the assassination of Horik, Godfred's son and successor, in 854.

The warrior-traders of the tribes whom Tacitus had called Suiones took an eastward route of expansion – out of what is now Sweden into the Baltic hinterland by way of the rivers of eastern Europe – to found the trading bases which became Novgorod and Kiev and carve out their own claim on the founding of medieval Russia. Warriors from Sweden appear to have formed a modest component of a later phase of the Scandinavian expansion, just as warbands from the Danish Baltic were overwhelmingly prominent in the land-seeking of the second half of the ninth century in Ireland and most especially in England, but the first 'fury of the northmen' – the sudden and savage viking phenomenon under principal consideration here – was launched from the land now known as Norway.

The various chronology and circumstances of the phases of the Scandinavian Migration Age would infer similarly variant regional responses to the wider background pressure of overpopulation throughout the northlands. That population pressure would have been aggravated – as Eldjárn and others have proposed – by the Scandinavian tradition of *odal* right of succession, which insisted that all the sons of a landholder inherited some portion of their patrimony. In Norway, where fertile land is spread so thinly, each son's inheritance from his father must have progressively diminished with every generation, even to the point of the most meagre subsistence farming. Such a progression would have become more swiftly apparent in the stern Norwegian landscape than in the more generous arable farmland of Denmark, which might well explain how the initial viking longships came to be launched from the western seaboard of Norway rather than out of the Baltic.

The longship itself, while it cannot be claimed as a 'cause' of the Scandinavian Migration Age, stands out as its most significant enabling component. It has a further significance in its reflection of the maritime tradition which, no less than their shared language and legend, bonded the common culture of the northmen. For the tribes settled in territories as various as the sea-girt Norwegian uplands, the dense Swedish forests, the rich Danish farmland and the islands of the Baltic, the sea served as the one great thoroughfare unifying their northern world.

'I shall say the names of the sea', wrote Snorri Sturlusson in his extraordinary saga-poet's thesaurus, *Skaldskaparmal.*

> Ever-lying, salt, ... flat one, dead calm and bay, resounding, overhang, empty one, brawler ... sucker, swallower, maelstrom and fjord ... tempest, depth, breaker ... flood and surf, sparkler, engulfer ...

The sea itself provided the impetus and facility for advances in marine technology. The sheltered lee of the islands of the Norwegian seaboard, no less than its creeks and fjords, were nature's testing ground for maritime innovation and there the northmen developed their longship with its clinkered hull of oak strakes and single great keel for unprecedented stability. The longship has been too extensively and authoritatively analysed, investigated and illustrated elsewhere to demand any detailed consideration here other than its recognition as the most significant technology of the viking phenomenon. There is, of course, no contemporary documentary evidence for the design of the vessel which carried the first viking raiders to Lindisfarne and Iona, but it would certainly have been the *hafskip*, the ocean-going longship of the Atlantic-faring northmen. The magnificent vessel excavated intact at Gokstad in Norway represents a 'state-of-the-art' longship of the mid-ninth century. If the Gokstad ship was close kin to a vessel which raided Lindisfarne more than fifty years earlier, it is fair to imagine an oak-built hull, some seventy-six feet in length with a beam of some seventeen feet amidships, and rising almost six and a half feet from keel to gunwhale. Its rowing benches could accommodate no more than three dozen men, effectively an ocean-going warband, who must have served alike as crew and oarsmen at sea and as fighting-men on landfall.

Carrying a sail a dozen yards broad, it was fast-driven by wind or oar, seaworthy on the open ocean and shallow in draught for the river passage, light enough to be carried overland by its crew and shaped to run ashore at speed on beaches of sand, shingle or rock. Whatever can be claimed for the longship as the vehicle of trade and exploration, the maritime historian Alan Binns has identified its greatest significance on European seaboards as that of 'a fast, efficient and reliable landing-craft', and such was to be precisely its role on Lindisfarne in 793.

These then were the vessels so widely celebrated in modern times as 'dragonships' and that name represents its own dark irony. The Scandinavian shipwright who so often carved the prow of his longship into the monstrous features of a dragon was to strike more terror than he could have imagined into monastic perceptions coloured by the foretelling of the *Revelation*.

> And they worshipped the dragon which gave power unto the beast: and they worshipped the beast, saying, Who is like unto the beast? who is able to make war with him?

A modern experiment with a replica vessel made the crossing from Bergen to Newfoundland in some twenty-eight days and the prowess of the longship is attested by the remarkable range of its seagoing, carrying Scandinavian expansion even as far as *Vinland* on the edge of the north American continent. The impression of bold northmen daring the seas which lay beyond the range of southern seafarers until the sixteenth century has great romantic appeal, but one that needs to be qualified in the light of the realities of early medieval seafaring, which steered customarily in sight of land. On closer examination of the geography of the matter, it might be proposed that the great majority of viking seafarers followed that custom more closely than might sometimes be made to appear.

The northmen assuredly had sufficient knowledge of sun and pole star, log line and dead reckoning to ascertain their latitude, especially if they had access to a 'sun-stone' of light-polarising calcite for use when the sun was obscured by grey northern skies. If longitude-finding was beyond their skills on the open sea without chart or compass, it was probably unnecessary for a navigator working from commonsense based on a wealth of sea-lore and seeking only the next landfall. Experienced observation of cloud and current, seabirds and sealife could make it possible to sense a landfall before it became visible and there were, in any case, no enormous distances of ocean to the west without sight of land.

The name of Norway is believed to derive from its maritime aspect as the 'North Way', whereby the sheltered waters of its western coastline was the north–south sea-road of Scandinavia. Viewed from that perspective, Trondheim lies within the same radius of Bergen as does Shetland, and the south of Denmark within the same radius of Stavanger as Orkney. The sagas do tell of ships and men lost at sea, but they offer no record of how many lives might have been sacrificed to unfamiliar waters before more fortunate seafarers confirmed the disposition of the northern isles of Scotland to the west of Norway. Human life was of no great price in those distant days Icelanders call the 'saga-time' and the uncharted loss of ships and crews was of little account beside the knowledge brought back by the luckier land-seekers. It is certain that by the last quarter of the eighth century the presence of the seventy-mile coastline offered by the Shetland archipelago less than two hundred miles west of Bergen was known to anyone planning viking enterprise from the Hörtha-land seaboard and no very remarkable navigational skill needed to find it.

For a vessel sailing south from Sumburgh Head at the tip of Shetland, the Fair Isle is soon visible and from there the northern-most point of Orkney on North Ronaldsay lies only fifty miles further south again. To the west of Shetland – and the sagas confirm that a course down that side of the islands was favoured to avoid the east coast fogs and the hazardous seas of the Sumburgh Roost – the Faroes lie no further distant than Shetland from Norway, no more than a twenty-four hour sailing given a good wind. By virtue of climatological providence, otherwise interpreted as Thor's blessing on the *Thor-faring*, 'good' winds were firmly on the side of the seasonal sea-raider. The prevailing easterlies of springtime carried him west toward Shetland and Orkney, just as the autumnal westerlies would carry him home with the plunder of his summer's viking.

The Irish monk Dicuil fled Iona after the viking raids and so lived to write his cosmography *Libera de Mensura Orbis Terrae* in a continental monastery in 825. In its pages he set down his recollections of island hermits telling him thirty years before of how they had, even by then, been driven from their summer retreats on Orkney, Shetland and probably also the Faroes 'because of northern pirates'. Dicuil's testimony confirms that the vikings were infesting the northern isles at least as early as the beginning of the last decade of the eighth century.

The northmen were initially summer pirates who stayed on to over-winter wherever they found themselves too far from home to attempt the return voyage at autumn's end. The future Norse *jarldom* of Orkney and Shetland must have hosted its first Scandinavian visitors by virtue of offering a winter roost in the earliest phase of what the Orcadian poet George Mackay Brown has called 'their hawkflight through history' and those over-wintering refuges were soon to serve as forward bases for further-flung sea-raiding. The cliffs of Caithness on the Scottish mainland could be seen to beckon across the Pentland Firth to longships venturing out of the natural ship-haven of Scapa Flow. A course – set still within sight of land – across the Pentland Firth and round Cape Wrath brought the longships into *Scotland-fjord,* the sea-road in the lee of the Outer Hebrides, down the whole length of the western isles. The name Hebrides is said to derive from the Old Norse *Hav Bred Eye,* 'islands at the edge of the sea', but to the Gael they were to be soon called *Innse-gall,* 'isles of the aliens'.

Steering eastwards out of Scapa would have brought a ship across the Pentland Firth towards and around Duncansby Head to turn south down the Scottish coast. The Northumbrian strand – and the holy island of Lindisfarne – lay some two hundred miles to the south on a course held always within sight of land. It is quite possible that seafaring at a venture fell entirely by accident on monasteries sited so vulnerably in its path, but later evidence of viking raiding does reveal a measure of forward planning. It is no less possible that the 'heathen men' who fell on Lindisfarne had some hearsay intelligence, passed perhaps between raider and trader, to lure them so far and so soon to the southward.

Missionaries from Northumbria, Ireland and Iona had long been venturing towards the Baltic fringe of continental Europe and it is not beyond any reasonable bounds of historical speculation to wonder what word of holy places at the edge of the sea, beloved of the White Christ and richly-endowed by kings, might have found its way north to the viking homelands in trader's tales from the marketplaces of the Baltic. However accurately or extravagantly – or even if at all – informed by any such intelligence, the vikings who had reached Orkney and Shetland soon discovered the holy places of Cuthbert and Columcille within the striking range of their longships.

While every technical aspect of those longships seems to have received the most extensive attention elsewhere, what might be seen as their spiritual significance has been largely overlooked. Until the advent of the sea-raiders, the monks of the west had believed the sea to be their own dominion. The warbands of Anglo-Saxon England had not passed for centuries along the sea-roads and, as in Celtic Ireland, the way of the warrior had – with only the rarest exceptions – long lain through river valley and mountain pass. The sea was the pilgrim's way, and across it such holy men as Cormac the sailor-monk and Brendan called 'the Navigator' followed the 'wave cry and wind cry' in their hide-hulled curraghs to seek their 'hermitage in the ocean'. The same tides whose breakers thundered against rocky islet retreats from Skellig to Rona and washed the slipways of the great monastic port of Bangor in Down ran also over the beaches of hallowed monasteries and shrines at the edge of the ocean. For the Celt the sea had been possessed of a spiritual significance of far greater antiquity than the Celtic Christianity it served as both shield and supply line. The same sea, with a terrible irony, placed the Celtic church directly in the path of the viking onslaught.

So it must have been that the first of the countless sacrileges inflicted by the northmen on the monks of the west was their irretrievable devastation of 'the deep peace of the running wave'.

Either as a pure accident of history or prompted by some discernible design, the impact of the Scandinavian Migration Age which was to reshape the passage of these islands into the medieval centuries fell first and with its greatest ferocity on their most sacred shrines.

Within little more than a decade of the first raid on the western seaboard, the *comarb** and community of Columcille had been driven from their holy island to seek sanctuary on the Irish mainland. Twenty-five years later, the monks of Lindisfarne had uprooted the shrine of Cuthbert and carried it to a temporary place of safety inland from the edge of the ocean. After what appear as decades of remission from their raiding on the eastern seaboard, the northmen descended on Northumbria in numbers described by the chronicler as a *micel here*, or 'great host', and what remained of the community of Cuthbert was finally driven to abandon Lindisfarne to its seals and seabirds.

While the raid of 793 serves as the landmark for the beginning of the viking age, no similarly precise date can mark the point when the escalating assault of freelance sea-raiders passed into the waves of invasion and land-taking which followed in its wake. Summer raiders were superseded by overwintering warbands who were succeeded in their turn by national armies of conquest under warlords acknowledged as kings. By the last quarter of the ninth century the northmen had been established in the northern and western islands of Scotland for at least a hundred years, Norse and Danish warbands

* *comarb*, pl. *comarba* (Old Irish). Literally 'co-heir' but meaning successor to the abbacy of the founding saint.

were entangled in the internecine warfare endemic to the Irish dynasties, and the Anglo-Saxon kingdom of Wessex stood alone against the *Danelaw* which dominated England to the north and west of Watling Street. Within eighty-five years of the first landfall of the longships on Lindisfarne, the viking age had been succeeded by the Scandinavian settlement.

Even for the church which had endured the longest and most injurious experience of the viking onslaught, the northmen were recognised – at least by such monastic communities as had survived into the last decades of the ninth century – as a fact of life, however disruptive and dangerous, rather than as sea-borne horsemen of the apocalypse. While their atrocities and outrages were still recognised as instruments of divine retribution, their reverses were increasingly attributed to the intervention of the saints avenging injuries inflicted on their own earthly dominion. The 'heathen men' had found their way into the church histories and lives of saints even if they were cast usually – yet not always – in the role of death-dealers of the red martyrdom.

By reason of the monastic monopoly of literacy and scholarship, the documentary record of the viking onslaught was set down exclusively by those on whom it fell. While that inevitable historiographical imbalance has prompted allegations of bias and hysteria – and even the dismissal of the earliest sources as 'the outraged gibbering of priests' – the disrupted and fragmentary form in which those early sources have survived provides its own index of the devastation they record. The sparse chronicle of the northern English in the centuries between the Bedan histories and the Norman historians of Durham attests the 'monastic desert' to which Northumbria had been reduced by the first decades of the second millenium. Similarly, the terse record of the Irish annals cannot represent a complete catalogue of the viking onslaught on the dominions of the Gael, while the evidence of the flood of scholar-monks and manuscripts from Ireland appearing in continental monasteries through the ninth century confirms the flight to sanctuary taken by the cream of Irish learning.

'The burning of the monastic library on Iona', suggests Alfred Smyth in his remarkable history of early Scotland, 'might have dealt a greater blow to western civilisation than the destruction of the entire town of Nantes in a viking raid of 863'. Firebrand and war-axe served to demonstrate the fragility of liturgy and learning preserved on vellum, but, however imbalanced and incomplete, the sole surviving historical record remains the sole surviving historical record.

Twelve centuries on, its account of the fury of the northmen reveals nothing less than a descent of prehistoric aliens on the holy places which had inspired and informed the high peaks of western civilisation in the sixth age of the world.

'such an inroad from the sea'

Northanhymbre, AD 793–800

In the year from the incarnation of our Lord seven hundred and ninety three – being the one hundred and seventh year from the death of father Cuthbert, and the eleventh of the pontificate of Higbald, and the fifth of the reign of that most wicked king Aethelred – the church of Lindisfarne was miserably filled with devastation, blood and rapine, and all but entirely and thoroughly ruined.

But before we speak of this destruction, let us make a few extracts from earlier writers descriptive of this locality.

The following passage occurs:- 'The island of Lindisfarne is eight miles in circumference, in which is a noble monastery, the resting place of the bodies of that excellent bishop Cuthbert, and others, his most worthy successors in the episcopate, of whom it may well be said in the words of the anthem, "*Their bodies are buried in peace, and their names shall live for ever.*"

'It takes its name of Lindisfarne from a stream about two feet broad called the Lindis, which here falls into the sea, and which is not perceptible except at low water.'

So much, then, as to the island itself. Its approaching destruction, and that of other holy places, was presaged by the appearance of fearful thunders and fiery dragons flying through the sky. Presently after this, and in the same year, a fleet of the pagans arrived in Britain from the north; and rushing hither and thither, and plundering as they went, they slew not only the cattle, but even the priests and deacons, and the choirs of monks and nuns.

On the seventh of the ides of June, they reached the church of Lindisfarne, and there they miserably ravaged and pillaged everything; they trod the holy things under their polluted feet, they dug down the altars, and plundered all the treasures of the church. Some of the brethren they slew, some they carried off with them in chains, the greater number they stripped naked, insulted, and cast out of doors, and some they drowned in the sea.

Symeon's *History of the Church of Durham.*

I T WAS Winston Churchill who described battlefields as 'the punctuation marks of history'.

What befell Lindisfarne in 793 could hardly be described as a battle such as Culloden or Waterloo where the clash of armies decided the end of an era. There is no suggestion of contest between aggressor and defender but, for all that, Lindisfarne must qualify as one of Churchill's 'punctuation marks' when it marks the point of entry of Scandinavian expansion into western European history. Its universal recognition as that chronological benchmark hinges on the precise identification of the year 793 as the occasion of the first viking raid on England, yet there are marginal notes on the historical record which might suggest such was not the case. The evidence of this marginalia is not remotely conclusive, but it has been sometimes taken as sufficiently authoritative to assign the first viking incursion on the English coast to a date some four years earlier than 793.

The source of that assertion is an entry in the earliest manuscript of the *Anglo-Saxon Chronicle* for AD 789.

> In this year king Beorhtric [of Wessex] took Eadburh, king Offa's daughter, to wife.
>
> And in his days first came three ships. And then the reeve rode thereto, and would compel them to the king's vill, for he knew not what they were, and they there slew him. Those were the first ships of Danish men that sought the land of the English race.

This entry in the 'A' text dates from the early 890s, but the incident it records was expanded with greater detail in the chronicle set down more than a hundred years later by the West Saxon *ealdorman* Aethelweard.

> A small fleet of Danes, numbering three fast ships came unexpectedly to

30

the coast and this was their first coming. Hearing of this, the king's official, then staying at the town called Dorceastre, leaped on his horse and with a few men hurried to the port, thinking they were traders rather than enemies, and imperiously commanded them to be sent to the royal vill, but he and his companions were immediately killed by them. The name of this official was Beadwheard.

For all his lively local detail, the nearest Aethelweard can offer by way of a precise date is to follow the *Anglo-Saxon Chronicle* with 'while the most pious king Beorhtric reigned over the western lands of the English'. Beorhtric succeeded Cynewulf as king of Wessex in 786 and reigned until his death in 802, so the West Saxon sources' 'first coming' of the homicidal traders – if it is accepted at all on such late and anecdotal evidence – can only be assigned to some point in that sixteen-year span.

The Wessex tale became inflated to the point of confusion in the eleventh and twelfth centuries when the 'A' manuscript of the *Chronicle* was transcribed into the variant texts of its 'northern recension'. Of these, the 'D' manuscript made at Worcester, the 'E' manuscript made at Peterborough and the bilingual Latin/English 'F' manuscript from Canterbury were all supplemented by additional material from the lost northern history. That northern material could not have included any reliable independent account of the Dorchester incident, yet this 'northern recension' of the *Chronicle* somehow supplements the 'A' manuscript's 'there came for the first time three ships' with a precise geographical point of departure.

There came for the first time three ships *of northmen from Haerethalande.*

While there is a Hordaland in Denmark, *Haerethalande* is believed to be an Old English rendering of Hörthaland around the Stavanger fjord and would identify Aethelweard's 'Danish men' as of Norse rather than Danish origin. None of which explains why transcribers writing two hundred and fifty years after the event should have access to a point of detailed information unavailable to a more local chronicler working almost a century closer to the incident he records, still less why Norse seafarers should have reached as far south as the coast of Dorset before they are anywhere recorded in Northumbria or the Scottish islands.

Nothing more can be sifted from this material than the probability

31

that the incident was of a later rather than earlier date and that it bore no comparison with the impact of the attack on Lindisfarne which is precisely dated to the year AD 793.

While the onslaught on Lindisfarne remains the first reliably dated viking raid on these islands, its far greater significance is best summed up by the historian F. Donald Logan as 'an attack on both the body and soul of Christian England'.

Tidings of such an attack spread swiftly and even as far as the court of Charlemagne, which the *Royal Frankish Annals* record in residence at Regensburg through 793 before moving on to Würzburg for Christmas. While Charlemagne himself was otherwise engaged on the defence of his own frontiers, where the Saracens were breaking through on his Spanish march and the Saxons rising in revolt on the Danube, the news of a sea-raid on far-off Northumbria commanded the most anxious attention of one eminent member of his Frankish court.

That distinguished scholar was the monk Alcuin, the most famous graduate of the great school of ecclesiastical learning at York who had been first a protégé of Egbert, the pupil of Bede who became the first archbishop of York, and later a pupil of Aelberht, Egbert's brother and successor to the arch-episcopacy. When Aelberht became archbishop in 767, Alcuin succeeded him as master of the school at York and made his first pilgrimage to Rome in the archbishop's company. Alcuin made a total of three journeys from Northumbria to Rome, all of them by way of the dominions of the Franks where he seems to have made so great an impression as to prompt a personal invitation from Charlemagne to join the company of Europe's intellectual élite which he had recruited to his court. Alcuin accepted the invitation in 782 and rose to such prominence, even in that remarkable circle, as to merit his appointment in 796 to the prestigious abbacy of the church of Saint Martin at Tours.

Through all his long years on the continent – from 782 to his death at Tours in 804 – Alcuin maintained the closest interest in English, and especially Northumbrian, affairs. There is no record of how he was first informed of the raid on Lindisfarne, other than collateral evidence of his correspondence with a priest of the monastery by the name of *Biutta*, but his response to the news was as prolific as it was urgent. It is preserved in the German sources in the form of no less than seven letters written home to England and this canon of impassioned correspondence survives as the single immediately contemporary written source for the sea-raid which marks the advent of the viking age.

These letters of Alcuin, responding to outrage with genuine consolation and anxious advice, are individually framed in subtly varied tones of ecclesiastical dignity and addressed to persons whose eminence serves as an indication of Alcuin's own stature, amongst them the kings Aethelred of Northumbria and Offa of Mercia, the monks of Wearmouth and Jarrow, the archbishop of Canterbury and, most urgently of all, to the successor of Aidan and Cuthbert in the see of Lindisfarne.

> To the best sons in Christ of the most blessed father, Saint Cuthbert the bishop, Bishop Higbald and all the congregation of the church of Lindisfarne, Alcuin the deacon sends greeting with celestial benediction in Christ.
>
> The intimacy of your love used to rejoice me greatly when I was with you; but conversely, the calamity of your tribulation saddens me greatly every day, though I am absent; when the pagans desecrated the sanctuaries of God, and poured out the blood of saints around the altar, laid waste the house of our hope, trampled on the bodies of saints in the temple of God, like dung in the street. What can we say except lament in our soul with you before Christ's altar, and say: 'Spare, O Lord, spare thy people, and give not thine inheritance to the Gentiles, lest the pagan say, "Where is the God of the Christians?"' What assurance is there for the churches of Britain, if Saint Cuthbert, with so great a number of saints, defends not his own? Either this is the beginning of greater tribulation, or else the sins of the inhabitants have called it upon them. Truly it has not happened by chance, but it is a sign that it was well merited by someone ...

No less evident than the outrage and sympathy of these letters is their note of incredulous bewilderment. Alcuin, like Bede sixty years before, sought the hand of God in all the affairs of men and perceived omens of divine intent in the extraordinary phenomena of the heavens. Through the lens of that world-view the descent of 'the havoc of heathen men' out of the void of the ocean could only be accounted divine retribution for sin, and no one was more aware of the manifold sins of the Northumbrian kingdom in decay than Alcuin of York.

Therein lies the source of Alcuin's incredulity, because the onslaught had not fallen on some extravagant royal estate. Neither had it ravaged the city of *Eoforwik* at York which had largely supplanted the ancient stronghold of *Bebbanburh* at Bamburgh as the royal capital of Northumbria, but had instead devastated the island shrine of Cuthbert, the most guiltless of all the lands of the northern English, and 'miserably destroyed God's church on Lindisfarne'.

It was of course possible, as Alcuin implies, that even on Lindisfarne there were individuals guilty of sins unknown to their community yet known to God and judged deserving of such stern chastisement. The literature of hagiography records more than one innocent monastic community suffering grievously on account of some offence by one of its number and there are hints elsewhere in his correspondence with Lindisfarne that Alcuin disapproved of what he discerned as the shortcomings of Bishop Higbald's standards of monastic discipline. Such thoughts prompted Alcuin to continue his letter, and at some length, with suggestions as to how the community might look further to the impeccable example they should present to a secular world beset by sin.

Whatever his views on the bishop's shortcomings, the accusatory tone of Alcuin's letter to the Northumbrian king reflects his trenchant disapproval of Aethelred as, if not quite the prime example of those *peccata mundi*, little better than a usurper thane with no legitimate dynastic claim on the kingdom. The tone of his letter is perhaps less dramatically significant at this point than its content, which remains the most substantial contemporary account of 'such an inroad from the sea'.

> Lo, it is nearly three hundred and fifty years that we and our fathers have inhabited this most lovely land, and never before has such terror appeared in Britain as we have now suffered from a pagan race, nor was it thought that such an inroad from the sea could be made.
>
> Behold the church of Saint Cuthbert spattered with the blood of the priests of God, despoiled of all its ornaments; a place more venerable than all in Britain is given as a prey to pagan peoples. And where first, after the departure of Saint Paulinus from York, the Christian religion in our race took its rise, there misery and calamity have begun. Who does not fear this? Who does not lament this as if his country were captured? Foxes pillage the chosen vine, the heritage of the Lord has been given to a people not his own; and where there was the praise of God are now the games of the Gentiles; the holy festivity has been turned to mourning ...
> Whoever reads the Holy Scriptures and ponders ancient histories and considers the fortune of the world will find that for sins of this nature kings have lost their kingdoms and peoples their country; and while the

34

strong unjustly seized the goods of others, they justly lost their own.

Truly signs of this misery preceded it, some through unaccustomed things, some through unwonted practices. What portends the rain of blood, which in the time of Lent in the church of Saint Peter, Prince of the Apostles, in the city of York, which is the head of the whole kingdom, we saw fall menacingly on the north side from the summit of the roof, though the sky was serene? Can it not be expected that from the north there will come upon our nation retribution of blood, which can be seen to have started with this attack which has lately befallen the house of God?

Consider the dress, the way of wearing the hair, the luxurious habits of the princes and people. Look at your trimming of beard and hair, in which you have wished to resemble the pagans. Are you not menaced by terror of those whose fashion you wished to follow? What also of the immoderate use of clothing beyond the needs of human nature, beyond the custom of our predecessors? The princes' superfluity is poverty for the people ... Where is brotherly love? Where the pity which we are admonished to have for the wretched? The satiety of the rich is the hunger of the poor. That saying of our Lord is to be feared: 'For judgement without mercy to him that hath not done mercy.' Also we read in the words of the blessed Peter: 'The time is that judgement should begin at the house of God.'

Behold, judgement has begun, with great terror, at the house of God, in which rest such lights of the whole of Britain. What should be expected for other places, when the divine judgement has not spared this holy place?

As befits the earliest documentary source for the first experience of the fury of the northmen written under the long shadow of the prophecies of the *Revelation*, these are communiqués from the sixth age of the world.

Nonetheless and for all their formality, Alcuin's letters, intended after all as personal communications, fall woefully short as any full historical record. They offer powerful testimony to the sacrilege of the raid, but no description of the raiders to bear comparison with the graphic image carved on the Lindisfarne grave-marker. They include a wealth of scriptural quotation, but no note of the precise date of the momentous event to which they respond. Historical detail of that order can only be sought in the fragments of other contemporary sources which found their way into later chronicles and histories. Historians have tentatively identified just two such seminal sources for Northumbria in the viking age and, while neither of these has survived in whatever might have been its original form, something of both can be discerned in the later documentary record.

The first is the historical material which was preserved, if largely in oral form, in the tradition of the church of Lindisfarne. This corpus of collective memory, blending anecdote with somewhat firmer historical record, was nurtured within the community of Cuthbert throughout its hundred and twenty years of wandering which led finally to Durham on the Wear in 995. It was at Durham that this Lindisfarne tradition was set down in documentary form but its earliest text is the *Historia de Sancto Cuthberto*, which has been traced back to the community's tenth-century interregnum at Chester-le-Street. It is essentially an inventory of land grants and holdings, but its greater importance lies in the rarity of the historical evidence included with them. For all that importance, the tenth-century *Historia* must concede precedence here to the twelfth-century *Historia Dunelmensis Ecclesiae*, Symeon's history of the church of Durham, which remains the principal narrative text of the Lindisfarne tradition.

Little is known of the historical Symeon of Durham, other than his personal attendance at the translation of Cuthbert's remains in 1104. He may have been the master of the scriptorium and certainly appears to have served in the role of 'official historian' at Durham in the decades on either side of the year 1100. There are a number of historical works attributed to 'Symeon the monk' of which he was only the compiler or editor, but the *History of the Church of Durham* is the one text of which he was assuredly the author. It draws on earlier written sources including the Bedan histories, but its account of the raid of 793* derived from the oral tradition of Lindisfarne, coloured in whatever degree by the retrospect of three centuries.

Symeon's precise date for the raid 'on the seventh of the ides of June' must consequently be taken to be the date engraved long and deep on the memory of the community of Cuthbert. However much the extent of savagery and sacrilege may have been exaggerated in retrospect, a fixed point in time remains absolute and Symeon's date has all the reasonable authority necessary for its acceptance as that of the first recorded viking raid. All of which makes the entry of a different date in the northern recension of the *Anglo-Saxon Chronicle* the more irksome for the historical record.

* See p. 29 above.

Ann. DCC.XCIII:- In this year dire forewarnings came over the land of the Northumbrians, and miserably terrified the people: these were extraordinary whirlwinds and lightnings, and fiery dragons were seen flying in the air. A great famine soon followed these omens; and soon after that, in the same year, on the sixth of the ides of Ianr, the havoc of heathen men miserably destroyed God's church on Lindisfarne, through rapine and slaughter.

In the Latin calendar, the *ides* was accounted the thirteenth day of all months, other than March, May, July and October when it fell on the fifteenth day. Consequently, Symeon's date of 'the seventh of the ides of June' was the seventh day before the thirteenth and thus June 7th in the modern calendar, while the *Chronicle* date for the same event would correspond to the eighth of 'Ianr', apparently January 8th.

As has already been indicated, the northern recension of the *Anglo-Saxon Chronicle* incorporates material from an earlier and no longer extant northern history. It was this history which has been identified as the second of the seminal Northumbrian sources and largely independent of the Lindisfarne material which had informed Symeon's *History of the Church of Durham*. The precise origin and provenance of the lost northern history is unknown but it most probably grew out of the *Continuatio Bedae*, a chronicle appended to his *Historia Ecclesiastica* at Jarrow in the decades after Bede's death. At some point in the second half of the eighth century, the original Jarrow chronicle would seem to have been continued at York and expanded into an immediately contemporary history of later Anglo-Saxon Northumbria. While this northern history cannot have escaped both the seizure of York by the Danish 'great army' of 867 and the ravaging of the north country by the Norman conquerors two hundred years later, something of its content did survive to inform the northern recension of the *Anglo-Saxon Chronicle*.

The authority of the *Chronicle* date of 'the sixth of the ides of January' for the Lindisfarne raid hangs then on nothing more than that tentative provenance and must be discredited in favour of Symeon's date on the most probable grounds of scribal error. The condition of the manuscript from which the chronicler transcribed the northern material was most unlikely to have been one of crystalline clarity and he might be forgiven for rendering '*vii ides iun*' as '*vi ides ianr*', even though almost every modern authority dismisses early January as the most improbable season for sea-raiding. Charles

Plummer, the eminent editor of Bede's histories, opts for Symeon's date in June because 'the vikings would not cross the sea at midwinter'. Nonetheless, and always depending on its point of departure, a January raid would not have been impossible – in the opinion of Alan Binns, the outstanding modern authority on the theory and practice of viking seafaring – given 'meticulous planning, excellent intelligence and independence of ordinary agricultural and fishing concerns'. Even so, Binns agrees that such a voyage would have been a highly unlikely venture when daylight was short and storm at sea so great a hazard.

Beyond the evidence of Alcuin, Symeon and the *Anglo-Saxon Chronicle*, any more detailed reconstruction of the assault on Lindisfarne can only be a matter of speculative deduction.

Both tradition and topography propose the sea-raiders landing on the golden curve of the sands on the north side of the island which presented a classically inviting point of entry for the longship specifically designed to run up a beach. Whether the crews would have surrounded their vessels with a defensive wall of shields dug into the sand – the customary tactic of later Scandinavian raids – in an assault on an obviously undefended island monastery is doubtful, but there is a real possibility that the north side of the island was then in much greater use than in modern times. Archaeological excavation has exposed farming settlement of the ninth and tenth centuries at the Green Shiel site on the north shore of Lindisfarne. If it had been in similar use as an eighth-century monastic farm, working monks or lay brothers would have given early warning of the raiders' arrival or even some semblance of resistance. In any case, a running charge of berserks wielding sword and war-axe would have swiftly broken through any such defence to reach and overrun the monastic settlement on the south-facing shore of the island in a matter of minutes.

The buildings – including two churches, a guesthouse and a dormitory, according to Bede – were 'constructed in the Irish manner of hewn oak'. The first monastery established by Aidan on much the same site would have been closely modelled on Iona, with an oratory of wood or even wattle surrounded by 'beehive' monastic cells and the whole enclosed with the physical and spiritual boundary of an earthen rampart known as the *vallum monasterii.* Aidan's church was replaced by his successor and fellow-Irishman,

Finan, with the more imposing structure described with real reverence by Bede.

> On the island of Lindisfarne, he built a church befitting an episcopal see, although he constructed it in the Irish manner entirely of hewn oak, not of stone, and thatched it with reeds, and it was later consecrated by the reverend Archbishop [of Canterbury] Theodore to the honour of the blessed apostle Peter.

This was the church still in use on Lindisfarne in Cuthbert's time until his successor, Eadbert, put the next stage of building work in hand.

> Bishop Eadbert of Lindisfarne had the thatch removed and the whole church, that is to say not only the roof but the walls as well, covered with sheets of lead.

Such must still have been the structure of the principal church on which the northmen fell in 793 and, however expansive the monastic settlement had grown, the most important buildings would have been situated close beside it on the south shore of the island.

There is, of course, no reason why the longships could not have rounded the island from the north and put in to what would have been some sort of landing place on the site occupied by the modern harbour. Such an approach would have given more certain early warning to the monastery from its watchtower looking out over the Farne Islands, the sea approach and the causeway visible at low tide across the sands from the mainland. It would have also brought the viking warband ashore directly on to the monastic settlement, where Symeon's account of the ensuing savagery and sacrilege can be interpolated into this speculative construction.

The shock of the assault does seem to outreach the extent of the devastation. While Alcuin's implication is supported by Symeon's account of the 'church ... miserably filled with devastation, blood, and rapine, and all but entirely and thoroughly ruined', his *History of the Church of Durham* confirms that the injuries of 793 were not fatal.

> Although the church of Lindisfarne had been thus ravaged and despoiled of its ecclesiastical ornaments, the episcopal see still continued therein; and as many of the monks as had succeeded in escaping from the hands of the barbarians still continued for a long time to reside near the body of the blessed Cuthbert.

The most celebrated evidence for the destruction inflicted by the 'heathen men' as mercifully less than total is the survival of the great gospel book of Lindisfarne, already some hundred years old in 793 and still to be seen today in the British Library. While Symeon insists 'they miserably ravaged and pillaged everything; they trod the holy things under their polluted feet, they dug down the altars, and plundered all the treasures of the church', not only the Lindisfarne Gospels but, more importantly, the uncorrupt remains of Cuthbert survived to guide his community's departure from Lindisfarne and accompany them to Durham two hundred years later. The eminence of those two significant survivals has prompted some modern historians to accuse Alcuin's contemporary letters and Symeon's monastic tradition of gross exaggeration, but the quality of the survivals cannot be reasonably recruited to diminish either the extent or excellence of the casualties. On the contrary, the celebrated manuscript and metalwork which have survived over twelve centuries serve as indices of what was lost to posterity by way of the melting moulds and grave goods of Scandinavia.

The monastery on Lindisfarne had been the royal church of Northumbria since 635. It had been founded by monks schooled in the Irish tradition where ecclesiastical metalworking had reached such peaks of mastery as the renowned chalices of Ardagh and Derrynaflan, fashioned from silver worked with gold and amber. The vast land-holdings of Lindisfarne were spread over the full extent of the kingdom from Yorkshire to the Forth and represented the great wealth endowed by three generations of the most powerful royal house in England. Its church ornament – if only on the evidence of the garnets set in the gold pectoral cross interred in Cuthbert's shrine – must have amounted to a treasury of impressive splendour. The Sutton Hoo burial hoard, perhaps the best-known example of Anglo-Saxon craftsmanship, can serve to indicate the quality of artistry of the gold and silver vessels so often mentioned by Bede and his contemporaries. The close kinship between the Sutton Hoo designs from East Anglia and the decoration of the Lindisfarne Gospel pages can be taken to confirm that the same quality of craftsmanship characterised the far greater wealth of the Northumbrian church and kingdom.

The attraction of the Lindisfarne Gospels for a sea-raider would have lain no deeper than a cover richly encrusted with precious metals, yet the only surviving example of seventh-century Northumbrian bookbinding is the embossed crimson goatskin covering the 'Stonyhurst' Gospel of Saint John. There is no evidence that the Lindisfarne Gospels were any more extravagantly bound in the eighth century and a trophy of decorated leather would have attracted far less attention from raiders than any sizeable item of altar silver. Similarly, Cuthbert's shrine on Lindisfarne – described in the twelfth-century account by Reginald of Durham as 'made entirely out of black oak ... carved with very admirable engraving' – would not seem to have offered the most obvious plunder to a viking warband.

Symeon's *History* records just one specific instance of viking destruction on Lindisfarne as an incidental reference in his account of the standing cross commissioned in 698 by Cuthbert's successor, Bishop Aethelwold.

> He it was who caused a stone cross of curious workmanship to be made ... the top of which was broken off by the pagans when they devastated the church of Lindisfarne at a later period; but it was afterwards reunited to the body of the cross by being run together with lead, and subsequently to this it was constantly carried about along with the body of Saint Cuthbert, and honourably regarded by the people of Northumbria out of regard for these two holy men. And, at the present time [c. 1104] it stands erect in the cemetery of the church of Durham and exhibits to all who look upon it a memorial of these two bishops, Cuthbert and Aethelwold.

Of much greater significance is the evidence for the Lindisfarne raid as the first example of a phenomenon which was to become ever more apparent with the escalation of the viking onslaught. 'Some of the brethren they slew,' writes Symeon, 'some they carried off with them in chains', and Alcuin also refers to 'youths who have been led into captivity by the pagans'. However rarely encountered in the modern emphasis on trading rather than raiding, the sources confirm that slaving was already a feature of viking activity as early as 793.

While the attack on Lindisfarne is customarily presented as a significant but isolated 'hit and run' sea-raid against a single island target, the sources might be otherwise interpreted as to the extent of the raiding. Symeon's *History*, for example, would seem to indicate it as the outstanding infamy of a wider-ranging onslaught.

41

Its approaching destruction, and that of other holy places, was presaged by the appearance of fearful thunders and fiery dragons flying through the sky. Presently after this, and in the same year, a fleet of the pagans arrived in Britain from the north; and rushing hither and thither, and plundering as they went, they slew not only the cattle, but even the priests and deacons, and the choirs of monks and nuns. On the seventh of the ides of June, they reached the church of Lindisfarne ...

There is a closely similar version of events to be found in the *Historia Regum*, 'History of the Kings', once attributed to Symeon of Durham but now shown to be at least a hundred years older and largely the work of Byrtferth of Ramsey around the year 1000. Byrtferth is the best example of the medieval authors whose historical writings incorporate often substantial fragments of the same lost northern history which had informed the northern recension of the *Anglo-Saxon Chronicle*. The entry for 793 from the *Historia Regum* was clearly among the sources on which Symeon drew in turn for his *History of the Church of Durham*.

In the same year, of a truth, the pagans from the northern region came with a naval armament to Britain, like stinging hornets, and overran the country in all directions, like fierce wolves, plundering, tearing, and killing not only sheep and oxen, but priests and Levites, and choirs of monks and nuns ...

Both of these accounts of events appear to run counter to the perception of a single, sudden sea-raid and they call for some attempt at explanation. Taken at cursory face value, both authors seem to propose a wide-ranging onslaught of sea-raiders and imply their ravaging the greater extent of Northumbria. While such a proposal cannot be categorically denied, it must be considered unlikely. All the recorded attacks in the decades on either side of the year 800 appear to have been 'hit-and-run' pirate raids by warbands numbering less than a hundred men in two or three longships, who were able to outflank any rudimentary defences by their advantage of speed and surprise.

The most convenient explanation of the medieval accounts is that their authors' perception was coloured by the experience of the wide-ranging 'great armies' of the mid-ninth century, and that they interpreted a sea-raid on the lines of those later and much more substantial incursions. While such an explanation can reasonably be applied to later medieval reworkings of the same material, it is rendered unnecessary when the precise terminology used by Symeon and Byrtferth is closely examined. Both authors specify a sea-borne force 'of pagans' who came 'from the north' to 'Britain', who 'rushed hither and thither' according to Symeon and 'overran the country in all directions' according to Byrtferth. Eighth-century sources always employ 'Britain' to mean the greatest extent of the mainland, but in practice, early medieval authors regularly use 'Britain' to distinguish Scotland – otherwise called *Alba* – from Ireland which would be known by the Latin *Hibernia,* the Gaelic *Erin,* or even *Scotia* if the north of Ireland is specified. It is in just that sense that Bede always refers to the settlement of Scotic Dalriada in Argyll as that of 'the Irish in Britain'. Similarly Adamnan, abbot of Iona and biographer of Columcille, describes the saint's voyage from Derry to Kintyre as a pilgrimage 'from Scotia to Britain'.

When Byrtferth and Symeon are read in that context, their eighth-century sources reveal a remarkable correspondence with the entry in the *Annals of Ulster* – the most ancient Irish annals deriving in part from an Iona exemplar – at the year 793.

> Devastation of all the islands of Britain by the heathens.

The form of words testifies to the antiquity of the entry which was certainly transcribed from the lost chronicle of Iona known as the *Chronicon Hyense.* The precision of its date is less than reliable when the Ulster annalist places events of that period one year earlier than the true date. The entry has nonetheless been generally interpreted by historians as recording a sudden eruption of viking raiding out of Orkney and Shetland and into the Western Isles around the date of the raid on Lindisfarne.

Northumbria cannot have been entirely uninformed of events on the western seaboard. Lindisfarne had maintained some form of contact with Iona, however disrupted by theological schism and unnoticed by the Bedan sources, since the mid-seventh century. When the monks of Iona finally agreed to adopt the Roman tonsure and church calendar in 716, they had been persuaded by the efforts of a Lindisfarne monk known as 'Ecgbert the Englishman'. The busy flow of monastic traffic across the Irish Sea – like 'bees after honey' according to Aldhelm, abbot of Malmesbury – is thoroughly documented and the ancient church at Whithorn in Galloway, well-placed on the sea-roads of the Irish world and still a Northumbrian bishopric until long after 793, served as a strategic westward listening-post. Set into that network of communications, the sources which informed both Symeon and Byrtferth serve to confirm the modern recognition of the Lindisfarne raiders as a 'splinter-group' of a greater viking force which was already striking into the Outer Hebrides from forward bases established in Orkney and Shetland.

The 'heathen men' who fell on Lindisfarne, then, were Norse vikings operating out of the northern isles, which must be the district and direction intended by Symeon's 'from the north' and Byrtferth's 'northern region'. Alone among the earliest sources and by reason of his continental viewpoint, it is Alcuin who should have been best placed to recognise the point of departure of 'such an inroad from the sea'.

The great implication of his choice of that phrase is Alcuin's assumption – and astonishment – that the raiders had crossed 'the Ocean' as he would have called the North Sea. He was unaware of the viking sea-road out of the northern isles and the question remains as to whom Alcuin believed capable of the accomplished seafaring which he assumed to have facilitated their sacrilegious piracy. The obvious answer points to the northmen of Jutland and the Baltic where Tacitus had long before proclaimed 'the sea was master'. Alcuin must certainly have known something of the Danes from the earlier mission of his own kinsman Wilbrord and also from Frankish sources, but he nowhere identifies them as the raiders on Lindisfarne. He was, of course, quite right not so to do because, although they were raiding the coast of Aquitaine by 799, Danish vikings did not follow the Norse sea-raiders as far as England until forty years after 793.

Alcuin's letter to King Aethelred includes his vague reference to the origin of the raiders – 'from the north there will come upon our nation retribution of blood' – but only to reflect the ominous portent of the rain of blood on York which 'we saw fall menacingly on the north side from the summit of the roof' of the church of Saint Peter. In his elegaic verses *De clade Lindisfarnensis monasterii* – 'On the destruction of the monastery of Lindisfarne' – he reverts by way of poetic licence to the vaguest form of location.

> How all must lament that day,
> When the pagan troop,
> Coming from the ends of the earth,
> Suddenly sought our shores by ship.
> Despoiling our fathers' venerable tombs of their splendour.

Just a few clues drawn from his letters suggest – if only to me – that Alcuin identified the raiders of Lindisfarne with the same peoples who were engaging Charlemagne's armies on the Danube in 793. In his letter to Aethelred, Alcuin makes reference to the three hundred and fifty years since his own Germanic forbears came to Britain. Alcuin knew that they had come as raiders as well as mercenaries and settlers. He knew that they had also come by sea and, significantly, that they had come from the same continental homelands around the Baltic where their own pagan Saxon descendants were in revolt against the militant Christianity of Frankish expansion. When Alcuin accuses the Northumbrian king of 'resembling the pagans' in his style of hair and beard, he can have had no realistic idea of the appearance of a Norse viking and little enough of a Danish warrior, but he would have had the best of information from the Frankish military as to the appearance of their Saxon enemies and may even have seen it at first hand among Charlemagne's prisoners-of-war.

The most strategic clue might be found in the last paragraph of Alcuin's letter to the bishop of Lindisfarne and the offer of his own good offices to seek the release of those enslaved by the sea-raiders.

> When our lord King Charles returns home, having by the mercy of God subdued his enemies, we plan, with God's help, to go to him; and if we can then be of any profit to your Holiness, regarding either the youths who have been led into captivity by the pagans or any other of your needs, we will take diligent care to bring it about . . .

This generous thought has been interpreted by some authorities as the intention to ransom any monks of Lindisfarne from the hands of Danish slave-traders with Frankish gold in the marketplaces of the Baltic. An alternative reading might suggest that Alcuin imagined the slaves to have been taken by Saxon sea-raiders and proposed to secure their freedom in exchange for prominent Saxon hostages hopefully captured in the course of Charlemagne's victory on the Danube.

All of which remains no more than speculation. If Alcuin suspected the sea-raiders to be Danes or, more probably, Saxons he was wide of the mark and he had no means of accurately recognising them as Norse. The fact of the matter seems to be that he had no firm notion as to their origins and the shock of 'such an inroad from the sea' reflects his instinctive outrage at the desecration of 'the deep peace of the running wave', no less sacred to Cuthbert of Lindisfarne than to the Celtic monks of the west.

Alcuin's reaction can also be shown to reveal a political dimension when, as an expatriate Northumbrian and counsellor to the most powerful warlord in Europe, he expressed anger and astonishment at the fact that the outrage had gone unpunished

For almost a hundred years, the kingdom of Northumbria had been the greatest military and political power among the Anglo-Saxon kingdoms. The dynasty established by Ida at Bamburgh in 547 had forged the vast territories *be northan Hymbre*, 'to the north of the Humber', into the unified Northumbrian kingdom by the first years of the seventh century in the time of Ida's grandson Aethelfrith. When Oswald and his successor Oswy, both of them sons of Aethelfrith and schooled on Iona, returned from exile to reclaim their father's kingdom they were accorded the status of *bretwalda*, overlords of all the English kingdoms with hegemony over the territories of the Picts, Scots and Britons beyond the Forth.

The century of decline from that high peak of the Northumbrian ascendancy began on the battlefield of Nechtansmere near Forfar where Egfrith, son of Oswy and last legitimate king of the line of Ida, was slain with the greater part of his army in a devastating defeat at the hands of the Picts. In the same year of 685 the monkish Aldfrith, Egfrith's illegitimate half-brother, succeeded to a greatly reduced kingdom, yet one entering its 'golden age' of literacy and learning. The succession of Aldfrith's son Osred, principally recorded as an infamous rapist of nuns, marked Northumbria's vertiginous descent into anarchy. As the middle English kingdom of Mercia superseded its northern neighbour as the great power in the land, the eighth century entered into history as the age of Mercian ascendancy.

Power to the north of the Humber passed into the successive hands of obscure rulers claiming the kingdom by right of descent from the founding dynast through semi-historical 'sons of Ida by concubines'. Alcuin's own disparaging assessment of such kings was expressed in a letter he wrote in 797.

> Scarcely anyone can now be found from the ancient stock of kings, and the more uncertain their origin, the more they lack valour.

Only one of those kings, Eadbert, who shared effective power with his brother Bishop Egbert of York, appears to have even temporarily stemmed the decline to the point where Alcuin looked back on his reign through the 740s and 750s as a resurgence of the 'golden age'. Eadbert abdicated to enter the church and in favour of his son, Oswulf, who 'during one year held, parted from, and lost, the kingdom; for he was wickedly put to death by his family' according to the *Historia Regum*. Northumbria fell to the thane 'Aethelwald who was also called Moll' by right of nothing more than his sword arm and ruthless ambition. Aethelwald 'Moll' lacked even the dubious claim of illegitimate lineage on the kingdom which he lost in battle near Durham to one Alcred described as 'a descendant, as some say, of king Ida'. This Alcred was himself driven into exile in Pictland in the year 774 by Aethelred, son of Aethelwald Moll. Within five years Aethelred was driven out in favour of Eadbert's grandson, 'the pious and upright' Aelfwald, who was 'miserably slain ... near the Wall' by a conspiracy of thanes in 788. When Aelfwald's successor Osred, son of Alcred, was forcibly tonsured and driven into exile, it was the signal for Aethelred's return, 'freed from banishment' to reclaim the kingdom in 790.

The epic saga of the Northumbrian warrior kings of earlier centuries had dwindled to this dismal cycle of usurper succeeded by assassin succeeded by tyrant which, even if it did not invite the descent of the 'great army' of the northmen, was to be snuffed out by it. Aethelred returned as a veritable 'lord of misrule' over a Northumbria engulfed by anarchy. Such were the king and his kingdom indicated by Alcuin when, only two years into Aethelred's second succession, sea-raiders struck with apparently entire impunity at the church of Lindisfarne.

As much as he must have recognised the impotence of that decayed temporal sovereignty in defending the shrines of its saints, Alcuin might reasonably have hoped for some divine retribution on the raiders. Even that seemed unforthcoming – on the evidence of his letter to Aethelred.

> What assurance is there for the churches of Britain, if Saint Cuthbert, with so great a number of saints, defends not his own?

Once again Alcuin's choice of phrase is revealing and here confirms the impressive stature which the hermit-bishop Cuthbert had achieved within little more than a hundred years of his death. By the last decade of the eighth century the cult of Cuthbert had already almost entirely supplanted that of the founding bishop Aidan on Lindisfarne and he was established as a patron saint for the northern English of a stature to match that of Columcille for the Gael.

The hagiographical sources all tell of Cuthbert's tending sheep in the Lammermuir hills and his vision of the ascent of the soul of Aidan which prompted him to enter the church at the daughter foundation of Aidan's Lindisfarne at Melrose on the Tweed in 651. There he was trained in the ancient Celtic tradition of Iona and, for all his tolerance of the winds of theological change, his spirituality was cast immutably in the Celtic mould.

Those winds reached gale force above the bay at Whitby in the year – according to Bede's reckoning – of 664. Oswy, king of Northumbria, had summoned the most eminent clergy to Whitby to resolve the 'Paschal Question' which had long divided the Roman and Irish orthodoxies over the theologically correct date for the celebration of the Easter festival. The learned churchmen would debate and the king, who was himself almost certainly illiterate, would decide because this 'Synod of Whitby' was, in reality, a matter of politics. It was a struggle between Canterbury and Iona for power in the *bretwalda*'s kingdom masquerading as a dispute over the church calendar and the style of monastic tonsure which Iona – in the person of Colman who had succeeded his fellow Irishman Finan as bishop of Lindisfarne – lost.

Colman returned with all his Irish monks and many of their English brothers to Iona and from there to the west of Ireland. Tuda, one of Aidan's pupils, was appointed as the new bishop but died within the year and the see of Lindisfarne was carved up into portions assigned to the churches of York and Ripon. Its much-reduced community was placed under the authority of Eata, abbot of Melrose, and with him came Cuthbert, initially as guest-master and later as prior when Eata was confirmed to the restored episcopacy of Lindisfarne.

Although the Benedictine Rule was applied throughout North-umbria before the year 800, it was still the practice in the third quarter of the seventh century for an abbot or prior to devise his own rule for his own monastery. So it fell to Cuthbert to set down a rule for a community still shocked and riven by the new orthodoxy imposed by the council at Whitby less than a year before. His remarkable personality somehow harmonised a formal submission to the Roman orthodoxy and the arch-episcopacy at Canterbury with his own essentially Celtic spirituality. He was assuredly the right man in the right place at the right time, possessed of the full measure of the extraordinary qualities which set those called *sanctus* apart from lesser humankind. Within little more than a twelvemonth, the royal church founded by Aidan had been effectively branded heretic, reduced to a shadow of its former numbers and notability, then restored as the bishopric which was soon to command the especial patronage – and generous endowment – of the new king when Egfrith succeeded his father Oswy in 671. This dramatic shift in its fortunes can only be attributed to the sanctity, skills and inexplicable charisma of Cuthbert of Lindisfarne who – in the assessment of Sir Frank Stenton, the Oxford historian of Anglo-Saxon England – 'belongs to the world of the ancient Irish saints'.

It was his personal Celtic leanings which drew Cuthbert out of the monastic community to the 'green martyrdom' of the Irish hermit tradition when he first took up a hermitage on the tiny tidal Hobthrush islet off Lindisfarne, but its close proximity to the monastery drew him – according to Bede's *Historia Ecclesiastica* – 'to a place of combat more distant and more remote from mankind'.

> Farne lies several miles to the south-east of this half-island, and is surrounded by the Ocean, very deep on its landward side and on its further side boundless.

There he was able to spend long hours on his knees in prayer enclosed within the walls of his oratory with no view but the mantle of the sky. This was the rigorously ascetic life of the island solitary lived out in company with the grey seals the Irish call 'the people of the sea' and the eider still known in Northumberland as 'Cuddy's ducks'.

When the warrior king Egfrith insisted that Cuthbert return to the world as his bishop of Lindisfarne in 684, he needed to take boat to Farne to overcome the determined reluctance of the holy man. The burden of that episcopal office was onerous in the extreme when the administration of the extensive estates endowed on Lindisfarne and the responsibilities of a royal counsellor were added to the pastoral duties of a bishop.

For Cuthbert, in his sixth decade but physically exhausted to the point of infirmity by his self-denying asceticism, it must have been almost intolerable. Within two years of Egfrith's death in battle in

Pictland and interment on Iona, Cuthbert was forewarned of his own passing. He chose to return to his island hermitage and Bede's prose *Life* records the saint's last wishes from the testimony of one of those who attended his death on Farne.

'It is my wish that my body should rest here where in a small way I have fought the fight for the Lord, where I desire to finish the course, and from where I hope to be raised up by a merciful Judge to receive the crown of righteousness. I also think it more convenient for you that I should rest here, because of the incursions of fugitives and malefactors of every kind. They are likely to take refuge by my body, because, unworthy as I am, the rumour has spread abroad that I am a servant of Christ; and you will very often have to intercede for them with the rulers of the world, and will find the presence of my body a great burden to you.' But we pleaded with him for a long time, assuring him that a burden of that kind would be welcome to us and light to bear; and at last the man of God spoke words of counsel. 'If you wish to override my plan,' he said, 'and take my body back there, it seems best to me that you should entomb it inside your church, so that you yourselves may visit my sepulchre when you wish, and it may be in your power to decide whether any visitors should approach it.'

Cuthbert the hermit-bishop died on the twentieth day of March in the year 687 'at the customary hour of the night prayer'.

We placed the father's venerable body on the boat and took it back to the island of Lindisfarne. It was received by a large crowd which came to meet it and by chanting choirs, and was buried in a stone sarcophagus, in the church of the blessed apostle Peter on the right of the altar.

The many miraculous omens foretelling Cuthbert's sanctity were confirmed when his remains were disinterred in 698. Symeon of Durham – who himself handled the same remains at the later translation in 1104 – records how they were discovered to be undecayed after eleven years laid in earth.

When eleven years had passed since the period of his death, the brethren opened his tomb, and found his corpse quite as fresh as if he had recently been buried. The limbs were flexible, and his whole appearance was more like that of a man who was asleep than of one dead: the vestments also in which he was clothed not only were entire, but they exhibited as marvellous a freshness and sheen as they had done when they were new. Seeing this, the brethren were immediately struck

50

with such great fear and trembling that they scarce dared to speak, scarce to look upon the miracle which was revealed to them, scarce did they know what to do ...

Having wrapped the body in new raiment and placed it in a new shrine, they deposited it, with the reverence to which it was entitled, upon the pavement of the sanctuary. But the brethren took a portion of his hair, that they might have something to give, as a relic, to such of his friends as asked for the same, or to show in proof of the miracle.

This dramatic revelation of the uncorrupt remains provided the great impetus for the burgeoning cult of Cuthbert. The scriptorium at Lindisfarne which had produced the great gospel books of Durrow, Echternach and Durham, responded with the work acknowledged as the manuscript masterwork of Northumbria's golden age and commissioned in the same year of 698. The Lindisfarne Gospels are remarkable not only for the splendour of calligraphy and decoration but for their dedication, which is inscribed not to the apostle Peter to whom the church was dedicated but instead 'for God and Saint Cuthbert'.

The first of the three principal Cuthbertan hagiographies, the 'anonymous' *Life of Cuthbert* commissioned by Eadfrith, bishop of Lindisfarne and himself accredited as the scribe of the great gospel book, was completed within five years of the disinterment. It was swiftly followed by Bede's 'Metrical' *Life* which prompted the Lindisfarne community to request a second hagiography from the scholar-monk of Jarrow, the masterly 'Prose' *Life* which is dedicated to Bishop Eadfrith. These two Bedan *Lives* were to establish the cult of Cuthbert far beyond the confines of Northumbria and a letter from the abbot at Jarrow to Lul, archbishop of Mainz, confirms that copies of 'the books about the man of God, Cuthbert, composed in verse and prose' had reached as far as the Rhine by 764. Less than twenty years later, when Alcuin was the outstanding luminary at the court of Charlemagne, all the evidence confirms that copies of the *Lives* were prominent in his personal library. For Alcuin, steeped in the Cuthbertan tradition, there was no hesitation in comparing the desecration of the 'church of Cuthbert' with the devastations of Jerusalem, Nineveh and Rome.

Lindisfarne's greatly enhanced stature in the decades after 698 carried with it greater wealth and its endowed landholdings, 'the patrimony of Cuthbert', extended over much of northern Northumberland, south into Yorkshire and north to the coast of Lothian. Its prominence as shrine and sanctuary inevitably entangled the holy island in the political turbulence which bedevilled the secular history of eighth-century Northumbria. When the warrior king Eadbert faced what appears to have been an attempted coup in 750, the bishop of Lindisfarne offered sanctuary to the pretender Offa, claimed as a son of the late king Aldfrith. Symeon betrays the sympathies of his sources when he records the summary brutality of royal retribution in his *History of the Church of Durham.*

> During the reign of Eadbert, who succeeded Ceolwulf, the bishopric of the church of Lindisfarne was held by Cynewulf for some considerable length of time, but under many annoyances and misfortunes. One of the royal family, named Offa, in order to escape from the persecutions of his enemies, fled to the body of Saint Cuthbert, but having been forcibly dragged away from it, he was wickedly put to death. Hereupon king Eadbert, highly displeased, laid hold upon bishop Cynewulf, and commanded him to be imprisoned in Bebbanburh ... until the king becoming appeased released Cynewulf from his confinement, and permitted him to return to his church.

Lindisfarne's long history as the royal church of the legitimate line of Ida enmeshed the monastery and its bishops in some strange alliances when the eighth-century kingdom became the tarnished prize of the squabbles between illegitimate lines of Idings.

Such a sympathy might explain Lindisfarne's sanctuary for the pretender Offa, son of Aldfrith, son of Oswy, as well as account for the hostility of Eadbert who claimed the kingdom through an illegitimate son of Ida. Symeon implies a similar Lindisfarne sympathy for the thane who contrived the succession of Osred, son of 'Alcred, as some say, a descendant of king Ida', when he slew Aelfwald, royal martyr and Eadbert's grandson.

> In the sixth year of [Bishop Higbald's] pontificate, the aforesaid king Aelfwold was miserably murdered by his thane Sicga at a place near the vill called Scytlescester, and was buried in the church of Hexham.

At the site of Aelfwald's murder – the old Roman cavalry fort of Chesters-on-the-Wall – 'light sent down from heaven was seen by many' confirming some local celebration of Aelfwald's sanctity and five years later Sicga the thane took his own life. The *Historia Regum* enters the burial – by whatever strange right of sanctuary – of Sicga, assassin and suicide, on Lindisfarne in 793.

In this year also, thane Sicga, who murdered king Aelfwold, died by his own hand; his body was carried to the isle of Lindisfarne, on the ninth of the kalends of May.

These secular turbulences which washed against his holy island would have been recognised as 'the incursions of fugitives' foretold by Cuthbert himself when he warned that 'you will find the presence of my body a great burden to you'. The sanctity of the saint and his shrine stood far above such disorders of the times and, in the event, the burial of Sicga survives as no more than a footnote to the more dramatic occurrence of the year 793.

'What should be expected,' asked Alcuin, 'for other places, when the divine judgement has not spared this holy place?'

His anxiety must have centred on another Northumbrian monastery which, more than any other, represented the intellectual wellspring of Alcuin's world. That church was the double foundation at Wearmouth and Jarrow, dedicated to Saint Peter and Saint Paul but already best renowned by the end of the eighth century as the monastic home of the Venerable Bede. Alcuin's anxiety prompted the urgent advice of his letter of 793 to the monks of *Wiuraemuda* and *In Gyrwum.*

> Keep most diligently to the life of the rule which your holy fathers, Benedict and Ceolfrid, decreed for you ... Consider whom you have as your defence against the pagans who have appeared on your coasts. Set not your hope on arms, but on God. Trust not to carnal flight, but in the prayer of your forefathers. Who does not fear the terrible fate which has befallen the church of the holy Cuthbert?
>
> You also dwell by the sea out of which this pestilence is come ...

The spiritual significance of Lindisfarne was mirrored in the realm of the intellect by Wearmouth/Jarrow where the Venerable Bede, described by Alcuin as 'the most noble teacher of our age', had been interred in 735. The esteem in which the whole of medieval Europe held the great scholar of Jarrow is well reflected in Symeon's eulogy from twelfth-century Durham.

> During his lifetime this Beda lay hidden within a remote corner of the world, but after his death his writings gave him a living reputation over every portion of the globe.

The library in which he had worked, rivalled only and later by York as the finest in England, and the accomplished scriptorium which had first set his works so splendidly on vellum were the legacy of the founding abbot, Benedict Biscop, and his successor, Ceolfrith.

Benedict Biscop was one of the most extraordinary personalities of Anglo-Saxon Northumbria. He was the first recorded English bibliophile and the first Northumbrian, even the first Englishman, to set foot in Rome since the end of the *Pax Romana*. He had been a thane at the court of Oswy at the height of the power of the Northumbrian kingdom until his intellectual interests took him on the extensive continental travels which inspired his future achievement. He visited seventeen monasteries throughout Italy and Gaul and entered holy orders at the island monastery of Lérins near Cannes in the mid-660s. On his return to Northumbria he made a great impression on Oswy's son and successor, Egfrith, who granted him lands at the mouth of the Wear for the foundation of his first monastery.

It was on those lands – around the modern town of Sunderland – that Bede was born in 673 and given, as a boy of eight, into the care of the monastery. His *Lives of the Abbots* provides the most authoritative contemporary account of the foundation, construction and decoration of the church of Saint Peter at *Wiuraemuda*.

This monastery was built in the year of our Lord 674.

Only a year after the foundation of the monastery, Benedict crossed the sea to Gaul, where he looked for stonemasons to build him a church of stone in the Roman style that he had always loved; and he hired some and brought them back. He displayed so much enthusiasm in the work of building the church, out of love of blessed Peter to whom it was to be dedicated, that within the space of a single year from the laying of the foundations the roof was in place, and you might have seen the solemn rites of the Mass being celebrated inside. As the work neared completion, he sent representatives to Gaul to bring back glass-makers, craftsmen as yet unknown in Britain, to glaze the windows of the church, its side-chapels and upper storey ... lamps for its living-quarters and vessels of many other kinds. In addition, Benedict's devotion led him to buy and have transported from overseas all the sacred vessels and vestments needed for the service of the altar and the church, because he could not obtain them at home.

Tireless in providing for his church, he determined that the means to adorn and protect it that were unobtainable even in Gaul should be brought from Rome; and after ordering his monastery under the life of a Rule, he completed his fourth journey there, and returned with a wealth of spiritual treasures more varied than ever before. First, he brought back a great number of books of every kind. Secondly, he brought a plentiful supply of relics of the blessed apostles and martyrs of Christ, to the future benefit of many English churches.

He brought back to adorn the church ... paintings of sacred subjects, a picture of the blessed Mother of God, Mary ever virgin, and of the twelve apostles, with which to span the central nave of the church from wall to wall on a wooden entablature; scenes from the gospels, to adorn the south wall of the church; and the visions of the Apocalypse of Saint John to adorn the north wall.

Within a decade of the foundation at Wearmouth, a further endowment of land from King Egfrith enabled Biscop's second monastic foundation at *In Gyrwum* where the Don flows into the Tyne at Jarrow. Bede's *Lives of the Abbots* describes the place where he came from Wearmouth as a boy of no more than ten and spent the remaining years of his life in the scholarly endeavours which were to mould the entire course of medieval learning.

King Egfrith ... seeing that the land he had granted him for building a monastery had borne good fruit, increased his gift by the additional grant of an estate of forty hides. A year later, with King Egfrith's approval, or rather, at his bidding, Benedict sent about seventeen monks there with the priest Ceolfrith as abbot, and built a monastery dedicated to the blessed apostle Paul, on the understanding that the two foundations should be united in the same spirit of peace and harmony.

The monastery at Jarrow was dedicated on 23rd April 685 and soon afterwards Benedict Biscop set out on his fifth journey to Rome from which he brought back 'a rich store of countless valuable gifts for his churches'. Sacred paintings for the decoration of Saint Paul's accompanied a quantity of books to lay the foundation of its library. Bede tells how Ceolfrith succeeded to the abbacy on Biscop's death in 690.

He then for twenty-eight years exercised enlightened rule over both monasteries, or to speak more accurately, over the one monastery of the blessed apostles Peter and Paul founded on two separate sites. All the splendid works of piety begun by his predecessor he set himself to complete with equal energy. He built more oratories, and he enlarged the stock of vessels for the altar and church and that of every kind of vestment. He doubled the number of books in the library of each monastery, with an energy equal to Abbot Benedict's urgency in founding them. For example, he had three pandects of the new translation of the scriptures copied to add to the copy of the old translation which he had brought back from Rome; and on his return to Rome in old age he took one of these with him among his gifts, leaving the other pair to the two monasteries.

The sole example of Ceolfrith's three great copies of Saint Jerome's Vulgate Bible to survive intact is the *Codex Amiatinus* intended as his gift to the Pope in 716 and preserved today in the Laurentian Library in Florence. Its calligraphy and decoration represent the Wearmouth/Jarrow counterpart of the Lindisfarne Gospels and its seventy-five pounds weight of calfskin vellum an enormous investment in time and money far beyond the resources of most monasteries. Benedict Biscop and his successor had not only created an intellectual powerhouse virtually unrivalled in Europe, but they had housed it in a splendidly-appointed dual foundation of enormous wealth.

Alcuin's anxiety for those 'who dwell by the sea' at Wearmouth and Jarrow is fully justified by the evidence of the northern recension of the *Chronicle* for the year 794.

> Ann. DCC.XCIV. ... And the heathens ravaged among the Northumbrians, and plundered Egferth's mynster at Donemuth; and there one of their leaders was slain, and also some of their ships were wrecked by a tempest, and many of them were there drowned, and some came to shore alive, and they were there slain at the mouth of the river.

For Symeon of Durham, describing these events as the conclusion to his chapter *Concerning the Destruction of the Church of Lindisfarne,* this was the divine retribution exacted for the 'havoc of heathen men' of the year before.

> Yet this was not unavenged; for God speedily judged them for the injuries which they had inflicted upon Saint Cuthbert.
>
> In the following year, when they were plundering the port of king Egfrith, that is, Jarrow, and the monastery which is situated at the mouth of the river Don, their leader was put to a cruel death; and shortly afterwards their ships were shattered and destroyed by a furious tempest; some of themselves were drowned in the sea, while such of them as

succeeded in reaching the land alive speedily perished by the swords of the inhabitants.

The historical substance of these accounts falls under the shadow of uncertainty cast by the dwindling documentary record of Northumbria in the viking age. Evidence for the existence of a comparatively obscure monastery also called *Donemuth* further to the south in what is now Yorkshire has prompted historians to wonder whether the raid entered by the chronicler actually fell on Jarrow at all. Even if it did, there remains the question of whether it fell only on Jarrow, or on Wearmouth, or on both. Symeon evidently believed it to have been a raid on Jarrow, but Joseph Stevenson, the editor and translator of both the *History of the Church of Durham* and the *Historia Regum*, suspected that *Wiuraemuda* rather than *Donemuth* had been intended by their long-lost earliest sources.

Symeon's account was undoubtedly coloured by what he knew to have been the condition of Wearmouth and Jarrow discovered by the post-Conquest churchmen who sought out the sites of Bede's monastery in the later twelfth century. They record nothing of whatever residual community might have survived at Jarrow, but their description of the ruins would well correspond to destruction by the northmen.

> The monastery of the blessed apostle Paul, which had been erected at Jarrow by its former abbot Benedict, the unroofed walls of which were alone standing, ... exhibited scarce any vestige of their ancient dignity.

> The monastery of the blessed apostle Peter, in Wearmouth, which had formerly been a noble and august fabric, as it is described by Beda, who had resided in it from his infancy; but at the period of which we are speaking, its original state could scarce be traced, in consequence of the ruinous condition of the buildings.

The more recent investigation of the same sites by Professor Rosemary Cramp sets the twelfth-century evidence into the context of modern archaeology. Evidence of the firebrand was found at both sites, including badly burnt fragments of architecture and ash at Wearmouth and floor surfaces blackened by fire at Jarrow. The Jarrow excavation turned up fragments of glass from the south windows and lead inside the south wall, all of them melted and distorted by heat.

Professor Cramp does not confirm whether these destructions were a result of viking raiding or of later eleventh-century attacks by the Scots, and, however likely the former, the historical evidence blames the invading northmen of the later ninth century rather than the raiders of 794. Symeon's evidence most firmly points to the onslaught of the 'great army' on Northumbria in 866–7 as the occasion of the destruction of Wearmouth/Jarrow.

> We may reckon that two hundred and eight years had passed from the time when the pagans had ruined the churches, and destroyed and burnt down the monasteries, in the province of the Northumbrians, until the third year of the pontificate of Walcher [1074], when the monastic mode of life began to revive in that province.

Whatever the extent of its impact, the first viking raid on Wearmouth/Jarrow did not mark the end of Bede's monastery. It was, moreover, evidently resisted and Alcuin's advice to 'set not your hope on arms' implied that the monks themselves had been prompted by the Lindisfarne experience to plan for their own defence. Beyond those observations, the further reconstruction of the raid of 794, even to the identification of the raiders' targets on Tyne and Wear, remains, as so often, a matter for speculation.

The *Historia Regum* specifies the 'pagans ravaging the harbour of king Egfrith ... at the mouth of the river Don' and indicates the natural harbour of Jarrow Slake to the west of the monastery. For all Bede's presentation of Wearmouth/Jarrow as 'one monastery in two places', there was no direct route between the two sites over the marshy ground to the south and east of Jarrow – from which incidentally its name *In Gyrwum* from the Old English *Gyrwas*, or 'marsh-dwellers', derived. Professor Cramp has suggested a probable monastic route along the road shown on early maps to run west of Wearmouth through Hedworth and Monkton – both later possessions of Jarrow – to join the Roman road from South Shields. The northmen would have been doing no more than anticipate their extensive use of Roman roads in later decades if they had used the monks' way to extend their attack from one monastery to the other.

It may even have been this hazardous extension of 'hit and run' raiding which delayed their escape until the weather worsened and allowed the mustering of some resistance, if not of armed monks then of a local levy. Whatever its historical value, local tradition associates the resistance to the sea-raiders with Wearmouth, where I was told of 'two Danish kings' who had been hung outside the church of Saint Peter. If such folklore needs be recruited to supplement the fractured formal history of the viking age in Northumbria, it might serve to indicate how suddenly the rich record of a hundred and twenty years of Biscop's foundation expires with the entry of the raid of 794.

The impact on the sea-raiders of their own injuries suffered in 794 is, of course, unrecorded, but there is only sparse evidence of any further viking onslaught on the northern English between 794 and the invasion of the great army more than seventy years later. That apparent remission from the northmen's fury must indicate an effective failure of either the nerve of the sea-raiders or of the northern historical record. There are, nonetheless, fragments of evidence for some persistence of raiding on the Northumbrian coast. The best example is found in the *Flores Historiarum* of the St Albans chronicler Roger of Wendover. Roger's 'Flowers of History', although sometimes discredited by its mis-attribution to the often unreliable Matthew Paris, must have been drawing on material from the lost northern history for its entry at the year 800.

> The most impious army of the pagans cruelly despoiled the churches of Hertenes and of Tinemutha, and returned with its plunder to the ships.

Bede confirms 'a monastery at the mouth of the Tyne' in the early eighth century which reappears as the post-Conquest priory at Tynemouth and this church must have been the target of the raid entered by Roger of Wendover. *Hertenes* is less firmly identified. It has been suggested as Hartlepool where Bede located 'the monastery named Heruteu, meaning the island of the hart ... founded by Christ's devout servant Heiu, who is said to have been the first woman in the kingdom of the Northumbrians to take the vows and habit of the religious life'. Recent archaeological investigation at Hartlepool has revealed no evidence for viking raiding and even indicates that Heiu's church had been abandoned before 800. The *Historia Regum* records a church in *Heorternysse* – or Billingham on the Tees to the south of Hartlepool – built by Egred, bishop of Lindisfarne, in 854 and this might well have been a restoration of the earlier foundation of *Hertenes* destroyed by vikings in 800.

Such construction on fragmentary survivals is once again largely speculation, although it can call on the support of Sir David Wilson – the eminent authority on the northern world and former Director of the British Museum – when he wrote that 'we may assume that during the whole period up to 834, a year which appears to be a turning-point in the history of the Vikings in England, the Scandinavians were present on the coasts of northern Britain'.

Whatever may have been the persistent but unrecorded presence of sea-raiders on the northern English coast, the tide of the viking onslaught was running fast against the islands of the western sea. Within twelve months of the year AD 794, it was to reach its first ferocious flood.

'vastatio i-columcille'

Islands of the Western Sea,
AD 795–825

'My mind and heart have been sore troubled', saith
Columcille, 'by a vision that hath been given me ...
for at the end of time men will besiege my churches,
and they will kill my monks and violate my sanctuary,
and ravage and desecrate my burial-grounds.'

*Betha Colaim Chille**

* *Betha Colaim Chille.* The 'Life of Columcille' compiled by Manus O'Donnell in
1532 from Columban traditions of great antiquity.

Vastatio omnium insularum Britanniae a gentilibus.

'The devastation of all the islands of Britain by the heathens' recorded under the year AD 793 in the *Annals of Ulster* is the first entry in a grim catalogue of the northmen's fury which was to dominate the historical record of Ireland and Scotland for the greater part of the following two centuries.

All the Irish annals are medieval or later compilations from earlier records and the *Annals of Ulster*, set down in Fermanagh in the fifteenth century, are accounted amongst the most authoritative by virtue of their meticulous transcription of sources of far greater antiquity including, most prominently for the eighth century and earlier, the lost chronicle of Iona. Thus, taking account of the Ulster annalist's dates being consistently in arrears by one year throughout this period*, the entry at '793' represents a sudden eruption of viking raiding on the western isles as it was recorded by the monastic community of Iona in the year 794.

The annals of Ireland are invariably sparing of descriptive detail, but the exceptionally imprecise entry in the *Annals of Ulster* reflects its own original source's record of events some distance from Iona. All the collateral evidence – from Dicuil's account of hermits driven from the northern isles by pirates to Snorri Sturlusson's description of *Orkneyjar* as 'a vikings' lair' – confirms that the sea-raiders had established their forward bases on Orkney and Shetland by the last decade of the eighth century.

The significant discovery by archaeologists at Skaill in Orkney of a spearhead in a style out of use after 800 confirms the testimony of both Dicuil and Snorri and – taken with the absence of evidence of eighth-century settlement – fully corresponds to the northern isles serving as winter roosts for viking warbands. The predominance of workshops in the celebrated Scandinavian settlement known - but only since the nineteenth century - as 'Jarlshof' at Sumburgh on Shetland serves to emphasise its origin as a 'service station' for viking longships. In this context, the sudden onslaught of sea-raiders entered in the English and Irish sources for 793/4 must represent a substantial viking fleet, having overwintered in the northern isles, rounding Cape Wrath and striking south into the islands of the Hebridean archipelago in the summer raiding season.

When the Norse king Magnus Olafsson called 'bareleg' made his

---

* All subsequent Irish annal references are given with *recte* dating to correspond with the true historical date for the annal entry.

'royal cruise' to enforce his sovereignty over the northern and western isles in 1098 he followed the same sea-road in much the manner of his viking forbears three hundred years before. King Magnus' *skald* Bjorn 'Cripplehand' celebrated the rapacious royal progress in vivid detail which might reasonably serve to reconstruct the surge of sea-raiding of 794.

> In Lewis isle with fearful blaze,
> the house-destroying fire plays,
> to hills and rocks the people fly,
> fearing all shelter but the sky.
> In Uist the king deep crimson made
> the lightning of his glancing blade;
> the peasant lost his land and life,
> who dared to bide the Norseman's stride.
> The hungry battle-birds were filled
> in Skye with blood of foemen killed,
> and wolves on Tiree's lonely shore,
> dyed red their hairy jaws in gore.

If the 'devastation of all the islands of Britain' followed this same viking course then it must have represented the plundering of countless homesteads and hermitages – none of them recorded in any detail by the annals – and the slaughter of unnumbered islanders. The ominous entry at 794 in the *Annals of Ulster* transcribed a tocsin sounding out for all the holy places of the saints of the western sea.

By the last decade of the eighth century the western seaboard of what is now Scotland had been an effective dominion of the Irish Gael for some two hundred years. This kingdom of Scotic Dalriada centred on Argyll had asserted various measures of independence from the Irish mainland since the last quarter of the sixth century and through the following two hundred years its territory extended north of the Clyde estuary, through Islay and Jura, Kintyre and Mull, even as far east as the Firth of Moray.

The ancient Strathclyde of the Britons still maintained its power base in the fortress of *Alcluith* on Dumbarton Rock as it had against the unrelenting pressure of Dalriada and Northumbria for four centuries. The Scottish mainland east of the Great Glen and the

Grampian range was still the territory of the Pictish tribes who had survived Roman and English invasions to remain 'the last men on earth, the last of the free' since prehistoric times. Pictland was finally to succumb by the second half of the ninth century to the eastward expansion of Scotic Dalriada and to be absorbed into the new Gael-dominated kingdom of *Alba*, the embryo of the Scottish nation.

So it was that the coming of the northmen in the west, which would play its own role as catalyst in that shaping of the Scottish nation, fell first on the seaboard of the Gael and there most furiously on the island monasteries of the Columban church as they were numbered by the Old Irish *Life of Columcille*.

> A hundred churches lapped by the wave:
> that is the number of his churches on the sea-coast.
> Or indeed, a hundred churches with perfect abundance.
> Mass-chalices in every church.

There is evidence for the west coast of Scotland as a prehistoric 'pirate coast' in folk-memories preserved in Scottish and Irish tradition recalling the predatory *Fomoire* who are believed to have been a proto-Pictish survival from the Bronze and Iron Age peoples of the northern isles. The early sources record punitive campaigns waged by warrior kings of Pictland and Dalriada against pirate warbands in the waters around Orkney through the sixth and seventh centuries, but when the annals and martyrologies entered 'the burning of the martyrs of Eigg by sea-pirates' in 618 they were recording an isolated atrocity blamed by tradition on a pagan Pictish queen.

There had also been sea-raiders among the Gael of Dalriada – the most infamous of them the renegade tribe of Loarn, son of Erc – and Adamnan's *Life* of Columcille tells of more than one confrontation of the saint with sea-robbers who were either thrown back in awe of the holy man born of a dynasty of warrior kings or doomed to suffer savage supernatural consequences.

It is a fact too rarely emphasised that the monks of the west bore the very least resemblance to the 'holy water priests' of medieval Chaucerian caricature. They were, of necessity, hardy islanders whose faith had been tempered by wind and wave. Just such is the theme of an ancient quatrain from the Old Irish *Life of Columcille*.

> Wondrous the warriors who abode in Iona,
> thrice fifty in the monastic rule.

> With their boats along the main sea,
> three score men a-rowing.

Their veins still ran with the blood of the fighting Celt and it had been less than a hundred years since the *Cain Adomnain* – the 'Law of Adamnan' proclaimed at Birr in 697 – had proscribed ecclesiastics along with women and children from active participation in 'hosting' for battle.

For all that background, nothing could have saved the holy men of the western sea from the onslaught of the northmen. The great seapower boasted by Scotic Dalriada in its sixth-century ascendancy had long declined and the once-mighty Pictish warfleets were no longer a power in the northern oceans. The island monasteries had been strategically sited on the seaways from Ireland just as the 'hermitages in the ocean' had been chosen for their remote seclusion at the world's edge. Now they found themselves directly in the path of an alien sea-raider skilled like no other in handling fighting ships and wielding war-axe, firebrand and long-bladed sword unrestrained by any recognition of shrine or sanctity.

The ninth tenet of the Rule of Columcille demanded of the holy man 'a mind prepared for the red martyrdom'. When the annals for the year 795 record the southward thrust of the northmen through the inner Hebrides, around Malin Head, and against the islands off the west coast of the Irish mainland, they leave no doubt that the time of that red martyrdom was at hand.

First the *Annals of Ulster* at the year 795:

> The burning of Rechra by the heathens
> and Sci was pillaged and wasted.

The annalist's 'Sci was pillaged' represents the longships striking down *Scotland-fjord* – as the northmen were to call their course in the lee of the Hebrides – towards the Isle of Skye. While there were foundations recorded on Skye itself, they were no more than outposts of either Iona or the important monastery at Applecross on the mainland peninsula across the Sound of Raasay. This was the *Apur Croscan* of Maelrubai, called 'the apostle of the Picts' by the *Martyrology of Gorman,* and was certainly the target of the sea-raiders of 795.

66

Maelrubai, abbot of Bennchair; he was of the Cenel-Eogain, and he blessed a church in Apur Croscan in Scotland.

Maelrubai was a close contemporary of Cuthbert of Lindisfarne, born into a clan of the Ui-Neill dynasty. He had been an alumnus and abbot of Saint Comgall's monastery at Bangor in County Down before he set sail in 671 from his native Ireland, as had Columcille a century before, to seek the 'white martyrdom of pilgrimage' in Scotic Dalriada. The foundation of his church at Applecross in the following year is entered in all the annals as is his death there fifty years later. Maelrubai's obituary is most fully entered at 722 in the authoritative annals set down by the monk Tigernach at Clonmac-nois in the eleventh century.

> Maelrubai rested in Applecross, after completing the eightieth year of his life, three months and nineteen days; on the eleventh day before the kalends of May, the third day of the week.

Tigernach's meticulous detail bears its own testimony to the stature of the saint who had evangelised the Picts across Skye and as far as Loch Broom near modern Ullapool. The success of his mission must have generously endowed his church at Applecross with Pictish silver, perhaps even bearing comparison with the eighth-century hoard found on Saint Ninian's Isle in Shetland. These twenty-eight items of silverwork – plaques, brooches and drinking bowls engraved with Pictish symbols – were buried in the sands of Saint Ninian's Isle to escape the northmen and await the archaeologist's spade, but whatever comparable treasure might have been plundered from Applecross disappeared aboard the longships as they sailed on towards the Irish mainland.

The late Donegal compilation known as the *Annals of the Four Masters* draws on the widest range of historical and traditional sources. Their entry at 795 adds independent detail to 'the burning of Rechra' recorded by the *Annals of Ulster.*

> The burning of Rechrainn by the plunderers; and its shrines were broken and plundered.

Rathlin, lying off the coast of Antrim and directly on the sea-road from Scotic Dalriada, was a daughter house of Iona and formed a part of the confederation or *paruchia* of monasteries founded by Columcille and his successor abbots. The *Annals of the Four Masters* enter its foundation at the year 635.

> Segine, abbot of Iona of Columcille, founded the church of Rechrainn.

Other than the note of its foundation virtually nothing more is recorded of Rathlin in the annals until the raid of 795, although Adamnan knew of it as *Rechrea insula* which lay beyond the 'whirlpool of Brecan' on the sea crossing from Iona to Ireland described in his *Life* of Columcille. There is no surviving record of whatever shrines were 'broken and plundered' by the northmen but they can be fairly assumed to have been reliquaries sufficiently richly-wrought to invite the sea-raider's attention. The church on Rathlin island evidently survived the raid of 795 and recovered to attract another raid by the northmen in 973 when the annals record the slaughter of its abbot Feradach 'crowned as a martyr by the Danes'.

For all the brevity of the annal record, the first raid on Rathlin was significant enough to merit entry in the Welsh 'Chronicle of the Princes', the *Brut y Tywyssogion*, as the first viking onslaught through the North Channel.

> 795 was the Year of Christ when the pagans first came to Ireland
> and Racline was destroyed.

The *Annals of Inisfallen* – an eleventh-century compilation numbered among the earliest of the annals of Ireland – chronicle what seems to have been a further wave of viking raiders down the western seaboard of Scotland and the Irish mainland in 795.

> Devastation of I-Columcille,
> and of Inis Muiredaig,
> and of Inis Bo Finne.

In just a dozen words the Inisfallen annalist sets down the sole surviving record of the first deep thrust of the northmen into the very heart of the Celtic church.

Ironically the island monastery of *Inis Bo Finne* – Inishbofin off the south-west coast of Mayo – had been founded by a former bishop of Lindisfarne and as a consequence of crisis in the seventh-century

Northumbrian church. The victory of the Roman over the Celtic orthodoxy in synod at Whitby in 664 marked the end of Lindisfarne as the 'Iona in the east' and prompted its bishop Colman to return with his monastic company to I-Columcille. Bede's *Historia Ecclesiastica* provides the most detailed account of the foundation of Inishbofin when it follows Colman's long road home, first to Iona – or *Hii* in Bede's Old English form – and on to Ireland.

Colman, who was a bishop from Ireland, left Britain and took with him all the Irish whom he had gathered on Lindisfarne; and also about thirty men of the English race, both groups being thoroughly instructed in the monastic way of life.

He went first to the island of Hii, from where he had been appointed to preach the word to the English. He then withdrew to a small and remote island off the west coast of Ireland, called Inisboufind, meaning the island of the white heifer. On his arrival there he built a monastery and housed in it the monks whom he had assembled from both races and brought with him.

They were unable to live in harmony with each other, as in summertime, when the harvest had to be gathered, the Irish left the monastery and strayed in different directions over the country which was familiar to them; yet they returned on the approach of winter, expecting to share in the supplies provided by the English. Colman, therefore, looked for a means of healing the dispute, and after searching everywhere far and near he found a place suitable for building a monastery on the Irish mainland, called in the Irish language Mag éo. He bought a small part of it on which to build a monastery from the nobleman to whose estate it belonged, on condition that the monks who settled there should offer prayers to the Lord for the provider of the land. The monastery was built at once with the help of the nobleman and all his neighbours, and Colman housed the English there, leaving the Irish on the island. This monastery is still occupied by Englishmen.

While Colman's foundation on the mainland became renowned among the Irish as 'Mayo of the Saxons' and had grown even by Bede's time 'from its modest beginning to a large monastery', Inishbofin retained the eminence of the mother church and remained the island shrine for the relics which Colman had brought from Lindisfarne. Bede tells how 'Colman on his departure for home took with him some of the bones of the most reverend father Aidan' and the *Annals of Ulster* confirm that he carried them with him when he sailed from Iona to Inishbofin in 668.

The voyage of Bishop Colman, with the relics of the Saints,
to Inis-bo-finde, in which he founded a church.

Relics of so esteemed a saint as Aidan of Lindisfarne could only have
been housed in the richest of reliquaries and the remains of Colman
– 'the praiseworthy bishop from the island of the white cow'
according to the eighth-century *Martyrology of Oengus* – would have
been similarly enshrined as befitted the founding father after his
death in the early 670s.

The sea-raiding northmen bold enough to venture so far down the
west coast of Ireland must have been rewarded with the finest of
plunder when the shrines were broken on Inishbofin.

For all their quest of slaves and silver, the viking crews had regular
need to take on board fresh water and revictual their longships. Such
was the purpose of the raiding for livestock and comestible plunder –
called *strandhögg* – which featured in every voyage west-over-sea and
it would have been excellently satisfied when the dragonships
descended on *Inis Muiredaig*. Inishmurray in Donegal Bay off the
coast of Sligo is still the outstanding example of a large and fertile
monastic settlement on the evidence of the extensive archaeological
remains which are considered amongst the most remarkable in
Ireland. They include an immense stone wall surviving from the
cashel which housed the monastery's great wealth of livestock, in
addition to a number of oratories surrounded by beehive monastic
cells and a series of cross slabs marking stations of pilgrimage which
propose *Inis Muiredaig* as an ancient and venerable foundation long-
established before the time of its most celebrated association with
the seventh-century saint Laisren.

Laisren is elsewhere known as Molaise, son of Deglain, and
venerated from Sligo to Arran. Although his obituary is reliably
entered at 639, his life is largely the stuff of legend and his cult was
centred on his enthusiastic endurance of thirty concurrent diseases
as an earthly purgatory for the expiation of sins. The cave hermitage
dedicated to him on Holy Island off Arran is traditionally associated
with his very Cuthbertan friendship with the local seal population,
but it is Inishmurray which has the greatest claim to be his spiritual
home.

Its founding father is more heavily shrouded in the mist of time.
Inis Muiredaig means 'Muredach's Isle' and there are innumerable

Muredachs to be found in the Irish sources, but tradition claims this *Muiredaig* to have been of the dynasty of the Ui-Neill and descended from the first high king of Ireland, Niall of the Nine Hostages. Muredach's anecdotal associations with Patrick in the fifth century and Columcille in the sixth do not help to clarify his dates, but they do confirm his legendary links with the *paruchiae* of both saints and attest the eminent ecclesiastical as well as political standing of his traditional foundation on *Inis Muiredaig*.

A raid on Inishmurray, then, would have been accounted as much an assault on the Columban and Patrician dominions as on the political dignity of the powerful Ui-Neill dynasty. For the northmen it would have represented little more than a chance to revictual their longships which – on the evidence of the *Annals of Inisfallen* – had already devastated the most sacred shrine of the western sea.

Vastatio I-Columcille. The stark Latin of the Inisfallen annalist seems even now to echo the terrible impact of the first 'devastation of Iona of Columcille' in 795.

It was Alcuin of York who had compared Lindisfarne with Jerusalem, but the same comparison might have been even more impressively claimed for Iona. Just as Jerusalem is considered a holy place for all the 'peoples of the Book', Christian, Muslim and Jew, so Iona had for centuries been held sacred by Pict, Gael and northern English since Columcille came ashore from Ireland at the Bay of the Coracle, as it had been hallowed by the pagan Celts in the era before Christ.

'To tell the story of Iona', wrote the nineteenth-century mystic William Sharp, 'is to go back to God and to end in God.' The pre-Christian druids customarily sought out the most ancient landscape for their hallowed places and geological science has confirmed that Iona is formed of the oldest rock of all the earth's crust. In the seventh century after Christ, Adamnan knew it as *Iou-a* – which was corrupted by medieval scribal error into 'Iona' – but it has long been called in the Gaelic simply *I*, which is most evocatively rendered as '*The* Island'.

In the Celtic cosmography of the Gael – as it is echoed in a rune of foretelling from the *Carmina Gadelica* collection of Hebridean tradition – I-Columcille was the first place on earth to be made and will be the last place on earth to be destroyed.

71

Seven years before the Day of Doom,
The sea will come over Erin in one watch,
And over Islay, green, grassy,
But float will Iona of Colum the cleric.

Such was the island chosen by Columcille for the foundation of his church when, 'in the forty-second year of his age [he] sailed from Ireland to Britain, wishing to become a pilgrim for Christ'. Much as their hillforts had served his warrior ancestors as symbols and centres of power, so Iona became the symbol and centre of the earthly dominion of Columcille and, when he was himself laid in its earth in the year 597, the charisma of the most awesome holy man of the Gael became fused with the ancient sanctity of his holy island. *I* was transformed for all time into *I-Columcille.*

Adamnan's *Life* tells how an angel bearing a scourge and book of glass came to Columcille in solitary retreat and commanded him to proclaim Aidan, son of Gabran, *Ri Albain*, 'king of Alba'. When the holy man consecrated the succession of Aidan mac-Gabran on Iona in 574, Iona was confirmed as the royal church of the Scots and northern Irish. Through succeeding centuries warlords and dynasts of Scotic Dalriada, of Pictish and Irish kingdoms, of Anglo-Saxon Northumbria and even – in the fullness of time – of the northmen themselves were borne along its Street of the Dead to lie among the tombs of the kings in the burial ground called *Reilig Odhrain.*

All of this Columcille had foretold in his last benediction on the island as it was set down in the concluding chapter of Adamnan's *Life.*

> Small and mean though this place be, yet it shall be held in great and unusual honour, not only by Scotic kings and people, but also by the rulers of foreign and barbarous nations, and by their subjects; the saints also even of other churches shall regard it with no ordinary reverence.

Such extraordinary reverence was not to emerge entirely unscathed from the temporal and theological power struggles of the seventh century and it was inevitable that the ecclesiastical imperium of I-Columcille would be diminished by the triumph of the Roman persuasion at the Synod of Whitby in 664. The kingdom of Northumbria had turned its allegiance away from Iona just as southern Ireland had chosen the Roman way thirty years before and the Pictish church was to adopt the calendar and custom of 'catholic unity' fifty years later.

Even on Iona itself, in the decade following Adamnan's death in 704, the Paschal schism had divided the monastic *familia* into two factions, each of them celebrating the festival of Easter under its own 'abbot' and according to its own persuasion. It fell at last to Egbert – the monk of Lindisfarne described by Bede as 'a most reverend and holy father and bishop, who had for long been an exile in Ireland for the sake of Christ and was most learned in the scriptures' – to bring the community of Iona into the fold of the *unitas Catholica*.

For all its submission to the letter of Roman orthodoxy, the spirituality of Iona, as of Cuthbert's Lindisfarne, was firmly cast in the old Celtic way. Its decades of isolation may even have served to enhance its mystique as the island at the edge of the world and the lodestar for all the monks of the west. Adamnan's *Life* of Columcille, written when Iona was on the brink of its greatest isolation from 'the whole Church of Christ', could still claim divine appointment for the Columban dominion.

Of what and how high honour in the sight of God our holy and venerable abbot must have been deemed worthy, how great and many were the bright visits of the angels made to him, how full of the prophetic spirit, how great his power of miracles wrought in God, how often and to what great extent, while yet he was abiding in this mortal flesh, he was surrounded by a halo of heavenly light: and how, even after the departure of his most benign soul from the tabernacle of the body, until the present day the place where his sacred bones repose, as has been clearly shown to certain chosen persons, doth not cease to be frequently visited by the holy angels, and illumined by the same heavenly brightness.

And this unusual favour has been conferred by God on this same man of blessed memory; that though he lived in this small and remote island of the Britannic Ocean, his name has not only become illustrious throughout the whole of our own Ireland, and Britain, the largest island of the whole world, but has reached even unto triangular Spain, and into Gaul, and to Italy lying beyond the Pennine Alps; and also to the city of Rome itself, the chief of all cities.

Some seventy years after Adamnan, the appointment of Bresal as the *comarb* or successor of Columcille marked a new high peak for the prestige of Iona among the Irish dynasties. During his three decades of abbatial office, two Irish kings – Nial Froissach, 'high king at Tara', and Artgal mac-Cathal, king of Connaught – retired to become monks on Iona and to be interred in the *Reilig Odhrain* on their

73

deaths in 778 and 791.

It is a sad irony of history that this remarkable abbot who presided over the new ascendancy of I-Columcille lived also to witness its first devastation, because it was in the twenty-fourth year of the abbacy of Bresal that the northmen first fell on Iona.

The Inisfallen annalist provides the only surviving record of the raid and he offers no further evidence for the season or circumstances of the 'devastation of I-Columcille' of 795. His entry of three 'devastations' indicates a viking voyage southward through the Hebrides to the coast of Mayo, but includes no number of slain monks or inventory of plunder. The raid on Iona appears to have been the landfall, even by chance and probably by no more than one or two longships, which served to alert the northmen to a prize of great prospect and to encourage their return to an island monastery entirely undefended and endowed by the generosity of so many Irish, Pictish and Anglo-Saxon kings.

The northmen were in the Hebrides and the North Channel again in 798 according to both the Ulster annalist's note of 'great devastations between Erin and Alba' and the fourteenth-century Munster compilation known as the *'Dublin' Annals of Inisfallen.*

The Hebrides and Ulster plundered by the lochlann.

Like the term *gaill* for 'aliens', *lochlann* – 'men of the lakes' – is often used by all but the very earliest Irish sources to identify the northmen and its precise derivation remains uncertain. It has been suggested as a recognition of 'vikings' as denizens of the fjords, in the sense of the Old Norse *vik* for 'creek' or 'inlet', but it is at least unlikely that the fjords would have been familiar to any scribe in ninth-century Ireland. It might have derived from the later viking stratagem of gathering fleets of longships on the Irish loughs as 'floating fortresses', but might just as probably reflect the sea-raiders infesting the lochs of the Scottish seaboard.

Such a form of usage would correspond – even in the absence of detailed place-names – to the annal entries as a record of sea-raids on Colonsay and Oronsay, Islay and Jura, even Kintyre and across the sea to the coast of Antrim. Against that backdrop the further and greater 'devastation' of Iona was no more than a matter of time when Bresal died in 801 to be succeeded for only twelve months by

Connachtach who is acclaimed as 'the best of scribes' in the *Annals of Ulster* obituary at 802. In the same year of Connachtach's passing the dragonships descended again on Iona, probably in greater numbers and certainly with the firebrand on the evidence of the *Annals of Ulster.*

> I-Columcille was burned by heathens.

Lest there be any doubt, the later *Annals of the Four Masters* attribute the burning to 'the gaill, that is the northmen'. No other viking raids are recorded by any annals for that year, which must indicate that the attack – whether launched from pirate bases in the northern or western isles – was directly targeted on I-Columcille.

All that now survives of the monastery on Iona is the *vallum*, or earthen rampart, which marked its boundary and indicates a monastic settlement centred on the site of the restored medieval priory on the north-east shore of the island. It would have enclosed at least one oratory surrounded by beehive cells, certainly a guesthouse, and a scriptorium which might well have also housed the monastic library. All of these buildings, and whatever lay accommodation was sited outside the vallum, would have been constructed in what Bede calls 'the Irish manner' of wood and wattle. Entirely fragile to the firebrand, their 'burning by the heathen' would have represented nothing less than the total devastation of the mother church of the western sea on the island believed to be indestructible until the Day of Doom.

For all the customary brevity of the annals, the dramatic and urgent response of the new abbot to the burning of I-Columcille provides a most impressive index of the severity of the onslaught. Cellach mac-Congal, who succeeded Connachtach as abbot, had evidently recognised that the northmen were infesting the western seaboard in ominous numbers and the days of the church and community on Iona were inevitably numbered. He resolved to evacuate his *familia* to the greater security of the Irish mainland and his acquisition of a place of sanctuary at Kells in Meath is confirmed by the *Annals of Ulster* in their entry – heavy with portents – at the year 804.

> Great thunder, with wind and lightning, on the night before the feast of Patrick, dispersing a great number of people, that is, a thousand and ten men, in the country of the Corco-Baccinn [in Co. Clare]; and the sea

THE FURY OF THE NORTHMEN

divided the Island of Fita [Mutton Island, off Co. Clare] into three parts.
   The giving of Cenannas [Kells] in this year, without dispute, to Colum-Cille the musical.

The unusual phrasing of the entry indicates its original source as other than Iona. 'Columcille the musical' is a reference to the remarkable quality of the holy man's singing voice celebrated by a quatrain in the Old Irish *Life.*

> The sound of the voice of Columcille,
> Great its sweetness above all clerics.
> To the end of fifteen hundred paces,
> Though great the distance, it was clearly heard.

'Columcille the musical' is not to be found in the known Iona sources and suggests the annalist worked from an Irish original, just as the reference to the 'feast of Patrick' must point to Armagh. The *paruchia* of Saint Patrick could justly claim to be the primacy of Ireland by the end of the eighth century and Cellach of Iona would have turned first to Armagh – whose extensive land-holdings included an outpost at Castlekieran just a few miles from Kells – in his search for a sanctuary on the mainland. Rivalries between Irish monastic *familiae* led often to litigation and even to conflict, but the grant of Kells to Iona was made 'without dispute'. There had been no rivalry between Iona and Armagh to bear any comparison with the long-standing contest over precedence and patrimony between the *paruchiae* of Patrick and Saint Brigid of Kildare and there would have been political advantage for Armagh in alliance with the powerful Ui-Neill dynasty so long the patrons of I-Columcille. Françoise Henry, the historian of early Irish art, has found evidence for Armagh's granting generous refuge to the church of Columcille in the inscription dedicating the ninth-century cross at Kells as the 'Cross of Patrick and Columba' and, even more impressively, by a marginal note in the gospel Book of Armagh – precisely dated to 807 – which enters the name *Cellach* against aptly-chosen verses in the Gospel according to Mark.

> See what manner of stones and what buildings are here!
> ... Seest thou these great buildings?

Having secured the grant of land at Kells, Cellach put swiftly in hand the construction of a church of stone to better withstand the firebrand than the timber oratory and wood-and-wattle monastic cells burned by the northmen on Iona. The *Annals of Ulster* confirm that the mainland refuge for the community of Iona was in progress by 807.

The building of a new monastery of Columcille in Cenannas.

But the sea-raiders out of the north moved at greater speed than the masons of Meath and the sanctuary of Kells was not completed in time to save many monks of Iona from the red martyrdom. A shadow of apocalyptic omen hangs over the entry at the year 806 in the *Annals of Ulster.*

> In which a great plague broke out in Ireland.
>   The community of Iona slain by heathens,
> that is, to the number of sixty-eight.

The *Annals of the Four Masters* add their own independent detail.

> I-Columcille was plundered by the gaill;
> and great numbers of the laity and clergy
> were killed by them, namely sixty-eight.

This was the great martyrdom of the *familia* of Iona of Columcille. The place of slaughter is still commemorated on the island in the local name for the beach of white sand on the eastern shore a short distance to the south of the modern landing-place on Saint Ronan's Bay. *Port nam Mairtir* translates as 'The Bay of the Martyrs'.

If a company of monks from the formal complement of 'thrice fifty in the monastic rule' had accompanied Cellach to Kells – and the abbot himself would have been in Ireland at the time of the raid – then at least half of those remaining on the island must have fallen victim to the northmen. Despite the fact that his new stone church in Meath was still under construction and yet some years from completion, Cellach could delay the plans for evacuation no longer and the survivors of the community on Iona appear to have been brought in the following year across the sea to the sanctuary of Kells.

Nonetheless, I-Columcille seems never to have been entirely abandoned and there is every indication of some residual brotherhood staying on to watch over the tombs of the kings and, more importantly, to stand guard over the shrine of Columcille himself. Cellach may well have intended Kells to serve as only a temporary refuge, even if of some years' duration. If such was his intention history had decreed otherwise. The raid of 806 which had stained with blood so much of the white sand of *Port nam Mairtir* marks the last chapter in the chronicle of Iona as the capital church of the Columban *paruchia*. All the future *comarba* of Columcille were abbots at Kells and the *Annals of Ulster* record how Cellach himself felt it necessary to relinquish the office of abbot before he returned in 814 to end his days on I-Columcille.

> Cellach, abbot of Ia, the building of the church of Cenannas being finished, resigned the abbacy; and Diarmait, foster-son of Daigre, was ordained in his place.

To which the *'Dublin' Annals of Inisfallen* add their entry by way of obituary.

> [In 807] Cellach, abbot of I-Columcille, came to Ireland after the slaying of his people by the lochlann; and the monastery of Columcille was constructed by him in Kells of Meath. And he was abbot there for seven years, and went back to I-Columcille and he was buried there.

The transfer of the community of Columcille from Iona to Kells was the first of the dramatic consequences of Scandinavian expansion in the west. It was an effective recognition of the alien wedge which had been driven between Scotic Dalriada and the Irish mainland and was to redirect the passage of both Alba and Erin through the following medieval centuries.

Against that wider historical canvas, the art history of the 'Insular' gospel manuscripts – so called by reason of their production in island monasteries – must represent little more than a footnote, but the specific case of the manuscript called by the annalist 'the great Gospel of Columcille' is of remarkable and ironic significance. The *Codex Cenannensis*, or Book of Kells, is acknowledged by every authority as the masterwork of the genre, yet had it not been for the fury of the northmen in the islands of the western sea, this 'Book of Kells' would have been known today as the 'Book of Iona'.

The manuscript preserved in the library of Trinity College, Dublin, comprises 340 folios of calligraphy, marginal decoration, and full-page illumination. Its wealth of symbolism, enigma and allusion is entwined within portraiture, zoomorphs, knotwork and spirals reflecting the various influences of Pictish, Celtic, Carolingian, Byzantine and Northumbrian art. Such a remarkable range of inspiration has prompted no less wide-ranging speculation as to the manuscript's place and date of origin, but the greater weight of opinion has settled on the scriptorium on Iona and a date around the year 800. That most probable genesis is confirmed by the annalist's title of the 'great Gospel of Columcille', to which must be added the correspondence of the accepted date of 'around AD 800' for the manuscript with the obituary of Connachtach in the *Annals of Ulster* at 802.

> Connachtach, finest of scribes and abbot of Ia, slept.

The exceptional description of an abbot as the 'finest of scribes' must indicate Connachtach's association with some outstanding work on vellum in the same way as the colophon of the Lindisfarne Gospels confirms that 'Eadfrith, bishop of the church of Lindisfarne, originally wrote this book, for God and for Saint Cuthbert'.

At least four individual artists have been identified as contributing folios to the Book of Kells and, whether or not he was himself its calligrapher, Connachtach must have been responsible for commissioning the book to be made. Beyond that, it is only possible to speculate why an abbot of Iona, who survived no more than twelve months in office and all of them under the real threat of the return of the vikings, should have commissioned a gospel book of such incomparable splendour from masters accomplished in the world's great schools of monastic artistry.

So extraordinary a work can only have been the product of extraordinary circumstances, but such were those surrounding the *comarb* of Columcille in the year 801 on the island foretold as the last place on earth to be destroyed. If Connachtach had not himself witnessed the fury of the northmen, he was at the head of a community which had only recently experienced viking onslaught. In the last months of his life lived out in such a world and time, it would have been a fitting benediction from 'the abbot of Ia and the finest of scribes' to call into being a masterwork on vellum as the last testament of I-Columcille for the sixth age of the world.

Whether by reason of Connachtach's demise or the northmen's fire-raid in the same year, it seems that the gospel book was not to be completed on Iona. It was carried with Cellach's community, probably in 807 or possibly even earlier, to the sanctuary of Kells and it was there, two hundred years later, that its remarkable survival merited the entry in the *Annals of Ulster* at 1007.

> The great Gospel of Columcille was wickedly stolen in the night out of the western sacristy of the great church of Cenannas - the chief relic of the western world, on account of its ornamental cover. The same Gospel was found after twenty nights and two months, its gold having been taken off it, and a sod over it.

The annalist does not identify the thief as a *gaill* or a Gael. He might have been either, or a felon of mixed bloodstock, because the once-alien northmen had, before the end of the tenth century, become inextricably entangled as a contesting dynasty in an Ireland they themselves had transformed into Hiberno–Norse society. Kells lay no great distance to the north of the Leinstermen who had been the first of the Irish to join with the invading Scandinavians and were every bit as capable of thieving the gilt cover from a gospel book.

Two hundred years earlier, Kells in Meath – once the stronghold of the high-kings on a hill above the Blackwater – lay far enough inland to provide some real measure of refuge for the community of Iona when the sea-raiders were preying ever more boldly around the coastline of Ireland on the eve of the ninth century.

Thus was fulfilled the prophecy set down in the Old Irish *Life* as it had been foretold by the druid seer Becc mac-Dé to Columcille beneath the great oak at Kells.

> 'O Becc, tell me,
> as regards spacious, grassy Cenannas,
> what clerics will inhabit it,
> what warriors will abandon it?'
>
> 'It is the clerics who are in this place,
> who sing the praises of the Lord's Son;
> its warriors will depart from its threshold;
> a time will come when it will be secure.'

The viking fleet which had raided the Hebrides and Ulster in 798 had thrust further south through the North Channel into the Irish Sea on the evidence of the *Annals of Ulster.*

> The burning of Inis Patraic by the heathens; and they carried off the tribute of the districts; and the shrine of Dochonna was broken by them; and other great devastations [by them] between Erin and Alba.

It is uncertain which 'Patrick's Isle' is meant by *Inis Patraic*, but there are two likely probabilities. One of the Skerries just off the Irish coast to the north of Dublin is called Saint Patrick's Island, but Peel Island off the Isle of Man might have lain more directly in the path of the sea-raiders. It was anciently known as *Insula Patricii* and must have been one of the hermits' retreats for which Man had earned the attention of the *Tripartite Life of Patrick.*

The reference to the plundering of the 'shrine of Dochonna' has confirmed Peel Island as *Inis Patraic* for those authorities who have sought to identify a *Dochonna* as an early bishop of Man, but the annalist's punctuation does not necessarily associate the shrine-plundering with the same raid as the 'burning of Inis Patraic'. The annalist refers to the shrine as if to that of a holy man still quite familiar in medieval Ireland, which might not have been the case for an obscure Manx ecclesiastic. The intended *Dochonna* is more probably identified as the *Tochonnu* listed by a twelfth-century manuscript of the Adamnan *Life* as one of the twelve monks who accompanied Columcille to Iona, but the whereabouts of his shrine are nowhere recorded.

The annalist's further note that the raiders 'carried off the tribute of the districts' has been suggested as the first reference of the northmen's extortion of the 'protection money' later infamous in the English sources as *Danegeld*, but his use of the word *boruma* might better support an alternative interpretation. *Boruma* is used elsewhere in the Irish sources for the tribute paid over to monastic foundations by their estates. It was usually paid in kind and often in livestock, which would have supplied fresh meat to victual the longships, and the northmen's 'carrying off the tribute of the districts' might be most realistically interpreted as a *strandhögg* akin to that inflicted on Inishmurray.

The documentary record of the Irish annals for the following thirty years is dominated by two recurring themes.

The first is the escalating onslaught of the northmen and the second the dynastic warfare endemic in a Celtic society where every hillfort served as the power base of the local king. The annals for the first quarter of the ninth century continue to enter the interminable sequence of triumphs and disasters of internecine blood-feuds just as they had done for hundreds of years. Aed, high-king of Ireland of the line of Niall, was warring with the men of Leinster and Ulster while the *Cenel Conaill* and *Cenel Eoghain* branches of his own Ui-Neill were fighting with each other, all of them seemingly oblivious to the viking noose tightening around the land of Erin.

By the second quarter of the ninth century, sea-raiding longships had encircled the entire coastline. While the annals cannot represent any complete record of viking incursions, the *Annals of Ulster* confirm that the northmen were striking all along the west coast from Mayo to Kerry in the year 812. In the same way, some number of annal entries of 'slaughter of the heathens' insist that the northmen could not expect to plunder at will without some measure of resistance. The annalists had long been accustomed to recording the eddying fortunes of warband conflict and the defeat, even the implied massacre, of longship crews cornered on land by a well-placed force of Irish fighting-men would be entered in the same terse and dispassionate style as any more familiar domestic conflict. The *Annals of Ulster* provide a characteristic example at 812.

> A slaughter of the heathens by the men of Umhall [Owles of Mayo].
> A slaughter of the heathens by Munstermen, that is by Cobthach son of Madduin, king of Loch Lein.
> A slaughter of the Conmaicni [of Connemara] by the heathens.

Less than a decade later the northmen were raiding on the east coast as far south as Wexford where the *Annals of the Four Masters* record the plundering of two islands in Wexford Haven. In the same year of 821, the *Annals of Ulster* enter the first record of viking slave-taking on the mainland when the longships struck at the Howth peninsula at the north point of Dublin Bay, where the Hill of Howth is still called by its Irish language place-name of *Benn-Etair*.

> The plundering of Etar by heathens;
> a great prey of women being taken therefrom.

The following year, the *Annals of the Four Masters* record the plundering of the coast of Cork and demonstrate that the vikings had fully encircled the mainland of Erin. Every monastery within sight of the sea was at hazard and their inmates must have looked

'The island of Lindisfarne is eight miles in circumference, in which is a noble monastery, the resting place of the bodies of that excellent bishop Cuthbert, and others, his most worthy successors in the episcopate'

Symeon of Durham

Lindisfarne.

'The sixth age of the world ... in which our Lord Jesus Christ will come to judge the living and the dead and the world through fire'

Nennius

Grave marker (obverse), Lindisfarne, 9th century.

'Never before has such terror appeared in Britain as we have now suffered from a pagan race, nor was it thought that such an inroad from the sea could be made ...'

Alcuin

Grave marker (reverse), Lindisfarne, 9th century.

'Seven years before the Day of Doom,
The sea will come over Erin in one watch,
And over Islay, green, grassy,
But float will Iona of Colum the cleric'
                                    Carmina Gadelica

Iona.

'AD 806 I-Columcille was plundered by the gaill; and great numbers of the laity and clergy were killed by them, namely sixty-eight'

                                    Annals of the Four Masters

The Bay of the Martyrs, Iona.

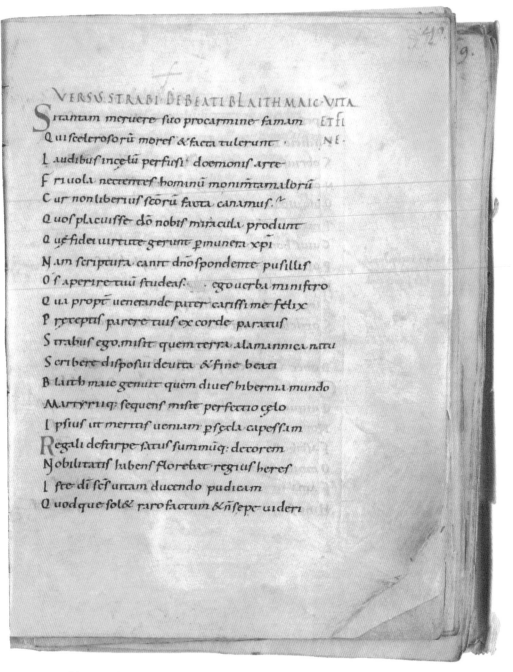

'A certain island lies on the shore of the Picts ... where the saint of the Lord, Columba, rests in the flesh. This island Blathmac sought under his vow to suffer the scars of Christ'

Walafrid Strabo

Walafrid Strabo's *Life of Blathmac*, 9th century: Stiftsbibliotek, St. Gallen, MS 899, f.49ʳ.

'The Arrest of Christ at Gethsemane'

Book of Kells: Trinity College, Dublin, MS A.I.6, f114ʳ.

'This mound was raised before Ragnar Lothbrok's ...'

12th century runic inscription, Maes Howe.

'They took the wooden coffin of Saint Cuthbert, in which till then he had laid at rest, and bore it with them, along with the church's other treasures, and so arrived at the seashore'
Historia de Sancto Cuthberto

Carved lid, Saint Cuthbert's coffin, 7th century.

'As the bearers of the sacred body were proposing to advance, always before their feet appeared a dry flow of sand and a level path for their journey ... So at last, treading safely, they reached the further shore, and on turning back their eyes to the island they saw the whole ambit of the sea flooded with its full volume of water'

Historia de Sancto Cuthberto

Lindisfarne across the pilgrim's causeway.

'Do not be alarmed by the sudden splendour of my appearance, and let not fear of the heathens' fury trouble you any longer ... My name is Cuthbert, a soldier of Christ ... henceforth I shall be your shield, and your friend, and the defender of your sons'

Historia de Sancto Cuthberto

Saint Cuthbert 'wearing episcopal regalia', 13th century wall-painting in the Galilee Chapel, Durham Cathedral.

anxiously at the sky and the seasons for omens of impending doom. It may thus have been that the severe winter entered in the *Annals of Ulster* at 819 was interpreted as such a portent by two prominent ecclesiastics from the east of Ireland when they evacuated the shrines of their saints to places of greater security further inland.

> Unprecedented frost and great snow from Epiphany to Shrovetide.
> Cuano, abbot of Lughmadh [Louth], went in exile to the land of Munster, with the shrine of Mochta.
> Artri, abbot of Ard-Macha [Armagh], went to Connaught with the shrine of Patrick.

For whatever reason, the *comarb* of Comgall at Bangor did not choose to follow the exemplary caution of his fellow churchmen at Louth and Armagh. Sited on the southern point of the shore of Belfast Lough, Saint Comgall's foundation at *Bennchor* was at the greatest hazard from the sea-raiders and the *Annals of Ulster* at 823 record their first assault.

> The heathens invaded Bennchor the Great.

By the first years of the ninth century, 'Bennchor in the Ards' offered, as did all the great Irish monasteries, a dramatic contrast to the remote hermitage of the old Celtic ideal. In the predominantly rural society of early medieval Ireland, the monastic settlement represented the only recognisable semblance of an urban centre. The emergence of the great monasteries from the simple foundations of the saints of earlier centuries is described in a fragment from the last years of the eighth century.

> The little places where hermits settled two or three together are now places of pilgrimage where hundreds, even thousands, gather.

Even before taking account of the supplementary populations of craft and farm workers who supplied their needs and worked their estates, the monastic *familiae* themselves had grown into communities of great numbers, not least at Bangor on the evidence of the *Litany of Irish Saints* set down around 800.

> Four thousand monks with the grace of God
> under the yoke [Rule] of Comgall of Bennchor.

Comgall – who 'kindled in the hearts of men an unquenchable fire of the love of God' according to the *Martyrology of Donegal* – was a contemporary and close personal friend of Columcille and is said to have accompanied the saint on his mission to the hillfort of Bruide mac-Maelchon, high-king of the Picts, near Inverness. Adamnan records a conversation in which the two holy men sadly prophesy the battle fought fifty years later at Dun Cethirn near Coleraine between 'thy kin and mine – that is, the people of the Cruithni and the race of Niall'. Those ancient allegiances of clan and kin are reflected in the comparable standing of Columcille with the Gael and of Comgall with the *Cruithne*, the 'Irish Picts' of Ulster.

Comgall was born the son of a warrior and, like Saint Martin of Tours, served in a 'hosting' before entering the church. Comgall has so much in common, as a soldier-saint, rigorous ascetic and remarkable monastic founder, with the great saint of Tours that his stature is best appreciated as that of the 'Martin of the Irish'.

His first monastery on Ely Island in Lough Erne was followed in 555 by his foundation of Bangor on Belfast Lough. Located at the hub of the sea roads to Dalriada and Pictland, Britain and Gaul, it grew swiftly into a great monastic port which provided the point of departure for the missions to 'Alba of the ravens' of the sixth-century Moluag of Lismore and Maelrubai of Applecross a hundred years later. It was from Bangor that Comgall's contemporary Columbanus set sail in 591 to follow with his companions the route of the wine-ships to Gaul in pursuit of 'voluntary exile for Christ' on the continent.

Bangor certainly encompassed an extensive settlement and the annalist's 'invasion' might be interpreted as a relatively small scale raid on the monastic estates. Whatever the impact of the first raid of 823, it evidently alerted the northmen to another prize of great promise. In the following year the vikings were back, this time to inflict the sacrilege which had been prophesied – according to the *Annals of the Four Masters* – by 'Comgall himself'.

The plundering of Bennchor by the gaill; the oratory was broken, and the relics of Comgall were taken from the shrine in which they were, as Comgall himself had foretold, when he said:
     It will be true, true,
by the will of the supreme King of kings,
     My bones shall be brought without defeat,
from the beloved Bennchor to Eantrobh [Antrim].

When Comgall died in 601, his remains – other than one arm carried as a relic to Leinster by the holy man Fiacre of Airard who had administered his last rites – were enshrined at Bangor. By the end of the eighth century, the shrines of the Irish saints had become symbols of the cultural and material wealth of their *paruchiae*. The relics of Ronan, son of Buite, were encased in 'a shrine of gold and silver' in 800, and the reliquary of so venerated a saint as Comgall would have been at least as richly-wrought when it was broken open in the raid of 824.

It is unlikely that there were any such riches to be plundered when the vikings fell on the archetypal 'hermitage in the ocean' of Skellig Michael in the same year. Having scaled the great rock some eight miles off the coast of Kerry, the sea-raiders won no greater prize than its unfortunate abbot whose martyrdom is entered in the *Annals of Ulster* at 824.

> Etgal of Scelig was carried off by the heathens,
> and died soon after of hunger and thirst.

The tone of the entry suggests that the mere fact of a raid on the great Skellig seems to have astonished the usually dispassionate annalist into adding an uncharacteristic measure of detail and not without reason. The tiny monastic foundation can be reached only in the gentlest of Atlantic swells and even then demands an ascent of the sheer rock face rising up out of the sea to a height of more than 700 feet. The substantial remains of stone-built oratory and beehive cells are still to be seen today, but only by the boldest pilgrim, because this must be the most remote survival of the Irish island hermitages. Nineteenth-century antiquarians found simple bronze crosses there, but it is almost impossible to imagine any great wealth of altar silver in so bleak a holy place, where subsistence must have depended precariously on fish, seabirds' eggs, and prayer.

It is similarly difficult to imagine what the northmen might have hoped to find in such an inaccessible target. A later source* from twelfth-century Munster supplements the annal entry with fragments from tradition telling of Etgal's capture by northmen, his 'escape' – probably meaning escape from the red martyrdom at their hands – and his death by starvation.

---

* *Cogadh Gaedhel re Gallaibh*, 'The War of the Gaedhil with the Gaill'. (See p. 97 below).

Scelig Michil was also plundered by them; and they took Etgal with them into captivity, and it was by a miracle that he escaped, and he died of hunger and thirst with them.

There is no record of its foundation or its founding father, because *Scelig Michil* is a holy place of the greatest antiquity. It had been hallowed, like Iona, in pagan prehistory and its naming for Saint Michael the Archangel – the Christian counterpart to the Celtic sea-god Manann mac-Lir – overlay a much more ancient sanctity.

It had been associated in Irish tradition with the wars of the hero Finn mac-Cumhall and found its way – albeit erroneously – into Hiberno–Norse tradition as the holy place where the Norse king Olaf Tryggvasson was baptised a Christian at the end of the tenth century. *Olaf Tryggvasson's Saga* records his conversion as taking place in *Scyllingar,* the Old Norse form of the Isles of Scilly which a medieval Irish scribe read as meaning the *Scelig.* The Munster source confirms the survival of the monks on Skellig Michael after the raid of 824. It was to be raided twice more by the northmen in the ninth century, but the 'abbots of Skellig' entered in the annals of the eleventh century were based at Ballinskelligs, 'the sanctuary of the rock' for the community which had abandoned the Skellig for the mainland.

In the following year of 825, the longships were off the coast of Down again to raid the easier and certainly more lucrative target of the church of Saint Finnian of Moville.

Nothing now survives of his foundation at *Magh-Bile,* 'the plain of the ancient tree' at the head of Strangford Lough, but it was a monastery renowned since the mid-sixth century as a centre of intellectual excellence. Finnian was said to have been of royal blood, certainly studied at Whithorn on the Solway, and is acknowledged as the outstanding Irish scholar of the sixth century. The *Martyrology of Oengus* calls him *sui,* or 'sage', in its reference to his bringing from Whithorn the first copy of Saint Jerome's Vulgate translation of the Bible to reach Ireland.

> A kingpost of red gold with purity,
> over the swelling sea with law,
> A sage whom Ireland mourns –
> Finnian of Magh Bile.

His monastery founded at Moville in the early 540s became established as an eminent school of learning, an intellectual centre in Ireland to bear comparison with Wearmouth/Jarrow in Northumbria a century later. It was to *Magh-Bile* of Finnian that Columcille came to begin his monastic studies and, almost three hundred years later, the northmen to burn what must have been amongst the very finest libraries of early Christian Ireland.

The *Annals of Ulster* at 825 record the year of plague and famine when the vikings fell on the churches of Downpatrick and Moville with fire and sword.

> A great pestilence in the island of Ireland ... a great famine and failure of bread.
> The plundering of Dun-lethglaise by heathens.
> The burning of Magh-Bile with its oratories by heathens, in which a great many were slain.

While 'a great many' monks were slain at Moville it is another, and more impressively attested, bloodletting which singles out 825 as a year indelibly marked by the red martyrdom. This most infamous of viking atrocities against the Gael is entered with characteristic brevity by the *Annals of Ulster* at 825.

> Martyrdom of Blathmacc, son of Flainn, by heathens in I-Columcille.

The same event is shrewdly placed in a modern perspective by the historian Barbara Crawford as the point where 'the Viking traders of recent history books and television series turn into the Viking raiders of yesteryear'.

Blathmac mac-Flainn was, like Columcille himself, of royal blood and born a prince of a branch of the Ui-Neill. He had been a warrior who had entered the religious life as the abbot of some unidentified monastic community, most probably one enjoying the patronage of his own dynasty in Ireland. Resolving with solemn deliberation to suffer 'the scars of Christ', he came from Ireland to join whatever monastic community remained on Iona to assume some form of abbatial authority over the shrine at greatest hazard from the sea-raiders. In so doing he confirms the strange new sanctity which surrounded I-Columcille in the decades following Cellach's transfer of the chief church of the Columban dominion to Kells. The most holy island of the western sea had passed into the viking age as the Golgotha of the Gael.

It remained the burial ground where lay the 'tombs of the kings' and, more importantly, where Columcille himself awaited resurrection when the sixth age came at last to its end. The exact whereabouts of Columcille's tomb on Iona had been shrouded in mystery since he was first laid in its earth in 597. Adamnan tells how miraculous meteorological intervention secured for his community the privacy of the saint's interment.

> 'None but the monks of my monastery will perform my funeral rites, and grace the last offices bestowed upon me.'
> And the fulfilment of this prophecy was brought about immediately after his death by God's almighty power; for there arose a storm of wind without rain, which blew so violently during those three days and nights of his obsequies, that it entirely prevented everyone from crossing the Sound by boat. And immediately after the interment of the blessed man, the storm was quelled at once, the wind ceased, and the whole sea became calm.

When the bones of other saints were translated into the reliquaries of gold and silver in the eighth century, it has been assumed that the remains of Columcille were similarly enshrined. The annals contain a sequence of entries for the early ninth century noting the voyages of Cellach's successors, the abbots Diarmait and Indrechtach, carrying the 'reliquaries' of Columcille between Kells and Iona. These have been taken to represent the physical remains of the saint regularly ferried between the two churches, but some closer examination of the Irish text of the annals suggests that this might have not been exactly the case. The annalists use two different Irish words in this context, both of which translate as 'relics' but each with its own more precise meaning. The word *martra* is used to represent the corporeal remains of a saint, while *mionna* generally identifies what might be called relics of association. A crozier or a habit worn by the saint, even lesser physical remains such as a fingernail or small bone separated from the body, were *mionna*, which is the word used by the annals for the relics of Columcille shipped back and forth between Erin and Alba. If those venerated items encased in gold and silver were not in fact his physical remains, then what remained of the earthly form of the saint would have stayed on Iona. Whether as a temporary or permanent arrangement, there is indisputable evidence that the enshrined remains of Columcille were on the island when Blathmac suffered his martyrdom defending them from the northmen in 825.

Whether by reason of his courage, his piety or, more probably, the grisly nature of his martyrdom, Blathmac's renown spread to the continent with the Irish monks seeking sanctuary overseas in ever greater numbers as the viking onslaught on Ireland intensified. It must have been one of these *peregrini*, most probably a surviving eye-witness of the event, who provided Walafrid Strabo, abbot of the Irish monastery at Reichenau in Switzerland, with the wealth of detail which informed his remarkable poetic elegy on the martyrdom of Blathmac. Abbot Walafrid's hexameter verses, written within twenty-five years of 825, survive as the most detailed contemporary narrative of a viking raid on the western seaboard. His continental viewpoint prompted him to identify Blathmac's assailants as 'Danes' when they were indubitably of Norse origin, but his account has every other hallmark – not least quotations of speech – of a first-hand testimony. It is also a text of great length and laden with pious homilies framed with scriptural quotation, so I have selected only those passages of especially significant relevance here.

A certain island lies on the shores of the Picts, placed in the wave-tossed brine; it is called Eo, where the saint of the Lord, Columba, rests in the flesh. This island he [Blathmac] sought under his vow to suffer the scars of Christ, for here the frequent hordes of pagan Danes were wont to come armed with malignant furies.

Blathmac, forewarned of the approach of sea-raiders, called his monks together to prepare them for the impending martyrdom. Those ready to endure that fate were to stay beside him, but those not yet ready were to take refuge elsewhere in the island. There seem to have been places of safety appointed and accessible by designated pathways for just such an occasion and it is reasonable to assume that some similar arrangement had been used during earlier raids.

The community, moved by these words, determined to act according to their strength. Some, with a brave heart resolved to face the hand of sacrilege, and rejoiced to have to submit their heads to the raging sword; but others, whose confidence of mind had not yet risen to this, took flight by a path to known places of refuge.
    The golden dawn dispelled the dewy darkness and the glittering sun shone again with glorious orb, when the pious cleric stood before the holy altar, celebrating the holy offices of the mass, himself a victim acceptable to God to be offered up to the thundering sword. The rest of

the brethren lay commending their souls with prayers and tears, when, behold, the cursed bands rushed raging through the unprotected houses, threatening death to those blessed men and, furious with rage, the rest of the brethren being slain, came to the holy father, demanding he give up the precious metals which enclosed the sacred bones of Saint Columba. But [the monks] had taken the shrine from its place and deposited it in the earth in a hollowed tumulus, or grave, and covered it with sods.

This was the plunder the Danes desired; but the holy man stood firm with unarmed hand, with a stern determination of mind; taught to stand against foes and to challenge encounter, unaccustomed to yield. He then addressed the barbarians in the following words:

'I know not of the gold you seek, where it may be placed in the ground, and in what recesses it may be hidden; but, if it were permitted by Christ for me to know, never would these lips tell it to your ears. Savagely bring your swords, seize their hilts and kill. O God, I commend my humble self to Thy protection.'

Hereupon the pious victim was cut in pieces with severed limbs, and what the fierce warrior could not compensate with a price, he began to seek out by wounds in the stiffened entrails. Nor is it a wonder, for there always were and always will arise those whom evil rage will excite against the servants of the Lord.

Thus the abbot Walafrid portrays the martyrdom of a 'servant of the Lord' in an account which indicates some greater significance than the summary despatch of a martyr to his crown.

The Irish calendars of saints record the date of Blathmac's death as 24th July, which falls into the later raiding season and suggests an attack made by a warband returning to the north after its plundering of Down and Moville. The reiterated references to 'rage' in Walafrid's account would suggest the raiders as *berserkr*, the blood-frenzied warrior-priests of Odin found throughout the Scandinavian saga sources. If the raiders of 825 were berserkers, then the grisly detail of Blathmac's martyrdom assumes a greater significance than the casual brutality of the sword, because Walafrid's account is quite consistent with the saga evidence for the ritual sacrifice to Odin, known across the northlands as the 'blood-eagle'.

The *Orkneyinga Saga* contains an impressive account of a 'blood-eagling' inflicted – some seventy years after the similar mutilation of Blathmac – upon Halfdan Haraldsson called 'long-leg' by Torf-Einar Rognvaldsson, the one-eyed *jarl* of Orkney, on the island of North Ronaldsay.

Then jarl Einar took to saying these words:

'I know not what I see on Rinansey, sometimes it lifts itself up, but sometimes it lays itself down, that it is either a bird or a man and we will go to it.'

There they found Halfdan Long-Leg, and Einar made them carve an eagle on his back, and cut the ribs all from the backbone and draw the lungs there out, and gave him to Odin for the victory he had won.

If such was the fate dealt out to Blathmac mac-Flainn, then the renown accorded his martyrdom might be explained in terms of its fearsome symbolism no less than its savage circumstances. It can only have represented the symbolic sacrifice of the White Christ before the shrine of Columcille to Odin battle-bringer.

No image from the pages of the insular gospel books is possessed of such ominous aspect as the folio from the Book of Kells portraying Christ at Gethsemane in the form of a Celtic holy man seized by two gnomic warriors. It would have appeared to the sixth age of the world as the foretelling on vellum of the red martyrdom of Blathmac on I-Columcille.

Less than a decade after the onslaught of the berserkers of 825, the course of Scandinavian expansion west-over-sea had changed from summer-raiding pirates to overwintering warbands. Now came the invasion of Erin by 'sea-cast floods of aliens'.

'sea-cast floods of aliens'

Erin and Alba,
AD 832–871 and after

In a word, although there were an hundred hard steeled
iron heads on one neck, and an hundred sharp, ready, cool,
never-rusting, brazen tongues in each head, and an hundred
garrulous, loud, unceasing voices from each tongue,
they could not recount, or narrate, or enumerate, or tell,
what all the Gael suffered in common, both men and women,
laity and clergy, old and young, noble and ignoble,
of hardship and of injury and of oppression in every house
from these fearless, wrathful, alien, pagan people.

The War of the Gaedhil with the Gaill.

THE LAND and the people of Ireland in the first decades of the ninth century were very little changed from those Saint Patrick had known four hundred years before.

Untouched by the Roman and Germanic invasions which had so reshaped the other lands of western Europe, Ireland remained the dominion of Celtic farmers whose homesteads and cashels were scattered across a landscape devoid of town or village. Their world was centred on the clan, the *tuath*, bound together by kinship and ruled by its chieftain from his *rath*, a ramparted hillfort, or from his *crannog*, a fortified lake-island, which had long been the symbols of power in the land. The overlord of these lesser kings was the *ard ri*, honoured as the 'high-king at Tara' long after that ancient royal fortress in Meath had been abandoned in the time of Columcille. The power of the high-king – even though there had never been a time when any *ard ri* could command the submission of all the clans and kingdoms of Ireland – had for centuries passed between the northern and southern branches of the Ui-Neill until the tenth century when the dynasty of Niall 'Nine-Hostager' was overtaken by the rising power of the Munster kings of Cashel. Political stability hung on a network of shifting alliances against a background of perpetual dynastic contest. The virtually unbroken continuum of conflict and cattle-raiding from the prehistoric myths and sagas into the battle and blood-feud entered in the annals confirms that so it had always been with the Irish Gael.

In that same context, the monastic *familiae* were the heirs to the ancient authority of the pre-Christian druids and drawn by their clan loyalties into every turbulence of secular politics. The monasteries which had grown up around the shrines and holy places of the saints reflected the wealth and pride of the patron clan, their abbots appointed almost without exception from the close family of the chieftain, and their communities even drawn into active service on the battlefield against rival *familiae*. Such hosting by clerics had been proscribed by the *Cain Adomnain* in 697, but the annals continue to enter transgressions of this 'Law of Adamnan' through the eighth century. The *Annals of Ulster* record Adamnan's shrine being brought from Iona to Ireland in 727 in an attempt to reinforce the saint's ordinance, but subsequent entries confirm the attempt as less than effective while secular conflict continued quite unabated.

There is no doubt that some of the interminable warfarings recorded by the annalist represent serious clashes of arms, of which the blood-fray involving Columcille himself 'in which 3,000 fell' at

Culdrevny in 561 is a prime example. It is equally clear that only a small proportion of these innumerable 'battles' can have been conflicts of that order. The great majority, and especially those involving monastic participation, must have represented ritual confrontation rather than real bloodletting. The honour of the clan was the issue at stake in every clash of Celt on Celt and even the most grievous passages of arms were fought out within the mutually-recognised bounds of time-honoured protocols. Even when a warlord is recorded as 'plundering' the monastic dominions of a rival clan the attack is always credited with stopping short of 'the door of the church'. There were also rights of redress and when these took the form of retribution in arms the victory was claimed for the intervention of the patron saint. Breaches of such ancient protocols spelled the doom of the offender be he even so mighty as the mythic hero Cuchulainn whose death, according to the legends, was brought about by his transgression of taboos.

All of these rites of rivalry in an enclosed society which had long before emerged largely unchanged out of pagan prehistory into the Christian era were swept aside by the viking onslaught.

The Irish fighting man was certainly no match for the superior weaponry and war-skills of the berserker, but such purely military comparisons are less significant than the fact that the northman of the viking age was the creature of a different world. He came with no recognition of the laws and loyalties which underwrote the way of the Gael, to plunder and pillage without thought of redress or the least terror of divine retribution. When the sea-raiders were followed by larger warbands thrusting deep into the interior of the Irish mainland who were followed in turn by overwintering armies, they wreaked such havoc as to transform the land and the people of Erin beyond all recognition.

Yet the most extraordinary aspect of each new onslaught of the northmen was its apparent failure to distract in any degree the Irish kings and high-kings from their internecine warfaring. This seemingly suicidal phenomenon can only be reasonably explained as a consequence of the primitive communications of an insular society. Tidings of summer raiding off the coast of Mayo need not have reached a Ui-Neill high-king in Donegal, just as news of a score of longships on Carlingford Lough and their crews rampaging through Ulster need have rung no alarm bells in the monasteries of the Shannon. It is only from the wider perspective of medieval compilations which draw together the range of earlier and immediately contemporary sources that the full extent of the invasion of Erin by the *gaill* is brought into retrospective focus.

While the Irish annals still remain the central source for the ninth century, they can be usefully supplemented for that period by a second documentary record. Unlike the annal sources, which note the progress of the northmen in much the same terms of dispassionate brevity as they enter the skirmishing of rival Irish warbands, the *Cogadh Gaedhel re Gallaibh* takes the form of an enthusiastic narrative chronicle of the 'War of the Gaedhil [Irish Gaels] with the Gaill' from the first raids in the western sea to the last great battle which broke the Scandinavian ascendancy at Clontarf in 1014. It was probably completed in the scriptorium at Clonmacnois around the year 1165 and intended, as was the first *Anglo-Saxon Chronicle*, as a work of propaganda. Much as the original *Chronicle* presents the Anglo-Saxon centuries from the perspective of the royal house of Wessex, so the *Cogadh* celebrates the Munster dynasty and above all its high-king *Brian Boruime*, 'Brian of the Tributes' popularly called 'Brian Boru', as Ireland's great champion against the *gaill*. It seeks always to diminish the achievement of the rival Ui-Neill and its narrative form does not easily synchronise with the chronological framework of the annals. The *Cogadh* must be handled with caution but its chapters concerning the 'sea-cast floods of aliens' of the ninth century can serve as an illuminating, and on occasion independently informed, companion to the annal record.

None of these sources explicitly identify the sea-change in the onslaught of Scandinavian expansion which can be discerned around the year 832 when the summer raids of smaller-scale pirate warbands were overtaken by more substantial warfleets numbering 'scores' of longships and directed by warlords recognised as 'kings'. These were the first semblance of the invasion forces who moored their ships on the loughs as 'floating fortresses' from which they could launch extensive campaigns of inland raiding. From this point on, the northmen were a progressively resident force and the 'viking age', in its most precise usage, was to give way within a decade to the Scandinavian settlement of Ireland. It would, nonetheless, be some years before the forces of invasion and conquest behaved very differently to the viking style of pirate warbands and no such change in military operation would have been at all perceptible to the great churches of Armagh and Kildare, Glendalough and Clonmacnois which were only now to suffer their first experience of the northmen.

The shift in strategy is most clearly indicated by the change in the names appearing in the sources. The *Cogadh* identifies 'royal fleets' which certainly represent something greater than the handful of longships implied in accounts of earlier raids, but the newly permanent presence of the *gaill* is most clearly confirmed by the references to personal names which single out prominent individuals from the earlier collective identities of 'heathens', 'pagans' and 'aliens'. It is possible to cautiously identify personalities from the variant names used for the same individual across the full range of Irish, English and Scandinavian sources. The annalists' Gaelic forms of Old Norse nomenclature – such as *Ivar* rendered as *Imhar* and *Olaf* as *Amlaibh* – can usually be translated with plausible accuracy, but the identity of the first Scandinavian name prominent in the Irish sources has long remained an enigma.

This *Turgeis* – or *Turgesius* – was the name by which the *Cogadh* identified the warrior king who brought the 'great royal fleet into the north of Erin' around the year 832. The name is generally accepted as a rendering of the Old Norse *Thorgisl* and it would seem to identify a chieftain of the Norse royal house of Vestfold. Snorri Sturlusson's *Heimskringla* claims one Thorgisl as a son of Harald Finehair who 'fell into a snare of the Irish and was killed', precisely as was Turgeis in 845. The distorted chronology of the saga tradition would have been quite capable of relocating a prince of the 830s to Harald's reign more than fifty years later, but J. H. Todd, the eminent editor of the *Cogadh*, has alternatively suggested Turgeis/Thorgisl as an identity of the legendary viking Ragnar Sigurdsson called *lothbrok*, or 'shaggy breeches', by the saga-makers. The historical Ragnar Lothbrok has been best distilled by Alfred Smyth from the super-hero of saga tradition as a sea-king with Norse as well as Danish royal connections and exotic associations with the pagan gods of the north. His rough hide leggings traditionally provided magical protection from injury until his inevitable death – in a snake-pit at York, according to the most imaginative saga tradition, or in Ireland according to more historically reliable Scandinavian sources. The 'sons of Ragnar' can be claimed as genuinely historical figures of great significance, but their father must remain too thoroughly obscured by his own legend to be historically identified with the warlord of the 'sea-cast floods of aliens' described in the *Cogadh Gaedhel re Gallaibh*.

There came after that a great royal fleet into the north of Erin, with Turgeis, who assumed the sovereignty of the gaill of Erin; and the north of Erin was plundered by them, and they spread themselves over Leth Chuinn ['Conn's Half', the north of Ireland].

A fleet of them also entered Lough Neagh, and another fleet entered Louth, and another fleet entered Loch Ree.

Moreover Ard-Macha was plundered three times in the same month by them; and Turgeis himself usurped the abbacy of Ard-Macha, and Forannan, abbot of Ard-Macha and chief comarb of Patrick was driven out, and went to Munster, while Turgeis was in Ard-Macha and in the sovereignty of the north of Erin. So Berchan, chief prophet of heaven and earth, prophesied when he said:-

> 'Heathens shall come over the gentle sea;
> They shall confound the men of Erin;
> Of them there shall be an abbot over every church;
> Of them there shall be a king over Erin ...
> There shall be of them an abbot over this my church,
> Who will not attend matins;
> Without Pater and without Credo;
> Without Irish, but only alien tongue.'

Columcille also foretold the same thing, when he said:-

> 'This fleet of Loch Ree,
> By whom are magnified the heathen gaill;
> Of them there shall be an abbot over Ard-Macha;
> It shall be the government of a usurper.'

The old Ciaran of Saighar foretold also the same – that the gaill would three times conquer Erin; that is, a party of them [in punishment] for the banishment of Columcille; a party of them for the insult to Ciaran [of Clonmacnois] at Tailtin; and a party for the fasting of the Apostles [of Ireland] in Temhair ...

And now these three predictions came to pass, and the prophecies were fulfilled.

J. H. Todd quite reasonably dismisses the prophecies as 'palpable forgeries', and it is unlikely that Ciaran of Saighar who lived before the time of Patrick, Columcille in the sixth century, or the

99

apocryphal eighth-century seer Berchan would have foretold the Scandinavian onslaught with quite such precision.

The real significance of these prophecies here is their indication of the changing role of the northmen in the view of the time. Foreknowledge had long been central to Irish spirituality and the foretellings of holy men were regularly recruited to sanction political ambitions and settle old scores. The interpolation of such dubious prophetic utterances into the historical record of the second quarter of the ninth century reflects the revised Irish perception of the northmen who had now been raiding the western seaboard for a full generation. They could no longer be regarded as the agents of imminent apocalypse descending out of a void and, while they were still called 'aliens', the term *gaill* had already begun to acquire the effective usage of a tribal name. The northmen were recognised as a hazardous, heathen, even satanic, force in the land but they had become a fact of life in ninth-century Ireland.

The paragraphs from the *Cogadh* telescope a long sequence of incursions through the 830s and link them together by their association with Turgeis/Thorgisl as 'sovereign of the gaill of Erin'. The annal record confirms the same sequence as a thirteen-year campaign which began with the raids on Armagh entered in the *Annals of Ulster* at 832.

The first plundering of Ard-Macha by heathens, thrice in one month.

The northmen had brought their longships on to Lough Neagh to strike, and strike decisively, at the episcopal church of the *comarba* of the Apostle of Ireland at Armagh, the *Ard-Macha* of Patrick.

This was the beginning of the devastation of 'the greater part of the churches of Erin' and in each succeeding year the annals enter new fleets on the loughs and rivers to inflict a catalogue of plunderings and burnings on the holy places of the saints of Ireland. The following year of 833 found the northmen raiding the church of Patrick's disciple Mochta at Louth and plundering a *rath* in the Derry of Columcille and the monastery at Lismore in Waterford. The next year they were raiding into Wicklow on the evidence of the *Annals of Ulster* at 834.

The plundering of Glenn-da-locha by the heathens.

Glenn-da-locha was the foundation of the holy man celebrated by the *Martyrology of Oengus* as 'Coemgen the chaste, the fair warrior in the glen of two broad lakes' at Glendalough in the Wicklow mountains. Although born of a line of Leinster kings, Coemgen was the archetypal Irish hermit-bishop and his life is inextricably entangled with legends of such a 'green martyrdom'. He is said to have fed his community on salmon brought to him by an otter and when a blackbird made its nest in his praying hands, Coemgen remained in prayer until the eggs were hatched and the young fledged. His community soon overflowed the confines of the Bronze Age rock tomb in which he had first founded his church and moved down the hillside to the more accessible site in the valley below.

Coemgen was believed to have been one hundred and twenty years old when he died in 618 – or 622 according to other sources – and his burial place was described two hundred years later by Oengus as 'the cemetery of the western world in multitudinous Glenn-da-locha'. His Irish *Life* explains how Coemgen's shrine became the centre of a great burial ground of sovereigns and saints.

> Many kings of Erin, and of Britain, chose to be interred at Glenn-da-locha for love of God and Coemgen. There are relics of apostles close by Coemgen's cell to go with him to the judgement of doom in the presence of the Lord.

So splendoured a graveyard offered a rich prospect to viking warbands already accomplished in tomb-breaking and the annals record a total of four raids by the northmen on Glendalough of Coemgen.

In the following year the monasteries at Clonmore and Ferns in Wexford were plundered and numerous churches in Meath burned. The south of Brega was ravaged 'for the first time' in 836 and raiders on the Shannon inflicted 'cruel devastation' on Connaught, but the greatest sacrilege of the year must be that blamed by the *Annals of the Four Masters* on the fleet from *Inbher Dea*, now called the Vartry estuary.

> Cill-Dara was plundered by the gaill of Inbher-Dea,
> and half the church was burned by them.

Cill-Dara, the 'Oak-Church' of Brigid at Kildare, was a holy place of an eminence in the Irish church to rank beside Armagh of Patrick and Iona of Columcille, but it was also the centre of a sanctity far more ancient than Christianity.

The obituary of the historical Brigid is entered at 525. She was the patron of the royal house of Leinster and Oengus calls her the 'chaste chief of Erin's nuns', but her deeper-rooted patronage of farming and farmers, the milking-stool and the ale-keg, confirm this 'Mary of the Gael' as the Christian incarnation of a Celtic goddess of fertility. If the Paschal flame kept burning through each year from Easter Day to Good Friday in the church at *Cill-Dara* had its most ancient origins in the pagan Celtic Beltane fires, its blaze was to be at last engulfed by the northmen's firebrand in 836.

The onslaught continued to escalate. The year after the burning of Kildare there were longships on the Boyne and the Liffey pouring warbands through Brega on the evidence of the *Annals of Ulster* at 837.

A fleet of three score ships of the lochlann upon the Boyne. Another fleet of three score ships on the Liffey. These two fleets afterwards plundered the plain of Liffey and the plain of Brega, between churches, and forts, and houses.

In the same year the northmen were raiding up the Shannon and the Erne and clashing with warbands of the Ui-Neill, but no event of 837 was so significant for the history of Ireland as that entered – and almost as an afterthought – in the *Annals of the Four Masters.*

The first taking of Ath-Cliath by the gaill.

Ath-Cliath, 'the ford of the hurdles', was nothing more than a crossing-point of the Liffey river until the northmen chose it as the site of their shore base for the repair and maintenance of the fleets moored nearby on the haven called *Dubh linn,* the 'black pool'. The longships were hauled aground into the protection of an earthen rampart which became the core of the fortified trading town beside the *Dubh linn* and the Four Masters' entry at 837 can be taken to mark the first foundation of the city of Dublin.

Similar onshore settlements began to appear around the coast and the Old Norse etymology of the modern names for Irish cities confirms their origin as overwintering bases for viking warbands, amongst them Wexford from *Veisuf jordr,* Waterford from *Vedraf jordr,* and Limerick from *Hlymrekr.* The only remotely comparable

102

settlements in Celtic Ireland were the monasteries where workshops
and farmsteads clustered around communities of clerics, scribes and
scholars, but these 'monastic towns' were essentially intellectual
centres and quite unlike the trading towns of the northmen such as
Hedeby on the Baltic and now *Dubh linn* on the Liffey. Dublin's pre-
eminence among the cities of Ireland grew out of its strategic
location on the sea-roads of Scandinavian expansion which brought
the longships south from Orkney and Shetland by way of the
Hebrides, and carried them later across the Irish Sea to the Danelaw
of northern England and south to the shores of Carolingian France
and Arabic Spain.

The *Cogadh* confirms the seizure of the 'ford of the hurdles' as the
first firm foothold of the *gaill* on the Irish mainland to serve them as
a haven for warfleets and a forward base for inland raiding on into
the 840s.

> After this came three score and five ships, and landed at Dubh linn of
> Ath-Cliath, and Leinster was plundered to the sea by them, and the plain
> of Brega.
> After this came great sea-cast floods of aliens into Erin so that there
> was no point thereof without a fleet.

There were fleets now on Lough Neagh, Lough Ree, and the loughs
of Strangford and Carlingford to reinforce the conquest of the north
of Ireland by 'Turgeis of Ard-Macha', and the entry in the *Annals of
the Four Masters* at the year 840 puts a date to his appropriation of the
abbacy of the *comarb* of Patrick as the prophesied usurper at Armagh.

> The burning of Ard-Macha, with its oratories and church
> by the aforesaid gaill.

The presentation of Turgeis/Thorgisl as a 'priest-king' over the
heathen *gaill* in Ireland may not have been entirely the invention of
monastic chroniclers. His seizure of Armagh as his power base might
be interpreted in terms of political symbolism or pagan sacrilege, or
indeed of both. It is even possible that *Turgeis* may have represented
a title associated with the god Thor, patron of the land-seeking
northman, rather than a personal identity. In that context, the
presence of such a pagan priest-king in the abbacy of Armagh would
have represented something more than a token of land-based piracy,
because *Ard-Macha* of Patrick was endowed with all the political, as

well as spiritual, authority of the primacy of Ireland. Indeed Saint Patrick's own pre-eminence as the 'Apostle of Erin' seems to have been itself a product of the contest of dynasties.

The original *Patricius* – the Briton of Strathclyde seized by Irish slavers in the early fifth century who escaped to freedom until prompted by a vision to return as the evangelist of the Gael – is a well-attested historical character, but the cult of Patrick which was centred on Armagh in the ninth century was a creation of later hagiography under the patronage of the southern Ui-Neill high-kings. The saint had been less widely venerated in Ireland than Columcille until the earliest *Lives* were set down at Armagh in the late seventh century. At that point the fifth-century prototype was furnished with all the foundations, shrines, retreats and holy places befitting the patriarch entered with due splendour at 17th March in the *Martyrology of Donegal.*

> Patraic, noble Apostle of the island of Erin, and head of the belief of the Gael, the first primate, and the first legate who was appointed in Erin; and it was he, moreover, who brought the people of Erin, both men and women, from the darkness of sins, and vices, and paganism, to the light of faith, and piety, and knowledge of the Lord.
>
> Three hundred and fifty holy bishops, and three hundred priests was the number on whom he conferred orders. Three hundred alphabets he wrote, and three hundred churches he built.

As the *comarb* of Patrick, the abbot at Armagh was the most political of churchmen and ever more entangled in the power struggle between the Munster kings and the dynasty of the Ui-Neill. Only a year before the first viking raid of 832, an ally of Fedlimidh of Munster had launched a night raid on Armagh to plunder the cattle herds of its Ui-Neill abbot, Eoghain. Shortly afterwards, Eoghain was succeeded by the abbot Forannan who seems to have been better disposed towards Munster, if only because it was there that he fled with the shrine of Patrick when Turgeis drove him and his community out of Armagh in 840. It took only five years – on the evidence of the *Annals of Ulster* at 845 – for the northmen of Limerick to get their hands on a refugee abbot carrying a precious reliquary.

> Forannan, abbot of Ard-Macha, was taken captive by the heathens ... with his reliquaries and his familia, and carried off by the ships of Limerick.

The *Cogadh* adds its own detail to the annalist's entry.

> Munster was plundered by the fleet of Limerick, who carried off
> Forannan, comarb of Ard-Macha ... and they broke Patrick's shrine.

While the 'comarb of Ard-Macha' was falling into the hands of the
vikings of Limerick, the pagan usurper at Armagh was carrying his
war on the saints of Ireland to the south-west.

> There came now Turgeis of Ard-Macha and brought a fleet upon Lough
> Ree, and from there plundered Meath and Connaught; and Cluain-mic-
> Nois was plundered by him, and Cluain-ferta of Brendan, and Lothra
> and Tir-da-glas ... and all the churches of Lough Derg.

The date of Turgeis's plundering of Connaught and Meath is
confirmed by the corresponding entry in the *Annals of Ulster* at 845.

> A host of the gaill with Turgeis ... burned Cluain-mic-Nois with its
> oratories, and Cluain-ferta-Brendainn, and Tir-da-glas, and Lothra.

The four churches singled out by the sources from the many burned
and plundered in the raids of 845 were all distinguished as
foundations of the sixth-century saints venerated as the 'Twelve
Apostles of Ireland', who had graduated together from the great
monastic school of Saint Finnian of Clonard. The passage of
fourteen centuries has relegated some of these holy men to obscurity
while perpetuating the fame of others, but tradition confirms all
twelve as of comparable eminence before the vikings came.

In 845, the now barely-known Colum of *Tir-da-glas*, Terryglass on
the shore of Lough Derg, would have been no less celebrated a local
saint in Tipperary than was Columcille in Donegal. Ruadhan of
Lorrha, anciently *Lothra*, is somewhat better recorded than his
neighbouring saint of Terryglass. Ruadhan was born of the royal
house of Munster and had been prominently involved in the
dramatic sixth-century confrontation of church and state remembered as 'The Cursing of Tara' when the holy men banished the
high-kings for ever from their ancient fortress on Tara hill in Meath.
The silver shrine believed to contain Ruadhan's hand was still
venerated at Lorrha until the Reformation, but other and no less
richly-preserved relics of the saint must have been carried off to the
melting-pots of the Scandinavian smiths in Dublin and Limerick.

The burning of *Cluain-ferta-Brendainn* was an assault on the shrine of one of the most remarkable saints of the Celtic church. Brendan of Clonfert, called 'The Navigator', was the great holy man of the west of Ireland, regarded above all others throughout his native Kerry and commemorated from Galway to the Garvellachs in the Firth of Lorn and Barra in the Outer Hebrides. The obituary of the historical Brendan is entered at 578, seventeen years after his foundation of the monastery of *Cluain-ferta* to the north of Lough Derg, but his cult is most remarkable for its accounts of his voyages by curragh under sail into the north Atlantic as far as Iceland and Greenland, and even North America. The spiritual roots of 'Brendan-Voyager' have been shown to lie much deeper in the Celtic folk-soul than his white martyrdom* of exile for Christ and have been traced as far into prehistory as the voyages of the mythological heroes who sailed beyond the setting sun in search of the land of the blessed called *Tir-nan-Og* by the pagan Celts.

For all their sacrilege, there is no obvious reason why these raids on holy places should have been motivated by anything other than pillage or that a pagan usurper in the abbacy of Armagh need be interpreted as anything more than a symbolic political challenge, were it not for the strange appendix to the *Cogadh* entry of the raid on Clonmacnois.

> And the place where Ota, the wife of Turgeis, used to give her answers was upon the altar of Cluain-mic-Nois.

This was something quite new in the Irish experience of the northmen – the deliberate profanation of a place of the most especial sanctity.

Cluain-mic-Nois was the great shrine of Ciaran on the Shannon where the round towers and high crosses still stand today as evidence of one of the most splendid of all the Irish monasteries. By the ninth century Clonmacnois had been long established as a foundation of wealth and prestige second only to Armagh and attracting the envy of ambitious Irish warlords, but its splendour was accounted only a pale reflection of the enigmatic charisma of its founder. Ciaran is entered in the *Martyrology of Oengus* as 'the wright's son beyond kings'. His Latin and Old Irish *Lives* tell how Brigid and Patrick had both foretold him, how Finnian of Clonard had called him 'Ciaran

---

* There were three orders of martyrdom in the Irish Celtic church: the white martyrdom of exile, the green martyrdom of the hermitage and the red martyrdom of the blood sacrifice.

half-Ireland' prophesying his dominion as greater than all others, and how the saints of Ireland, with the sole exception of Columcille, had prayed out of jealousy for his early death.

The annals are at variance on his exact dates, but hagiographical tradition insists that he was born in 512 and died just seven months after the foundation of Clonmacnois in 545. The same tradition claims Ciaran was born the son of a carpenter who had fled to Connaught to escape the oppressive tributary demands of the Ui-Neill kings, that 'thirty-three years was his age when he yielded his spirit to heaven', and that three days later his spirit 'came again into his body' to take communion from Coemgen, newly-arrived from Glendalough. The New Testament parallels are too explicit to be ignored as testimony of the Christ-like sanctity attributed to Ciaran of Clonmacnois and, while his monastery had been burned and plundered three times by the northmen in 834, 835 and 842, the sacrilege of 845 went beyond anything inflicted by fire and sword.

The evidence of the *Cogadh* can only be interpreted as a portrait of 'Ota' – probably representing the Old Norse *Utta* – in the role of a *vala* or pagan priestess reading the runes 'on the altar of Cluain-mic-Nois'. The ritual casting of heathen symbols of power – closely associated by skaldic tradition with Odin himself – before the shrine of Ciaran 'the wright's son beyond kings' must surely have been intended as a sacrilege inflicted in full knowledge of its profanity.

The profanation of Clonmacnois of Ciaran, the usurping of the primacy at Armagh, or the wider war on the saints of Erin might have equally enraged the Irish to wreak vengeance on the northmen. There is no record of just what it was that so suddenly provoked the new *ard ri*, Maelsechnaill of the Ui-Neill, to action in 845 but the *Annals of Ulster* do at least record the fact of the matter.

> Turgeis was taken prisoner by Maelsechnaill; and the drowning of Turgeis subsequently in Loch-Vair [Lough Owel].

The *Cogadh* records the restoration – probably by ransom – of Forannan and his reliquary to Armagh in the following year.

> Now, when Turgeis was killed, Forannan, abbot of Ard-Macha, went out of Munster and the shrine of Patrick was repaired by him.

The death by drowning in Lough Owel of the warlord of the *gaill* marks a definite turn of the tide in favour of the Irish.

This new resistance can be credited in some measure to the efforts of the high-king Maelsechnaill taking military advantage of the rivalries which were appearing among the northmen themselves. Their move towards onshore settlement had sacrificed the advantage of speed and surprise formerly enjoyed by the sea-raiders, and Irish warbands seized on the greater vulnerability of these new 'viking towns'. Cerball, king of Ossory, besieged one such settlement for a fortnight in 846. He slaughtered two hundred of the *gaill* of Dublin in the following year, when Maelsechnaill slew seven hundred more in a rout near Lough Skreen. An alliance of Munster and Leinster kings inflicted a similar defeat at Castledermot in Kildare in 848 while the Munster king Olchobar destroyed the newly-established Scandinavian settlement at Cork, but the great breakthrough came in 849 when Maelsechnaill joined with the warlords of south Brega to storm *Ath-Cliath of Dubh linn*.

For all its sudden energy, this resurgence of the Gael against the *gaill* had come too late and the *Annals of Ulster* enter the arrival of a new invasion fleet soon after the attack on Dublin.

> A fleet of seven score ships of the people of the king of the gaill came to take sovereignty of all the gaill who were there before them, and they ravaged all Erin afterwards.

Further fleets followed 'and the greater part of Erin was plundered by them' according to the *Cogadh*.

> There came after that a fleet of three score ships of the lochlann upon the Boyne; and Brega and Meath were plundered by them. Another fleet came and settled on Lough Neagh, and these plundered all before them to Ard-Macha. Another fleet came and settled on the river of Liffey, and the plain of Brega was plundered by them, both the country and the churches.
>
> There came after that a very great fleet into the south of Ath-Cliath, and the greater part of Erin was plundered by them; also I-Columcille, and Inishmurray ... and Glenn-da-locha ... and to Lothra where they broke the shrine of Ruadhan, and they spoiled Cluain-mic-Nois.

The Irish warlords had already begun to follow the example of the northmen. One Irish warband is described by the annalist as 'a great band of the sons of Death, who were plundering the districts in the manner of the heathen'. Others had taken to joining with the *gaill* in viking enterprise, even as early as 842 according to the entry in the *Annals of Ulster.*

Comman, abbot of Dundalk, was wounded and burned
by the heathens and Irish.

Cinaed mac-Conaing, king of north Brega, entered into alliance with the northmen to make war on his neighbours in southern Brega and their ally, Maelsechnaill. His punishment – after the manner of the late Turgeis – is entered in the *Annals of Ulster* at 851.

Cinaed, king of Cianachta, turned against Maelsechnaill, through the assistance of the gaill, so that he wasted the Ui-Neill, both churches and territories.
[He] was drowned in a pool, a cruel death, by Maelsechnaill ... with the approval of the good men of Erin, and of the comarb of Patrick especially.

The northmen were now 'aliens' in name only and well enough established among the warrior dynasties of Ireland to be subject, like their native counterparts, to the vengeance of the saints. The death of the Munster king Fedlimidh in 847 was said to have been inflicted by the crozier of Ciaran, who had risen from his tomb to avenge the Munsterman's harrying of Clonmacnois in the previous year, and the *Cogadh* records similar divine retribution inflicted on two viking *jarls* after their defeat by Olchobar in 848.

Earl Baethbarr escaped with many of the routed army to Ath-Cliath. Afterwards he was drowned at Ath-Cliath, through a miracle of Ciaran.
It was in that year that Earl Tomar was killed by Saint Brendan, three days after he had plundered Cluain-ferta.

To all of which rich mix of havoc was added, in the year 851, a new invasion by the ferocious northmen called by the *Annals of Ulster* the *dubh-gaill.*

The coming of the dubh-gaill to Ath-Cliath, who made a great slaughter of the finn-gaill, and they plundered the fortress, both people and property.

These were Danes who had come from their Baltic homeland around Jutland first as pirates on the coast of Frisia and eastern

109

England through the 830s and then into battle with the kings of Wessex through the next decade, until the *Anglo-Saxon Chronicle* for 851 entered their first overwintering in England.

> And the heathen men, for the first time, took up their quarters over winter in Thanet.

The sea-road west through the Channel and north into the Irish Sea brought the first warfleet of the Danes against the capital fortress of the Norse kings in Ireland at *Ath-Cliath*. From this point on the Irish sources differentiate between two tribes of the northmen as the *dubh-gaill* and *finn-gaill* and this new terminology calls for some note of explanation.

It has always been the custom for editors of the early sources to translate the Gaelic *dubh* as 'black' and *finn* as 'white' despite there being no obvious reason why the Danes should have been identified as 'black' and the Norse as 'white'. There is clearly no variance in racial type to justify such a nomenclature, but it has been suggested that the 'black' and 'white' might have indicated, if not the colours of the ships, the colours of the war-shields racked on their gun-whales. There are references in the sagas to red and white shields distinguishing two warfleets in battle, but nowhere is there any evidence in the English or continental sources of black and white colour-coded battle-gear and uniformity was never a characteristic of any Germanic warband in the viking age or earlier. The most convincing solution is that offered by Alfred Smyth* who has found evidence in Irish etymological scholarship for *Finn* as a personal name-form for 'the elder' and *Dub* for 'the younger', which would very well correspond to the usage of *finn-gaill*, 'old aliens', for the longer-established Norse vikings and *dubh-gaill*, 'new aliens', for the Danish newcomers. It had been Norsemen who had first raided the western seaboard, occupied the northern and western isles of Scotland and made such extensive inroads into Ireland and the Danes who came after them more than half a century later.

So it was that the first shock of northman on rival northman came about in Ireland and the Irish sources recording the fearsome slaughter seem almost to reel back from the clash of titans. The *Fragmentary Annals of Ireland*, compiled largely from traditional

---

* *The Black Foreigners of York and the White Foreigners of Dublin*, see bibliography under Smyth, A. P.

sources, tell horror stories of triumphant Danes lighting their campfires on great heaps of Norse corpses and record the Danish looting of 'the women, the gold, and all the property of the lochlanns' in terms of an act of divine retribution.

> Thus the Lord took away from them all the wealth which they had taken from the churches, and sanctuaries, and shrines of the saints of Erin.

The impact of the *dubh-gaill* onslaught might be more realistically attributed to the same advantages of speed and surprise which had accompanied the first Norse raids of fifty years before than to divine intervention. *Ath-Cliath* was little more than a fortified settlement of craftsmen and shipwrights which would have easily fallen to a sudden attack by battle-hardened Danish vikings. Immediately after their sack of Dublin the Danes sailed north along the coast and into Dundalk Bay to plunder the Norse settlement of *Linn-Duachail* at Anagassan with 'great slaughter'. At that point the *dubh-gaill* disappear from the annals for 851, as they probably pressed on through the North Channel and into the Hebrides to raid the islands now settled as the Norse outposts of *Innse-gall.*

They were back in Ireland – and in the Irish annals – the following year and moored on the great sea lough of Carlingford, called *Snamh-Aignech* by the *Annals of Ulster*. There the Danish fleet faced a ferocious attack by a hundred and sixty Norse warships sent to drive them out of Erin in the epic sea-fight on Carlingford Lough.

> A fleet of eight score ships of the finn-gaill came to fight against the dubh-gaill, to Snamh-Aignech.
> They were three days and three nights fighting; but the dubh-gaill were successful, that the others abandoned their ships to them.

This, indeed, was the battle of the titans. The *Cogadh* records one Norse warlord beheaded and another put to flight in a murderous rout when the Danes 'killed five thousand of the finn-gaill at Snamh-Aignech'. The *'Dublin' Annals of Inisfallen* confirm the Danes as the victors and now also as the new lords of the *gaill* in Ireland.

> They fought together for three days and three nights and the rout was on the finn-gaill; and the dubh-gaill enjoyed from then on the dwellings and the place of the finn-gaill.

In the event, 'from then on' amounted to no more than twelve months. Their vast and valuable dominions of the western sea were not to be so easily abandoned by the Norse dynasty of *Vestfold* which had sent Turgeis/Thorgisl in the vanguard of successive 'royal fleets' to enforce its sovereignty over the *gaill* in Ireland and the isles.

The *dubh-gaill* were a-viking in the Irish Sea – and plundering Anglesey according to the entry of *Mon vastata* in the *Welsh Annals* – when a new overlord appeared in Dublin to reclaim Norse dominion over Erin and Alba. The *Annals of Ulster* enter the arrival of *Amlaibh, mac ri lochlann*, 'Olaf, son of the king of the Norse', at 853.

> Amlaibh, son of the king of the lochlann, came to Ireland, and the gaill of Ireland submitted to him, and tribute was paid to him by the Gael.

The *Cogadh* adds that *Amlaibh* brought with him 'a prodigious fleet' and confirms that 'he assumed sovereignty over the gaill of Erin'.

The certain identity of this Olaf has been clouded by the variant name-forms used by the early sources but it is, once again, Alfred Smyth – in his ground-breaking study, *Scandinavian Kings in the British Isles* – who has most convincingly identified the man called *Amlaibh mac ri lochlann* by the Irish sources as Olaf Guthfrithsson, king of Dublin of the royal house of Vestfold.

Olaf was a figure of the greatest importance in the Hiberno-Norse world of the ninth century. He was the viking warlord whose twenty-year reign at Dublin marked the effective end of the Irish 'viking age' and shaped much of the future course of Scottish history, yet he owes his most enduring celebrity to the archaeological discovery of his burial-ship. Scandinavian sources record Olaf buried at Geirstadir which lies close by the site of the celebrated Gokstad ship-burial and provided the justly fitting dragonship-tomb for the man called by *Eyrbyggja Saga* 'the greatest warrior king of the western sea'.

Olaf began his first decade in Ireland by imposing his royal authority on the independent viking warbands of both *dubh-gaill* and *finn-gaill* and went on to pursue his war against the high-kings, first Maelsechnaill and, after 862, his successor Aed Findliath. Olaf's 'kingdom' of the *gaill* centred on Dublin was by now as effectively an 'Irish' dynasty as the Munster kings at Cashel and, in the way of all contenders in Irish dynastic warfare, he sought alliances with whichever warlord might be suitably sympathetic to his purpose of the moment. His staunchest ally and apparently joint-king of Dublin was *Imhar*, who is called Olaf's 'brother' in the Irish sources but identified by Smyth as the Ivar numbered among the 'sons of Ragnar Lothbrok' and called 'the boneless'.

Ivar is first recorded fighting beside Olaf in 857 and six years later the two were engaged – in company with Audgisl, 'a third king of the heathen', and an Irish ally – in the extraordinary raid on the prehistoric tombs of the Boyne valley entered in the *Annals of the Four Masters* at 863.

> Amlaibh, Imhar, and Auisle [Audgisl], three chieftains of the gaill; and Lorcan, son of Cathal, king of Meath, plundered the land of Flann [north Brega].
>
> The cave of Achadh-Aldai [Newgrange]; the cave of Cnoghba [Knowth]; the cave of the grave of Bodan over Dubadh [Dowth]; and the cave of the wife of Gobhan at Drochat-atha [Drogheda] were broken and plundered by these same gaill.

The great megalithic tombs of the Boyne valley in Meath – most prominent among them Newgrange with its ninety-foot-long entrance passage and the 286-foot-high mound at Dowth – date from before 3000 BC and are prized by archaeologists as the outstanding Irish examples of the neolithic 'passage tomb' form. These huge stone-built chamber-mounds are carved with the enigmatic ring and spiral art which is later reflected in the decoration of the insular gospel books of the Christian era.

Already four thousand years old when Olaf and Ivar broke into them – 'which had not been done before' according to the *Annals of Ulster* – these cavernous domains of the dead were possessed of a sanctity for the Celtic folk-soul akin to, yet more ancient than, that of the Reilig Odhrain on Iona. The pre-Christian kings at Tara had been buried in the precincts of these outposts of the otherworld where dwelt the pagan god of power and his wife, the goddess Boanna. The tombs of the Boyne had been revered as portals of the otherworld by the Irish Celt since prehistoric times. Entry through the narrow stone tunnels into their dark interiors was barred by ancient taboos, and whatever grave goods they contained had lain undisturbed for at least a thousand years.

The plundering of these dwelling-caves of the gods represented a grievous offence against shrines hallowed since prehistory and the horrific retribution inflicted by the high-king Aed Find on the Lorcan who had aided the northmen in their sacrilege reflects the gravity of his crime as it is entered in the *Annals of Ulster* at 864.

113

Lorcan, son of Cathal, king of Meath, was blinded by Aed, son of Niall.

Ivar, the 'son of Ragnar Lothbrok', seems to have been especially associated by the northmen with the plundering of megalithic mausolea, an association which is commemorated in runes cut into the wall of the 5,000-year-old chambered tomb of Maes Howe in Orkney. Most of the prehistoric buildings in the northern isles had been entered by the northmen for one purpose or another before the twelfth century when a runemaster, sheltering there for three days from a storm, added his inscription to the runic graffiti left by the northmen on stone walls older than recorded time.

> This mound was raised before Ragnar Lothbrok's ...
> His sons were brave, smooth-hide men though they were ...
> It was long ago that a great treasure was hidden here.
> Happy is he that might find that great treasure.

Alfred Smyth has suggested that Olaf and Ivar had been 'reduced to raiding the houses of the dead' as a result of the diminishing returns on viking activity in Ireland. The northmen now had their own settlements, storehouses and herd cashels to defend, while the losses suffered by their warbands increasingly involved in the Irish internecine wars had set back any ambitions Olaf might have nurtured for his greater conquest of Erin.

He was soon to turn his attention north towards Alba and launch his onslaught on the Picts, while Ivar disappears from the Irish sources after the raids on the Boyne to lead 'the sons of Ragnar Lothbrok' on their conquest of Northumbria.

More than half a century of experience of Scandinavian expansion had left its indelible mark on an Ireland barely touched by any force from the world outside since the coming of Christianity more than four hundred years before.

The northmen had established its first secular towns, placed it on the trade-routes of the northern world, and re-introduced Irish warriors and merchants to the sea which had been so long the exclusive preserve of pilgrims and holy men. It is, perhaps, most remarkable that the great monasteries survived relentless viking raiding in any form at all, and the fact that those same foundations endured as important centres of the medieval Irish church pays

114

tribute to their extraordinary powers of recovery. The annals record ten raids on Clonmacnois, nine on Armagh, five on Kells, four on Glendalough, and sixteen on Kildare, but even these totals very probably represent only a proportion of the real onslaught. Their buildings, constructed largely of wood, could be rebuilt and replenished with sufficient speed to make them worth raiding again after a restorative interval. The round towers so characteristic of Irish monastic architecture were creations of the ninth century and later, when raiding had become an uncomfortable fact of monastic life in Hiberno-Norse society, and intended as fireproof fortified sanctuaries for treasured manuscript books and holy relics. Despite the remarkable resilience of the monasteries, their communities can only have been desperately demoralised by life under constant threat of viking raid, a stress Françoise Henry has compared to the experience of those living in British cities during the Blitz of the Second World War.

The monasteries of the north, which had endured the longest duration of viking onslaught, clearly suffered the greatest impact. The *Ulster Cycle* of Cuchulainn legends, which had been first set down at Bangor, survives only in later manuscripts from the important scriptorium at Clonmacnois which also continued the annal record begun on Iona in the centuries before the northmen burned its library and slaughtered its scribes. All the monastic communities were drastically depleted by the growing numbers of monks, the élite of Irish literacy and learning, who took flight overseas to find sanctuary on the continent. There had been a prominent Irish presence in the monasteries of Switzerland, France and Italy since the time of Columbanus in the sixth century. Irish scholars had been attracted, like Alcuin of York, into the orbit of Charlemagne's empire and Irish monks were drawn to the shrines of Fursa at Peronne, Gall on Lake Constanz, Kilian at Würzburg, and Columbanus himself at Bobbio. Irish abbots presided over churches and communities along the pilgrim roads trodden by their compatriot *peregrini* throughout the seventh and eighth centuries. By the mid-ninth century those roads had been pressed into service as escape routes for monastic refugees driven out of Ireland and the Hebrides by the widening viking onslaught.

The best-documented of these fugitives was Saint Findan of Rheinau who had been betrayed by his Irish enemies into captivity by a viking warband around the year 850. He escaped in Orkney and fled into Pictland before setting out for Rome on a pilgrimage of

115

thanksgiving. On his return, Findan found sanctuary among an island community of Irish hermits on the Rhine where he lived until his death in 879.

While Hiberno-Norse Ireland emerged out of its viking age, Pictland and the Britons of Strathclyde were about to suffer the northmen's fury when Olaf of Dublin went a-viking into Alba in the year 866.

For all the inadequacies of the documentary record, it may be possible here to construct some outline of the impact of Scandinavian expansion on what is now Scotland by the mid-ninth century. The dominance of place-names derived from the Old Norse to be found on the modern map of the northern and western highlands and islands provides its own irrefutable testimony. From the Pentland Firth – *pettlands fjordr*, or 'Pictland's Firth' – around Cape Wrath, the *hvarf* or 'turning point', down to the *Ilasund* between Islay and Jura, almost every place-name on the seaboard bears the hallmark of Old Norse etymology. People do not easily admit foreign names for places long known in their own tongue, other than at the insistence of the swordblade of the land-seeker, and the place-names of the coastline from Shetland down to Kintyre confirm the impact and extent of invasion and conquest by pirate overlords from the northlands.

Orkney and Shetland – *Orkneyjar* and *Hjaltland* – had served the first vikings as their forward bases for piracy until Olaf forced them under formal Norse sovereignty in 853. Olaf granted the *jarldom* of *Orkneyjar* to Rognvald of Moer who passed it to his brother Sigurd called 'the mighty' as the first of a long line of Norse *jarls* who ruled Orkney and Shetland until the islands were ceded to Scotland as a royal dowry in the fifteenth century. Even today Orkney, where the local vernacular tongue called *Norn*, derived from Old Norse, was spoken until relatively modern times, and Shetland still retain their close affinity with Scandinavia. Anywhere across the Pentland Firth is 'The South' to an Orkneyman, just as the Outer Hebrides were called *Sudreyjar*, 'the southern isles', by the northmen of the viking age and Sutherland in the far north of the Scottish mainland derives from the Old Norse *Sudrland*, 'the land to the south'.

By the time the longships had reached the Hebrides their crews were so far from their Scandinavian homelands as to need more substantial accommodation than pirate camps fit only for the summer raiding season. So it must have been that the northmen won

116

swift command of the *vesthafr*, as they called the western sea, recruiting men of the isles to their warbands and island women to their beds. Raiding and settlement went hand-in-hand in the Hebrides to drive a permanent wedge between the Irish mainland and Argyll where the precarious foothold of Scotic Dalriada came under hostile pressure along the length of its western seaboard. In response to that pressure, the royal house of Dalriada had moved its power base eastward from Dunadd in Kintyre over the Spine of Britain and into the Pictish territory of *Fortriu* around Tayside within the first decades of the ninth century.

What appears to have been their custom of matrilinear succession provided the Picts with a long list of kings sired on Pictish queen mothers by northern English, Strathclyde Briton and Dalriadic Gael royal fathers, and the Picts had needed to reassert their independence time and again from the hegemony of Northumbria, Strathclyde and Dalriada. Eventually the Pictish king-lists came to be dominated by men bearing Gaelic names and born of the royal house of Dalriada, but ruling from a new seat of power in the Pictish heartland of Tayside.

The warlord who erupted into this fragile political scenario was the man who was to forge its symbiosis of Pict and Gael into the new dominion of Alba. He was the *Cinaed mac Alpin* – now more familiar as Kenneth mac-Alpin – who had been foretold by the *Prophecy of Berchan*.

> A son of the clan of Aidan [mac-Gabran] will take the kingdom of Alba by force of strength; a man who will feed ravens, who will overcome in battle; conqueror will be his name.
>
>   He is the first king from the Irish in Alba who will reign over the east, by the strength of spears and of swords, after violent deaths, after violent slaughter ... in Scone of the high shields.

Kenneth, son of Alpin, remains the great central enigma of early Scotland. Constructions of his genealogy are apocryphal, anecdotal accounts of his seizure of power fictional traditions, and even the chronology of his overlordship of Alba has been constructed largely by deduction. He was not the first ruler of both Pict and Gael, neither was he the first Gael to rule in Pictland, but Kenneth mac-Alpin has been too long and well established to be challenged as the founding dynast of the Scottish nation.

Historians agree that he succeeded as king of Dalriada around

117

840, extended his sovereignty to the Picts seven years later, died at Forteviot and was buried on Iona in 858. Whether or not he did slaughter Pictish kings trapped between feasting benches as tradition insists, or 'deceived the fierce men of the east' as Berchan prophesied, he most definitely ensured the succession of his sons to a kingdom of Alba dominated by his own Gaelic clan, church and culture. He was, like Brian of Munster and Alfred of Wessex, one of the new native warlords who seized their power in the vacuum left by older dynasties destroyed by the northmen. His kinship to the royal house of Aidan mac-Gabran must have lain in one of its more obscure lineages with lands in the north of Argyll around the head of the Firth of Lorn, where his rise to power would have depended on well-judged alliance with the warbands of the Hebridean vikings.

The *Annals of Ulster* confirm Kenneth already on the move in the west and involved in just such an arrangement by 836.

> Godfraidh mac-Feorghus, chieftain of Airgialla, went to Alba to strengthen Dalriada at the request of Cinaed mac-Alpin.

The annalist has provided here some crucial evidence for the nature of the northmen in the western sea before 840.

The name *Godfraidh mac-Feorghus*, 'Guthfrith son of Fergus', confirms a warlord of Norse/Gael bloodstock as his *Airgialla* must represent the viking dominion in Argyll. These were already the people soon to be identified as *gall-gaedhil*, 'alien Gaels', in the Irish sources. They were long believed to have been warbands of Irish origin and mixed Norse/Dane/Irish stock, but the annal evidence clearly identifies the *gall-gaedhil* as Hebrideans of mixed blood. The northmen had been in the western isles for at least forty years by 836, while there is no evidence for their first overwintering, far less settling, on the Irish mainland until after 832. *Gall-gaedhil* can thus be safely taken to mean Hebridean-Norse, and Guthfrith mac-Fergus to have been their warlord when Kenneth mac-Alpin sought him as his ally on the Scottish mainland in 836.

Three years later, the Picts – called 'the men of Fortriu' by the *Annals of Ulster* – were to suffer their first viking onslaught.

> A battle of the heathens over the men of Fortriu, in which fell Eoganan, son of Oengus, and Bran, son of Oengus, and Aedh, son of Boant, and others beyond counting were slain.

The term 'battle' was customarily used in the Irish annals to indicate

118

a major defeat and the 'battle over the men of Fortriu' must represent a devastating massacre which numbered Eoganan, king of Picts and Scots, his brother Bran, and Aedh, sub-king of Dalriada, among the slain 'beyond counting'. The annalist does not specify the 'heathen' warband responsible, but the *gall-gaedhil* of Guthfrith mac-Fergus striking east out of Argyll into Tayside are clearly the most likely aggressors. Kenneth mac-Alpin made his sudden and dramatic seizure of power in the year immediately after the massacre and Guthfrith mac-Fergus is already confirmed as Kenneth's ally, so the key role played by the northmen in the ascendancy of Alpin's son cannot remain in any serious doubt.

Guthfrith himself appears to have been an independent pirate king of the western sea and such a sovereignty could not long survive the arrival of Olaf in 853. It is no accident that the *Annals of the Four Masters* enter 'the death of Guthfrith mac-Fergus, chieftain of the Innse-gall' in the same year that Olaf's longships reached the western isles on their sea-road to Ireland. Guthfrith's dominion passed to Ketil Bjornsson called 'flat-nose' – who knew the western sea, according to saga tradition, 'for in his youth he had harried there far and wide' – appointed sub-king over the Hebrides under Olaf at Dublin. Their alliance would have been sealed by Olaf's marriage to Ketil's daughter – Aud, called 'the deep-minded', who will yet have her own remarkable part to play in north Atlantic land-seeking – and to have been doomed to a short life by Ketil's own viking inclination.

While Olaf established his kingdom on Dublin and pursued his ambitions for greater conquest of Erin, Ketil led his *gall-gaedhil* a-viking on his own account. He was fighting as an independent ally of Olaf's rival Maelsechnaill in 856 and the saga sources claim he was unwilling to pay the tribute demanded by his overlord. Ketil had clearly crossed Olaf of Dublin once too often by 857 and, whether the annalist's *Caittil Find* should translate as 'Ketil the White' or more probably 'Ketil the *finn-gaill*', the fact of his downfall is left in no doubt by the *Annals of Ulster.*

> A victory by Imhar and Amlaibh over Caittil Find
> with his gall-gaedhil in the territories of Munster.

At which point Ketil Flat-nose disappears from the Irish sources. The *Cogadh* claims he 'was killed with his whole garrison' by the same

Olaf who, according to the saga's boast, 'ruled far and wide over the western sea'.

It would seem that Olaf had brought Ketil's Hebridean northmen under his personal authority and when they appear again – as the '*gaill* of Alba' in the *Annals of Ulster* at 866 – they are, indeed, led by Olaf of Dublin in his viking war on Pictland.

> Amlaibh and Auisle went into Fortriu, with the gaill of Erin and Alba, when they plundered Pictland and brought away their tributes.

If the Saint Ninian's Isle treasure and the heavy, solid silver chains of Pictish origin can be taken as any kind of measure of their wealth, the Picts presented a rich prize for the northmen. Whether it was paid in silver or in slaves, the tribute of Pictland was so much more lucrative than the plunder of the Boyne valley tombs that Olaf was loath to share it with Audgisl, the 'third king of the heathens', who was 'slaughtered in treachery' the following year according to the *Annals of Ulster*.

It is also evident that Olaf invaded Pictland as an ally of the mac-Alpin dynasty, especially when his marital history is taken as an index of his political ambitions. His marriage to Aud the Deep-minded had not survived his quarrel with her father, Ketil, and he had married the daughter of an Irish king when the Dublin Norse were jostling with the Irish dynasties. By the time he turned his attention to Alba, Olaf had taken a daughter of Kenneth mac-Alpin as his queen. The annalist specifies that he '*went into* Fortriu' and that he '*plundered* Pictland' (my italics), so Olaf must have arrived in Alba as an ally, or at least with the approval, of his brother-in-law Constantine, Kenneth mac-Alpin's son and reigning king of Alba since 862. It may have been that Olaf plundered the territories of the Picts north of the Tay who were resisting the expansion of Alba and thus helped further the ambitions of the mac-Alpin dynasty, but he certainly installed himself, on the evidence of the *Fragmentary Annals*, as overlord of the Picts.

> Pictland was ravaged and plundered by the lochlann and they carried off many hostages with them as pledges for tribute, and they were paid tribute for a long time afterwards.

The annalist's 'long time afterwards' in fact amounted to some three years and Olaf was not to reappear in the Irish sources until 869, in fact precisely on 17th March of that year. The date on which he chose to return to Ireland is confirmed by the eleventh-century Scottish *Chronicle of the Kings* as 'the Festival of Saint Patrick' when he reappears in the *Annals of Ulster* at 869 with the entry of his raid on Armagh.

> The plundering of Ard-Macha by Amlaibh, when it was burned with its oratories. Ten hundred persons [taken] captive and slain; and a great depredation besides was committed.

The timing of Olaf's raid was certainly anything but accidental. The festival of the patron saint, and most especially of Patrick at Armagh, attracted great numbers of pilgrims to his church. It offered the most propitious date in the church calendar for a slave-raid and Olaf of Dublin will soon appear as the most accomplished of slavers when he returns from his war on the Britons of Strathclyde.

It was in the following year of 870 that he led his warfleet across the North Channel to join forces with his old ally Ivar, fresh from his own ravaging of Northumbria, for their siege of Alcluith, the ancient fortress of the Britons on Dumbarton Rock.

By 870, the Britons of Strathclyde had been a formidable power in the north country for over five hundred years. Their kingdom had been founded on the Celtic-Britons of the *Dumnonii* as a bulwark against the Picts and Gaels on the north-west frontier of Roman Britain. It had won its ascendancy out of the sixth-century power struggles of the north Britons under its greatest warlord Rhydderch Hael, patron of Saint Kentigern and friend of Columcille. When the Celtic kingdoms of *Rheged* in Cumbria and *Manau* around the Forth collapsed in the seventh century under the expansion of the northern English, Strathclyde alone endured as the last fastness of the north Britons.

A king of Strathclyde had slain the last fierce warlord of Scotic Dalriada at Strathcarron in 642 and exerted shifting degrees of dominance over Gael and Pict in Alba thereafter. A prince of Strathclyde had become the high-king of the Picts who had broken the Northumbrian war-machine at Nechtansmere and forced the northern English back to the south bank of the Forth in 685. The royal fortress of Strathclyde at Alcluith had stood fast, surviving even against the full-scale onslaught of the last Northumbrian royal

121

warlord Eadbert in 756, until Olaf and Ivar came from Dublin to lay it siege.

Alcluith of the Britons held out against the viking blockade for fully four months in 870, a duration remarkable if not unique in the military history of the Dark Ages, and then – according to the *Fragmentary Annals* – collapsed only by the sabotage of its water supply.

> Having wasted the people who were in it by hunger and thirst, by wonderfully drawing off the well they had within, they [the northmen] entered [the fortress] against them.

The conquest of Alcluith by Olaf and Ivar was so crushing a blow to the north Britons as to merit entry in the Britonic–Welsh sources and both the *Welsh Annals* and the *Brut y Tywyssogion* record 'Caer Alclut broken by the pagans'. Rather more detail is entered in the *Annals of Ulster* at 870.

> The siege of Alcluith by the lochlann; that is, Amlaibh and Imhar, two kings of the lochlann, besieged it, and at the end of four months destroyed and plundered the fortress.

Thus fell the last dynasty of the *Gwyr y Gogledd*, the 'Men of the North', whose ascendancy had emerged out of the twilight of Roman Britain, resisted the unrelenting 'Oppression of the Saxons', and been finally broken by the fury of the northmen.

Olaf of Dublin, who had earlier crushed the last embers of Pictish resistance for his brother-in-law Constantine of Alba, had served the ambition of the kingdom of the Scots once again. Artgal, king of the Strathclyde Britons, was slain in the year after the siege of Alcluith, at the instigation of Constantine mac-Cinaed. Within thirty years what remained of the north British nobility had fled to Wales and Strathclyde was annexed by the new Scottish nation.

While history records the siege of Alcluith as the last stand of the north Britons, it would appear to have been little more than an epic slave-taking for Olaf on the evidence of his return to Dublin entered in the *Annals of Ulster* at 871.

> Amlaibh and Imhar came again to Ath-Cliath from Alba, with two hundred ships; and a great spoil of people, English, Britons and Picts, were brought by them into Ireland in captivity.

122

The northmen had been raiding for slaves as well as silver in these islands since the first longships had struck at Lindisfarne eighty years before. 'A great prey of women' had been taken from the Howth peninsula in the first wave of viking raids on the Irish mainland, and such prominent churchmen as Forannan of Armagh had been taken as captives for ransom, but nowhere in the Irish sources had there been any record of slave-taking on the scale of Olaf and Ivar's 'great spoil of people' brought to Ath-Cliath in 871.

'Two hundred ships' represented a slave-cargo of at least a thousand captives and possibly over twice that number. It was the plunder in humankind from Olaf's looting of Pictland, Ivar's pillaging of Northumbria, and their combined devastation of Strathclyde. If any further evidence of Olaf's Scottish alliance were needed, it can be found in the absence of the Gael among the 'English, Britons and Picts' brought in chains to Dublin by the fleet of 871.

Olaf disappears from Irish history immediately after his return from Strathclyde, when he was summoned home to the aid of his father, the Vestfold king Guthfrith beleaguered by his own enemies in Norway, but his departure marks a new phase in the development of Scandinavian Ireland and, especially, of Scandinavian Dublin.

It is a grim fact of the history of Dublin town that its ascendancy as the Irish capital was built – as was the booming prosperity of Bristol and Liverpool some nine centuries later – very largely on its importance as a market place for the slave-trade. The Ath-Cliath of the northmen had no estates like those of the monastic towns with which to support its population, but it was described by the medieval Danish historian Saxo Grammaticus as a city 'filled with the wealth of barbarians'. It stood at the major western junction of the sea-roads of the northern world and thus, by the last quarter of the ninth century, at the hub of the inter-continental Scandinavian slave trade.

The trade of the Scandinavian expansion depended almost entirely on no more than three commodities. Amber, the fossilised resin of primeval conifers called 'the gold of the north', and the furs of wild creatures were brought by the northmen out of the great forests of their homelands, but slaves were the stock-in-trade harvested from their settlements in the western sea. There was certainly little demand for slaves from Scandinavia itself, where over-population had provided a major stimulus to the viking and land-seeking phenomena. While slave labour would be needed in the new north Atlantic settlement on Iceland by the later ninth century, the most lucrative market for the Scandinavian slave trade lay in the Islamic world of the Mediterranean and further east.

Against that backdrop, the 'great spoil of people' brought by Olaf and Ivar provided the first injection of working capital for Dublin's slave markets from where human cargoes were bought and sold, shipped out and sold on again to further-flung centres of the trade. Iceland lay on the sea-road to the north by way of Orkney and the markets of the Arab world were reached by way of Hedeby in the Baltic and the Russian rivers or Cordoba and Moorish Spain. Nor was it a one-way traffic. Saga tradition claims the 'sons of Ragnar Lothbrok' were a-viking on the Spanish and North African coast shortly before they invaded Northumbria and independent Muslim sources confirm raids by northmen – although named only as *majus* rather than Ragnarssons – reliably dated between 859 and 861. These were certainly the same raiders whose return to Ireland with their extraordinary human cargo is entered in the *Fragmentary Annals*.

> They brought a great host in captivity with them to Ireland.
> These are the 'blue men', because Moors are the same as negroes ...
> Long were these blue men in Ireland.

Norse, Dane, or Swede, the merchant-marauders out of the north were entered throughout the Christian and Muslim early sources as dealers in just one principal commodity, to the point where Alfred Smyth, who has most thoroughly investigated the Scandinavian slave trade, can describe the northmen as 'seen by their contemporaries primarily as heathen slave-raiders who preyed on western Christendom'. Such a thriving export trade demanded a steady supply of raw material and nowhere is that harvest so fully-documented as in the Irish sources. From Olaf's plundering of Armagh in 869 on through the tenth century, the annal record of monastic raiding enters the taking of captives with a new regularity and in much greater numbers than before. These were raids to supply the slave markets of Dublin and they were planned and executed with cynical, even 'industrial', premeditation.

The sparse and scattered nature of settlement in Ireland meant that monasteries – or, more realistically, monastic settlements – had represented the only substantial permanent populations at the outset of the viking age, but they had been plundered for silver and slaves for almost fifty years before the last quarter of the ninth century. Their monastic complements had been too drastically diminished to supply the numbers, much less the variety, of slaves needed to feed the demand of the markets. For that reason slave-takers who now had market forces to satisfy timed their raids on monasteries to coincide with the feasts of patron saints and other festivals of the church calendar. Such occasions were the most populous social gatherings to be found in early Christian Ireland, when pilgrims gathered in their many hundreds at the shrine of the saint and with them numbers of tradespeople and stallholders bringing food, drink and other wares to supply a ready market. In an atmosphere akin to a fairground in a monastic setting, they provided ideal targets for slave-raiders and, of even greater value, they were held on the same days every year.

This strategic importance of monastic centres as regular sources of slaves may, when viewed in retrospect, have ensured the survival of the great monasteries of Ireland. While the Danes who occupied England north of Watling Street as their Danelaw from the mid-ninth century had almost entirely destroyed the monasteries of Northumbria and Mercia, the *gaill* in Ireland, Norse and Dane alike, plundered the churches only to a point some way short of extinction. This must have reflected a deliberate policy of calculated 'harvest-ing', because the destruction of the Irish monasteries on the same scale as Northumbria would have amounted to the effective destruction of the slave trade of the northmen in Erin.

So it was that when Olaf timed his return from Pictland to raid Armagh on the feast of Patrick his warband was assured of the most profitable haul of human plunder, as many as 'ten hundred persons between the captives and the slain' on the annalist's evidence. Guthfrith, Ivar's grandson, seems to have paid especially assiduous attention to the calendar of saints when he planned his slave-raiding. The *Annals of the Four Masters* at 926 enter his raid on Kildare 'on the festival day of Saint Brigid'. Eight years earlier the *Annals of Ulster* had noted his choice of 'the Saturday before the feast of Saint Martin' to plunder Armagh where Martin was especially honoured – according to the ninth-century *Tripartite Life of Patrick* – because 'it is he that conferred a monk's tonsure on Patrick'.

Christmas Eve – or 'Christmas night' as it was called in the early sources – is more than once identified as the date of a slave-raid. Christmas, then as now, was the most popular season for church

125

attendance and selected for that reason by the Danes of Dublin a-viking in the Hebrides for their raid on Iona entered in the *Annals of Ulster* at 986.

> I-Columcille was plundered on Christmas night, when they killed the abbot and fifteen of the learned of the church.

It was the last raid by the northmen on Iona of Columcille, but it did not go unavenged by the saint on the evidence of the *Annals of the Four Masters* at 987.

> A great slaughter was made of the Danes who had plundered I[-Columcille], for three hundred and sixty of them were slain through the miracles of God and Columcille.

Whether by reason of the savagery of its slaughter or the sacrilege of its occasion the raid has been marked with an especial notoriety in Iona tradition. The place where the abbot and his brothers were cut down on the nine hundred and eighty-sixth anniversary of the eve of Christ's Nativity was the long beach of white sand at the north end of the island. It is still called in the Gaelic *Traigh ban nam manach*, the 'White Strand of the Monks'.

The evidence of the raid of 986 confirms that some form of monastic community remained on Iona and seems to have done so since the transfer of the seat of the *comarb* of Columcille to Kells in 807. The monks who had accompanied the martyred Blathmac in 825 were evidently on the island as guardians of the shrine of Columcille, but such could not have been the task of the community of 986. A sequence of entries in the annals for the first half of the ninth century records the transport of the 'relics' between Ireland and Iona but, apart from the note of the 'shrine' brought to I-Columcille by Diarmit the abbot at Kells in 818, it is uncertain whether the annals referred to the corporeal remains of the saint.

There appears to have been some division of the relics of Columcille in 849 when the *Annals of Ulster* enter their removal from Iona to Kells.

> Indrechtach, abbot of Ia [at Kells], came to Ireland with the relics of Columcille.

It was in the same year, according to the *Chronicle of the Kings,* that Kenneth mac-Alpin similarly endowed his royal church at Dunkeld.

> In the seventh year of his reign, [Kenneth] transported the relics of Saint Columba to a church that he had built.

Historians generally agree that relics of Columcille were divided between Kells and the new centre of the Columban church in Scotland at Dunkeld. The saint's *bachall*, his highly-esteemed crozier, was certainly in Scottish hands in 904 when the *Annals of Ulster* record 'Ivar, Ivar's grandson, killed by the men of Fortriu'. Ivar, the grandson of Olaf's ally and now himself king of Dublin, had raided Dunkeld the previous year and when he fell in battle at Strathearn the *Fragmentary Annals* confirm that the crozier of Columcille led the host of Alba to their victorious vengeance.

> Columcille's bachall ... was therefore called *Cathbuaid* ['battle-victory'] from that time on. It was a just name because they often won the victory in battle through it, even as they did on that occasion, when they placed their faith in Columcille.

Nonetheless, the crozier was not a corporeal relic, and neither is there any record of the bones of Columcille being enshrined at Kells. The possession of such bodily remains, the *martra* of the saint, carried with it the authority of the mother church of his *paruchia* and both Kells and Dunkeld would have been equally anxious to enforce their claims for at least some portion of them. While it is possible that Columcille's remains were apportioned between the two churches in 849, it is also possible that they were allowed to remain on Iona and the entries at 849 referred only to the *mionna*, just such non-corporeal relics as the crozier.

With the northmen infesting the *Innse-gall*, striking into the Scottish mainland, and based on the loughs of Ireland, there was no place of safety in any part of the Columban *paruchia*. The Norse fleets which plundered 'the greater part of Erin' from Dublin after 845 had raided the most important of Columcille's Irish foundations at Durrow and the sanctuary of the Iona community at Kells before the coming of the Danes in 851. Kenneth mac-Alpin's new church of Columcille at Dunkeld was not to suffer a raid until Ivar of Dublin went to war on Tayside in 903, but Iona had been attacked by a fleet out of Dublin in 849 according to the *Cogadh*.

127

The *Annals of Ulster* clearly record the 'shrine of Columcille and all his *mionna*' brought to Ireland in 878, so the community on Iona in 986 must have remained on the island as custodians of the Reilig Odhrain, which served as the burial ground for the kings of Alba and medieval Scotland as it had for the kings of Dalriada, Pictland and the northern Irish dynasties for more than four hundred years. Kenneth mac-Alpin was entombed there in 858 as was his son Constantine in 877 and their successor kings of Scots for centuries after. Most remarkably, Olaf Sitricsson called *cuaran* or 'sandal', king of the *gaill* of York and Dublin, had retired as a monk on Iona and became the first of the northmen to be interred in its hallowed ground on his death in 981.

I-Columcille had, after all, been foretold as the last place on earth to be destroyed and its ancient sanctity was somehow preserved by the holy men who clung on to the 'deep peace of the running wave' in the islands of the *Innse-gall.* It was they who must have administered the earliest baptisms to the *gaill* and their first convert recorded in the sources was Aud, daughter of Ketil and queen to Olaf of Dublin.

Whether or not her cognomen, the 'deep-minded', can be taken as evidence of a profoundly spiritual nature, Aud is confirmed by saga evidence as having become a Christian, almost certainly during her time in the islands following her separation from Olaf. After the death of her father in 857, Aud took refuge with her son, Thorstein Olafsson called 'the red', in Caithness. Thorstein the Red does not appear in the Irish sources but was nonetheless an historical character. He had 'become a warrior king and allied himself to Sigurd the Mighty', according to *Erik the Red's Saga*, 'and they conquered Caithness and Sutherland, Ross and Moray, and more than half Scotland'. Just as Sigurd was Olaf's *jarl* in Orkney, so Thorstein must have been his sub-king over *Katanes* and *Sudrland* until around 875 when 'the Scots betrayed him and he fell in battle'.

On the death of her son, Aud commissioned a longship to be built 'secretly in the woods' for the crossing of the Pentland Firth to Orkney. From Orkney she set sail again, with her grandson Olaf Thorsteinsson and 'twenty freemen' on a course by way of Foula and the Faroes to the new Norse outpost on Iceland. Her landfall there, as it is entered in the Icelandic *Landnamabok*, or 'Book of the Settlements', was almost exactly that of a Celtic holy man founding his hermitage in the ocean.

Aud made her home at Hvamm and a place for her devotions at Krossholar, where she had crosses raised, because she had been baptised and clung to the Christian faith.

Aud's voyage to Iceland is the more remarkable for its parallel with the seafaring of Brendan the Navigator and Cormac of the Sea.

The northmen who settled Iceland in the last quarter of the ninth century have been shown to have come there by way of the northern and western isles following the same course first explored by the voyager saints some three hundred years before. Setting out from the west of Ireland and using Iona as a forward base, Cormac had reached Orkney and the Faroes, while Brendan sailed on to Iceland, Greenland and, very probably, North America. Generations of hermit-monks followed in their wake from Iona to Orkney each February to spend the summer in retreat on the Faroes, Iceland and Greenland before making the return voyage when the prevailing winds shifted to the west in August. The presence of the holy men on retreat in the north Atlantic is confirmed from Norse tradition by the Icelanders' 'Book of the Settlements'.

> Before Iceland was settled from Norway, there were men there whom the Norse called *papar*. They were Christians, and men say that they must have come from the islands of Britain, because there were left there by them Irish books, bells, and croziers, from which it might be thought they were westmen.

They were indeed 'westmen', the monks of the western sea who had followed in the wake of Cormac and Brendan. It was they who had told Dicuil on Iona of 'islands in the ocean to the north of Britain which can be reached from the northernmost British isles in two days and nights sailing with full sails and a fair wind'. These holy men were called in Old Norse *papar* and their island landfalls can still be identified along the northern seaways by place-names incorporating the elements *papa* or *papay*.

Alfred Smyth has shown that all the Norse who settled Iceland had come there by way of the Hebridean *Innse-gall* and the saga accounts confirm the presence of Irish Celts – both freedmen and bond-men – throughout the north Atlantic settlement. Norse forms of the Irish names Niall and Cormac are clearly preserved in the titles of both *Njal's Saga* and *Kormak's Saga* and it might even be suggested that the Icelandic saga form had its deepest roots in the ancient Irish sagas, themselves the oldest vernacular literature in Europe. Dr Tim Severin, the maritime historian who retraced Brendan's course from Kerry to Newfoundland in a replica hide-hulled curragh under sail, is convinced that Irish seafaring monks had reached the north American *Vinland* four hundred years before the northmen. *Erik's Saga* describes Irish scouts guiding the northmen in *Vinland* and Severin suggests that they might well have also served as pilots aboard the longships.

He points to 'a Christian seagoing culture which had sent boat after boat into the North Atlantic on regular voyages of communication and exploration' and had clearly shown the way to the land-seeking northmen. Aud and her kind had learned as much of wind and wave as of *pater* and *credo* from the voyager-monks whose sea-road they followed to Iceland and, another hundred years later, to Greenland and beyond.

There is a strange irony in Eirik Thorvaldsson, more familiar now as 'Erik the Red', setting sail from Iceland to retrace Brendan's voyage to Greenland in the same year of 986 when Danish vikings out of Dublin inflicted the last fury of the northmen on I-Columcille.

More than a hundred years later, Magnus Bareleg, king of Norway, came to I-Columcille. His voyage to reassert Norse hegemony over the northern and western isles was conducted in the old viking way – on the evidence of the *Heimskringla* – until his longships put into Saint Ronan's Bay on Iona.

> [From Orkney] King Magnus, with his followers, proceeded to the Sudreyjar, and when he came there began to burn and lay waste the inhabited places, killing the people, and plundering wherever he came with his men ...
>
> King Magnus came with his forces to the Holy Island [of Iona] and gave peace and safety to all men there. It is told that the king opened the door of the little Columb's Kirk there, but did not go in, but instantly locked the door again, and said that no man should be so bold as to ever go into that church hereafter; which has been the case ever since.
>
> From thence King Magnus sailed to Islay, where he plundered and burned; and when he had taken that country he proceeded south around Kintyre, marauding on both sides of Scotland and Ireland.

The strange homage paid by Magnus Bareleg at the shrine of Columcille reflects the fact that kings of Norway had been Christian for more than a hundred years when he came west-over-sea in 1098 and I-Columcille had become a 'Holy Island' for the northmen of the White Christ.

The conversion of the northmen had been a gradual process brought about by their contact with Christian civilisation, but their Christianity long bore its own distinctly pagan aspect. The pagan polytheism of the northern world – in .stark contrast to the monotheistic commitment of Islam – was not closed to the admission of a new man-god and the pre-Christian roots of Celtic spirituality carried their own specially persuasive force. Only one generation separated Aud the Deep-minded from Utta the *vala* who had cast her runes on the altar at Clonmacnois and no high crosses on an Iceland shore could dissuade later generations of land-seekers from turning back to Thor when faced with crisis. Neither is it entirely accidental that the day of the week on which Columcille was born, still called in the Hebrides 'Thursday of benign Columcille', was the same day named 'Thors-day' for the northmen's lord of the harvest and the thunder.

The formal adoption of the White Christ by the Norse kings began with Olaf Tryggvasson who led the northmen into battle at Maldon before he made peace with Aethelred, king of the English and great-grandson of Alfred of Wessex, and accepted baptism from a hermit of the Scilly Isles in 994. In the following year, Olaf sailed north up the western seaboard to claim the dominions and the kingdom of his grandfather Harald Finehair for himself and to enforce his new faith, if needs be at sword-point, on all who called him lord.

When Olaf Tryggvasson reached Orkney, he brought his longship into Osmundwall at the southern tip of the islands and summoned the *jarl* Sigurd on board for the summary conversion recorded in the *Orkneyinga Saga*.

'It is my will that thou let thyself be baptised and all those that serve thee, else thou shall die here at once and I will fare with fire and flame all over the isles.'

When the jarl saw into what a strait he had come, he gave himself up into the king's power. The king then let him be baptised and took as a hostage his son ... then all the Orkneyjar became Christian.

While Olaf was so forcefully imposing Christian baptism on his jarldom of Orkney, the community of Cuthbert walked the last miles of their wanderings which had brought them to Durham on the Wear. There they laid the carved wooden coffin of their saint into the earth and there, another century on, was raised the last and greatest cathedral church of Cuthbert of Lindisfarne.

Their long journey to that place had begun a hundred and twenty years before in a Northumbria 'harassed by the heathen host' ...

'harassed by the heathen host'

Northanhymbre, AD 865–877 and after

'And I would have you know and remember
that if necessity compels you to choose one of two evils,
I would much prefer you to dig up my bones from the tomb
and take them with you and leave this place,
to dwell wherever God ordains, than that you should make
any compromise with wickedness.'

Bede's prose *Life of Cuthbert.*

B Y THE year 865, seven decades of Scandinavian raiding, invasion and settlement had entirely transformed the Celtic north and west of these islands. Norse vikings had seized the northern isles and claimed the western sea as far south as Man. Warlords of the *finn-gaill* and the *dubh-gaill* had carved out their own dominion on the Irish mainland and cast their long shadow over the newly-emergent Scottish nation. Now it was the turn of the English mainland to be engulfed by the flood-tide of the Scandinavian migration age.

The skeletal outline of England's history through the seventh, eighth and greater part of the ninth centuries is a sequence of ascendancies of kingdoms.

In the first decade of the seventh century the ancient English settlement of Deira, between the Humber and the Tyne, had been unified with its outcrop expansion of Bernicia, centred on Bamburgh and extending from the Tyne to the Forth, into the vast kingdom of *Northanhymbre*. Three of its seventh-century kings were ranked as *bretwalda*, the English counterpart of the Irish high-king, but the decline of the Northumbrian royal dynasty after 704 gave way to the Mercian ascendancy which reached its peak in the decades before the death of Offa in 796.

The long-established kingdom of the East Angles, centred on modern Suffolk, had flourished in the early seventh century – from which period the Sutton Hoo treasure attests its wealth and power – yet sustained its own independent line of kings, if under the shadow of Northumbria and Mercia, until it was swept into the Scandinavian settlement in 870.

In the south the kings of the West Saxons were already moving into the ascendant before the mid-ninth century. Alliances with Mercia sealed by royal marriages and the submission of the Northumbrian king to a West Saxon overlord in 829 left Wessex to shoulder the role of the great power in the land on the eve of its invasion by the northmen. By the end of the ninth and into the tenth century, the West Saxon royal house – in the person of Alfred and his line of successors – stood alone as kings of all the English and the last bulwark of the Anglo-Saxon Christian civilisation. It is an especially ninth-century irony that the West Saxon ascendancy – like that of the Munster kings of Ireland and Kenneth mac-Alpin's new kingdom of the Scots – was a direct consequence of Scandinavian expansion into the land.

While it had been the northern English who had felt the first shock of the viking age, the Norse out of Orkney and Shetland who first struck at the Northumbrian monasteries were to veer their course along the western seaboard in subsequent raiding seasons. The next wave of the Scandinavian onslaught came by a different sea-road and was not to reach the English coast until four decades after the first raid on Lindisfarne. These were the Danes out of the Baltic and they were already on the move before 800, raiding the coast of Aquitaine in 799 and Frisia in 810. It was the sack of the great trading centre at Dorestad in 834 which signalled the launch of their full-scale assault on the Frankish empire and their longships were across the Channel in the following year.

The first recorded Danish attack on England is entered in the *Anglo-Saxon Chronicle* for 836.*

In this year heathen men ravaged Sheppey.

For the next four decades the English early sources seem almost to groan under the weight of the escalating assault on southern and eastern England. Raiding from the sea gave way to land-based incursion when the first warband of Danes overwintered on the Isle of Thanet in 850 and another made its winter camp on Sheppey in 854, and yet throughout all this period Northumbria might appear to have been entirely untouched by the new viking onslaught. The *Anglo-Saxon Chronicle* records 'slaughter by the heathen' as far north as Lincolnshire in 841, but even its northern recension includes no reference to any return of the vikings north of the Humber through the sixty-five years after the raids on the Tyne and the Tees in 800.

The fact that no raids were recorded cannot be taken as any guarantee that none occurred, especially when Sir Frank Stenton admits that 'Northumbria throughout this period lies almost outside recorded history'. The lost northern history, which had informed both the *Historia Regum* attributed to Symeon of Durham and the northern recension of the *Anglo-Saxon Chronicle*, appears to expire between 801 and 810 and yet a few later fragments from it or from a similar source found their way into Roger of Wendover's thirteenth-century *Flores Historiarum*. One such note indicates a viking attack on Northumbria in 844 when the king Raedwulf – whose reign is firmly attested by coin evidence – was killed in 'a battle with the pagans'.

* All subsequent *Anglo-Saxon Chronicle* references are given with *recte* dating to correspond to the true historical date for the chronicler's entry.

There is also the evidence of the sixteenth-century antiquary John Leland who drew on Northumberland tradition to claim that the battle at *Carrum* – identified by the *Anglo-Saxon Chronicle* for 836 as Carhampton in Somerset – was in fact fought in Northumbria and won by the Danes at Carham on the banks of the Tweed.

There is more evidence of viking incursion north of the Humber, and at around the same time, in a Scandinavian source, the *Krakumal*. This 'Lay of Kraka' is a skaldic war-song placed in the voice of a wife of the legendary viking Ragnar Lothbrok and set down in the Hebrides in the twelfth century. It tells how Ragnar fought and won a battle 'in the morning' in *Northimbra landz* before he 'hewed with the sword' across the Hebrides and Ireland through the 840s and early 850s. It is only such fragmentary survivals in history and tradition which indicate that the northern English did not entirely escape the Danish onslaught described by all the sources as directed against the southern English kingdoms in the first half of the ninth century.

By contrast with the fractured record of secular Northumbria, the consecutive history of Lindisfarne was preserved by the Durham historians of the twelfth century and it is their transcription of the records and traditions of the community of Cuthbert which remains the sole unbroken thread of Northumbrian history throughout the age of Scandinavian expansion.

For all that, the impressive canon of Durham sources seems to have told something less than the whole story. Symeon's *History of the Church of Durham* records the survival of the church on Lindisfarne in the decades after 793 in unremarkable terms of the succession of its bishops, but other evidence suggests that nothing was ever the same again on the holy island after the 'inroad from the sea' of 793. Alcuin's letters deplore the further decline in standards of monastic observance and the eminent Bedan scholar A. Hamilton Thompson has discerned a corrosive legacy left by the first impact of the northmen on the Northumbrian church.

> There can be no doubt that the first ravaging of northern monasteries in 793 and 794 marks a dividing line in their history: weakened by plunder and massacre, the diminished communities relaxed a discipline for which no adequate guidelines were left.

While there is no evidence of any further attack on Lindisfarne until the second half of the ninth century, the very real fear of one must have been an ever-present anxiety for the community. The monastery had long maintained its contacts with the churches of Ireland and Iona and cannot have been uninformed of the devastation being wreaked along the western seaboard.

The clearest evidence for the insecurity of the church of Cuthbert – and also for a substantial viking incursion north of the Humber after 832 – occurs among the historical material annotating the inventory of Lindisfarne land-grants in the *Historia de Sancto Cuthberto*. This anonymous text was set down in the mid-tenth century, when the community was settled at Chester-le-Street after the evacuation of Lindisfarne and before the final move to Durham. Symeon's *History* enters the accession of Bishop Egred in 832 as the occasion of his gift of estates, amongst them the *vill* at Norham on the Tweed, to the landholdings of Lindisfarne.

> He was a man of noble birth, and energetic in his proceedings, taking care to enrich and honour the church of Saint Cuthbert with donations of goods and property. For he built a church at Norham, and dedicated it in honour of Saint Peter the apostle, and Cuthbert the bishop, and also of Ceolwulf, formerly a king [of Northumbria, 729–37], but afterwards a monk; and he translated there the body of that same God-beloved Ceolwulf.

The same land-grant and church-building was recorded in the *Historia de Sancto Cuthberto*, but with the very significant additional note of the translation of Cuthbert's remains from Lindisfarne to Norham.

> And he translated there the bodies of Saint Cuthbert and King Ceolwulf and gave to the holy confessor that same vill.

The removal of the shrine of Cuthbert from its appointed resting-place had been sanctioned by the saint's own last words – recorded at first-hand in Bede's prose *Life** – but was never lightly undertaken and only in the face of the greatest danger. Consequently – and assuming the accuracy of the tenth-century source – the translation to Norham provides evidence for the recognition of a serious threat of viking attack on Lindisfarne at some point during the episcopacy of Egred between 832 and 850. The threat must have passed,

* See p. 133 above.

presumably with the departure of the sea-raiders, and Cuthbert's shrine been restored to Lindisfarne from its temporary place of safety. Symeon's *History of the Church of Durham* confirms the saint's remains were back in the monastery before 875 when the shrine was taken up again to accompany the community of Cuthbert on the long road which finally led to Durham.

Whatever the extent of viking activity in Northumbria represented by these fragments of evidence, it can only have been driven – as elsewhere in England – by plunder-taking rather than land-seeking.

The shift from raiding to settlement is first evident in 865 when the *Anglo-Saxon Chronicle* records the arrival of the *micel haethen here*, the 'great heathen host', in East Anglia.

> And in the same year, came a great heathen host to the land of the English people, and took winter quarters among the East Angles, and were there horsed, and the East Angles made peace with them.

Other than the seventh-century laws which define a *here* as a 'host' of more than thirty-five fighting men, there is no more precise contemporary indication of the size of this 'great heathen host'. Modern estimates vary dramatically, but the range and impact of the invasion could not have been accomplished by a force numbering less than a thousand warriors and twice that number would not be an unreasonable speculation.

Symeon of Durham describes 'an immense fleet [of] Danes, Frisians, and other nations' and his list of its commanders confirms the host as a coalition of the warbands of Ivar, Halfdan and Ubba, sons of Ragnar Lothbrok, with those of their lesser ally *jarls*.

> An immense fleet, under their kings and leaders, Halfdene, Inguar, Hubba, Baegseg, Guthrum, Oscytell, Amund, Sidroc, and another leader of the same name, Osbern, Frana and Harold.

First amongst these warlords, according to Aethelweard's *Chronicle*, stood 'the tyrant Inguar' who was to lead the host on five years of campaigning through Northumbria, Mercia and East Anglia. *Inguar* disappears from the English sources after his murder of the king of the East Angles in 870, at which point the similarly named *Imhar* reappears in the *Annals of Ulster* laying siege with Olaf, king of

Dublin, to Dumbarton on the Clyde. The same *Imhar* had disappeared from the Irish annals after his raid on the tombs of the Boyne valley in 863 just two years before *Inguar* appears in command of the 'great host' which had landed in East Anglia and would soon seize York.

It must be stated here that historians are far from unanimous in accepting the identification which I have adopted, but the coincidence of the chronologies satisfies me that they are following the career of one and the same man: Ivar Ragnarsson called 'the boneless', tomb-plunderer and slave-trader, son of the legendary Lothbrok and king of the northmen at both Dublin and York.

Although the host had landed in East Anglia and there over-wintered, its ambition lay further north and to that end it took the Danegeld in the form of cavalry mounts from a region still today renowned for the quality of its horsebreeding. The extortion of *Danegeld* – payment in money or in kind to buy off the fury of the northmen – was already recognisable as a stratagem of Danish warbands on the continent where Charles the Bald, king of Franks, had bought peace for 7,000lb of silver from the Danes who had plundered Paris in 843. Danegeld was an attractive prospect when it enabled a pirate warband to load their longships with plunder without the need to fight for it. It might have been devised, although no saga says as much, by the wily Odin himself, especially when there was nothing to prevent raiders from taking the Danegeld and then reneging on the agreement to their greater profit. Just such a ruse was employed by the warband which overwintered on the Isle of Thanet in 864 – and may well have joined Ivar's coalition in the following year – on the evidence of the *Anglo-Saxon Chronicle.*

> In this year a heathen host took up their quarters in Thanet, and made peace with the men of Kent; and the men of Kent promised them money for the peace; and during the peace and the promise of money, the host stole away by night and ravaged all Kent to the eastward.

Similarly, the great host which took horses from the East Angles as their Danegeld in 865 returned to raid East Anglia just five years later. For all its viking tactics, this was no over-sized raiding force, but a full-scale army of invasion whose departure from its winter camp and advance on Northumbria is entered in the *Chronicle* for 866.

In this year the host went from the East Angles, over the mouth of the Humber, to Eoforwic [York] in Northumbria.

All the English sources record the seizure of York in similarly summary terms and it is left to the Anglo-Norman metrical *L'Estorie des Engles* written by Geoffroi Gaimar in the twelfth century to provide the most detailed account of the northern progress of Ivar's army.

> Then they took horses,
> And the best of their men,
> And most of them went in ships
> As far as the Humber, sails set.
> More than twenty thousand* went on foot ...
> At Grimsby they passed the Humber,
> And those on foot likewise.
> Great plenty they had of men;
> And those who were with the ships
> All went to York.
> Both by water and by land,
> They waged great war at York.
>   Those who came by water
> Sailed as far as the Ouse;
> But directly the sun was hidden
> The tide turned,
> And they then quartered themselves there;
> Some on the water, some in tents;
> But the chief men, the lords,
> Went into houses in the town.

Geoffroi's account confirms that the host moved north in their longships up the east coast as well as overland, mounted as cavalry and following the old Roman roads.

The road network built to carry the legions north more than seven hundred years before served the viking host as it had long served armies of Britons and Anglo-Saxons. The modern historian F. Donald Logan has shown how vital were the Roman roads to the Scandinavian invasion of England and has convincingly traced the route by the Fen Road west to Ermine Street which brought Ivar's

---

* Geoffroi's estimate is wildly extravagant for the ninth century. 'More than twenty thousand' is equivalent to twice the manpower of the invasion force brought to England by William of Normandy in 1066.

warriors to the south bank of the Humber. The land host would have there made contact with the longships to ferry its men and horses across the estuary – more probably at Brough than Grimsby suggested by Geoffroi – and the entire great host advanced up the Ouse to York.

The *Eoforwic* of the Anglo-Saxons had grown up on the foundations of *Eboracum*, the military capital of Roman Britain, where what remained of the fortifications of the Sixth Legion would have provided some defensive accommodation for Ivar and his host. Outside the Roman walls, the longships would have been brought ashore into newly-raised earthen ramparts – just as they had been at Dublin – and Scandinavian skill at raising effective defences at speed would have swiftly restored the decay of the Roman defences in the space of their first winter in Northumbria.

The seizure of York against apparently little resistance is best explained as a result of Northumbria's effective state of civil war prevailing in the year 866. What little is known of the seven decades of political history of the northern English between the first raid on Lindisfarne and the arrival of Ivar's host must be constructed from the evidence of Symeon of Durham and Roger of Wendover. It amounts to little more than a list of the names of 'kings', all of whom were warrior thanes struggling to hold together a vast kingdom beset by the conspiracies of their rivals. These thanes, none of them with any indisputable claim to royal lineage, are largely lost to history in any greater detail than their names and reign lengths varying between twenty-seven days and three decades.

So it was that the northmen found Northumbria bitterly divided by endemic warfare between claimants to the kingdom. Indeed, it may have been prior intelligence of this civil war which had attracted the invader north of the Humber, but the date of Ivar's arrival was certainly no accident. Symeon confirms it as 'the kalends [1st] of November' and Roger of Wendover as 'on All Saints' Day', when the city would have been filled with crowds of Yorkshire folk drawn to its *mynster* for the Feast of all the Saints amidst the last market fair before the onset of winter. Ivar the Boneless was already beginning to harvest his 'Saxon' contribution to the slave-cargo he was to ship into Dublin with Olaf in 871.

Symeon's *History of the Church of Durham* confirms that Ivar further

142

followed the established Irish strategy when he used York as the inland base for his devastations north of the Humber.

> The said army of the pagans, after having taken York on the kalends of November, spread themselves over the whole country, and filled all with blood and grief; they destroyed the churches and the monasteries far and wide with fire and sword, leaving nothing remaining save the bare, unroofed walls; and so thoroughly did they do their work, that even our own present generation can seldom discover in those places any conclusive memorial of their ancient dignity, and sometimes none.
>
> Upon this occasion, however, the barbarians advanced no further north than the mouth of the river Tyne, but returned from thence to York.

Roger of Wendover's sources did not provide him with the clearest chronology, but his listing of the monasteries ravaged by Ivar does expand on Symeon's evidence.

> The most noble monasteries along the sea-coast are said to have been destroyed ... a monastery of nuns at Tynemouth, another of monks at Jarrow and Wearmouth, another of nuns at Strenaeshalc [Whitby], founded by the most blessed abbess Hild, who gathered many virgins there.
>
> These relentless chiefs then passed through Yorkshire, burning churches, cities and villages, and utterly destroying the people of whatever sex or age, together with the spoil and the cattle.

The double foundation of monks and nuns at *Strenaeshalc*, the site of the great synod of 664, was the rich shrine of the saintly abbess Hild and Edwin, the first Christian king of Northumbria, and would have been a natural target for plunder-taking. The monastery was certainly destroyed by the northmen and 867 is the generally and authoritatively accepted date for their raid. Indeed its Old English placename *Strenaeshalc*, 'the bay of the lighthouse', was replaced by the Old Norse *Witebi*, 'the white bay', supporting the substantial archaeological evidence for a Scandinavian settlement at Whitby.

This ravaging of Northumbria presented its rival native kings with a common enemy and prompted them to join forces for an attempt to reclaim York from the northmen in the following year. The battle fought on the Friday before Palm Sunday is entered in all the early sources for 867 but the *Historia Regum* provides the most illuminating

143

introduction to the tactics which won the day for the 'great heathen host'.

> At the same time, a very great strife was kindled among the Northumbrian people; for he who loves strife shall find it.
>
> In those days the Northumbrians had violently expelled from the kingdom the rightful king, Osberht, and had placed at the head of the kingdom a certain tyrant named Aella. When the pagans came upon the kingdom, that dissension was allayed by divine counsel and the aid of the nobles. King Osberht and Aella, having united their forces and formed an army, came to the city of York; on their approach, the multitude of the shipmen immediately took to flight. The Christians, seeing their flight and terror, found that they themselves were the stronger party. They fought on each side with great ferocity ...

At this point, where the *Historia Regum* moves to an abrupt conclusion, the *Anglo-Saxon Chronicle* provides a more detailed account of the final phase of the conflict.

> They stormed the city, and some got within, and there was immense slaughter made of the Northumbrians, some within, some without; and both kings were slain; and the survivors made peace with the host.

Ivar's forces had deployed the old ruse of feigned battle-rout. The warriors manning the ramparts around the longships – called 'the shipmen' by the *Historia Regum* – pretended flight to draw the attackers through the Roman walls and into Ivar's fortress, where they were trapped, overwhelmed and massacred when the retreating enemy, now reinforced by superior forces within, turned on the Northumbrians. *Eboracum* of the Romans and *Eoforwic* of the English had been baptised in blood as *Jorvik* of the northmen.

Lindisfarne tradition – as it is preserved in Symeon's *History of the Church of Durham* – records the same events in very different terms of divine retribution on the Northumbrian kings. He also enters the most probably accurate date for the battle as the 21st March, which was the Friday before Palm Sunday in the year 867.

> They assaulted York, upon the twelfth of the kalends of April ... and the conflict was waged on both sides with great ferocity. It ended, however, in the death of the two kings, who fell along with the greater part of their followers; and thus they were deprived at once of life and kingdom, and so paid the penalty for the injuries which they had previously inflicted

upon the church of Saint Cuthbert: for Osberht had dared with sacrilegious hand to wrest from that church Warkworth and Tillmouth, and Aella had done the like for Billingham, Cliffe, Wycliffe and Crayke.

In fairness to the two dead kings, their 'injuries inflicted on the church of Saint Cuthbert' would have been motivated by military necessity rather than by land-hunger. A king recruiting a conscript warband, called a *fyrd*, was forbidden to levy such troops from church lands. Northumbria must have been long drained of manpower, certainly by civil wars and probably also by resistance to viking incursion, so the seizure of monastic estates might well have represented the last resort in the recruiting campaign of desperate warlords.

The death of Aella was also accounted an act of retribution by Scandinavian saga tradition. The twelfth-century *Ragnar Lothbrok's Saga* concludes with a grisly account of his death in a snake-pit at York at the hands of Aella, thus allowing vengeance for their father's death as the motive for the invasion of Northumbria by Ragnar's sons. Aella had been king for only a matter of months when the great host arrived at York and the historical Ragnar had been killed fighting in Ireland more than ten years before. The saga story is an entire fiction, which originated in Anglo-Danish Northumbria and accommodated the Ragnar of folklore into a snake-pit borrowed from elsewhere in Scandinavian tradition.

The killing of Aella by Ivar is, by contrast, confirmed by both English and Scandinavian sources. More remarkably, no less than three Scandinavian texts confirm Aella slain by the same ritual sacrifice of the 'blood-eagle' as Blathmac on Iona forty years before. The earliest such evidence is that of the *Knutsdrapa*, an eleventh-century elegy on Cnut, the Danish king of England.

> And Ivarr
> who ruled at Jorvik,
> Cut an Eagle
> on the back of Aella.

The *Thattr of Ragnar's Sons*, appended to *Ragnar Lothbrok's Saga*, goes into more precise anatomical detail.

> They caused the blood-eagle to be carved on the back of Aella, and they cut away all of the ribs from the spine, and they ripped out his lungs.

145

Alfred Smyth's investigation of the historical blood-eagle ritual has shown that it was a practice especially associated with Ivar the Boneless. Ivar has been implicated in the similar execution of an Irish king who broke faith with the northmen and suffered death, according to the *Cogadh*, when 'his back was broken on a stone'. There is evidence also that Edmund, the sainted king of the East Angles – whose red martyrdom will repay further consideration below – suffered a similar fate at the hands of Ivar the Boneless in 870.

The ritual slaughter of Aella of Northumbria cannot be satisfactorily explained as historical retribution for mythical injury. It can only have been a sacrifice to Odin to mark the battle victory at Jorvik and dedicate Ivar's conquest of the kingdom of the northern English to the god of the warband. Ivar had established York as his new capital fortress, the English counterpart of Dublin, and the northmen were now the new overlords of the former Northumbrian sub-kingdom of Deira with their own client ruler – identified by Symeon of Durham – placed over the other sub-kingdom of Bernicia.

> Upon the death of these two persons [Osberht and Aella], the Danes appointed Egbert as king over such of the Northumbrians as survived, limiting his jurisdiction to those only who resided upon the north of the river Tyne.

With its conquest secure to the north of the Humber, the great host moved back to the south and into the kingdom of the Middle Angles. The *Anglo-Saxon Chronicle* for 868 describes its progress.

> In this year the same host went into Mercia to Nottingham and there took up their winter quarters.
>
> And Burhred, king of the Mercians, and his council begged of Aethelred, king of the West Saxons, and Alfred, his brother, to help them that they might fight against the host.
>
> And then they went with the West Saxon fyrd into Mercia as far as Nottingham, and there met with the host within their fortifications and besieged them therein: but there was no great battle; and the Mercians made peace with the host.

Thus passed the first encounter between the northmen and the English warlord who – a decade later and as Alfred, king of Wessex – was to become their most formidable foe.

The host returned to Northumbria in the spring of 869 and went south again later in the year to overwinter in East Anglia. The *Chronicle* suggests they 'rode' overland, but Roger of Wendover describes them sailing out of the Humber. The great host seems again to have travelled both on shipboard and horseback, just as it had first come north in 866, to East Anglia where it wreaked the devastation best detailed by the chronicle of Roger of Wendover.

> Advancing thence they destroyed all the monasteries of monks and virgins that were in the marshes, and slew their inmates.
>
> The names of these monasteries are Croyland, Thorney, Ramsey, [Medes]Hamstede, which is now called Peterborough.

The northern recension of the *Chronicle* confirms Roger's account with additional material from its own sources to identify Ivar and his brother Ubba at the head of the great host.

> In this year the host rode over Mercia into East Anglia, and took winter-quarters at Thetford, and in that winter Edmund the king fought against them and the Danes gained the victory, and slew the king and subdued all that land, and destroyed all the monasteries which they came to. The names of the chiefs who slew the king were Inguar and Ubba.
>
> At the same time they came to Medeshamstede, and burned and broke it down, slew the abbot and monks, and all that place which was before full rich they reduced to nothing.

The monastery of *Medeshamstede* at Peterborough is one of the best-recorded monastic foundations of seventh-century England. It was begun by Peada, the first Christian king of Mercia, with the encouragement of the *bretwalda* Oswy of Northumbria, in 654 and its ceremony of dedication 'to the glory of Christ and the honour of Saint Peter' attended by an impressive company of kings and bishops is detailed in the *Anglo-Saxon Chronicle* for 656. *Medeshamstede* was richly endowed with 'gold and silver, land and property, and all that is needed for it', which must have offered the richest of prospects for Ivar's warband.

For all the plundering of wealthy monasteries, the great sacrilege of the campaign in East Anglia over the winter of 869–70 was the ritual slaughter of its king Edmund, of which the earliest account is the *Passio* written by Abbo of Fleury in the later tenth century. Abbo drew on the first-hand testimony of Edmund's standard-bearer for his description of the royal martyr captured by the northmen,

147

refusing to deny his faith or submit to Ivar, then lashed to a tree and shot with arrows.

> And as he continued to call upon Christ, the villainous Inguar commanded an executioner to cut off his head at once. Edmund was half-dead, the warmth of life barely throbbing now in his breast, when the executioner swiftly pulled him from the bloody stake with the inner parts beneath the ribs laid bare by repeated stabbings, as if he had been torn on the rack or tormented with savage claws.

Whether or not Abbo recognised as much, his evidence echoes other accounts of the ritual slaughter by the 'blood-eagle'. The decapitation of the king of the East Angles following the conquest of his kingdom would have been as apt occasion for ritual sacrifice to Odin as had been the slaughter of Aella at York.

There is a further curious similarity between the deaths of the two kings in that both of them are implicated by Danelaw tradition with the killing of Ragnar Lothbrok and their brutal deaths consequently justified as the vengeance of Ragnar's sons. The medieval legend of Ragnar and Edmund – preserved by Roger of Wendover and the fifteenth-century chronicler John of Brompton – tells of Ragnar shipwrecked in East Anglia and murdered by Edmund's huntsman, who was then cast out to sea in an open boat and blown across to Denmark. There the murderer falsely accused the innocent king of his own offence and prompted Ragnar's sons to their vengeance.

Edmund's Christian heroism swiftly elevated him to the status of an English saint within thirty years of his martyrdom and Alfred Smyth has shown the Ragnar tale to be a medieval contrivance which originated in the Danelaw of the eleventh century. By which time the Anglo-Danish settlement had long been converted to Christianity and devised the story by way of an apologia for their forbears' cruel murder of a royal saint. It was just such a reworking of pagan history into Christian tradition as the skaldic concoction set in a snake-pit and devised in the Northumbrian Danelaw to justify the 'blood-eagling' of Aella.

To which might be added a postscript entered under the year 1014 in the twelfth-century chronicle of Florent of Worcester. It tells how Edmund rose up, almost a hundred and fifty years after his martyrdom, to wreak vengeance on another Danish king, Swein Haraldsson called 'forkbeard', who had given him offence in the course of an attempted conquest of England.

The tyrant Sweyn, after having committed innumerable and cruel atrocities, both in England and in other countries, filled up the measure of his damnation by demanding a large tribute from the town [apparently *Bedricsworth*, now Bury St Edmunds] where rests the uncorrupted corpse of the precious martyr Edmund, a thing which no one had dared to do since the town was given to the church of that saint. He threw out frequent threats that if it was not speedily paid he would certainly burn the town and the townsmen, raze to the ground the church of the said martyr, and torture the clerks in various modes. Moreover he frequently dared to deprecate the martyr in many ways, and with profane and sacrilegious mouth to bawl out that he was a person of no sanctity. But because he would not curb his malice, divine vengeance did not suffer his blasphemy to last any longer.

As he was reiterating his threats, towards evening, in a general muster he was holding one day at Gainsborough, and surrounded by very dense ranks of Danes, he alone saw Saint Edmund coming armed against him. He was terrified at the sight, and began to cry in a very loud voice, 'Help, my comrades, help! Saint Edmund is coming to kill me.' As he was speaking, the saint ran him through fiercely with a spear, and he fell from the stallion whereon he was sitting, and remaining in great agony until twilight, he died miserably on the third of the nones of February.

John of Brompton's chronicle tells how Ivar appointed Guthrum as the northmen's king in East Anglia before setting out with his warband by way of Dumbarton Rock on what was to be his last journey to Dublin.

And on his way he destroyed the abbey of the holy maidens of Ely and the nuns that served God therein did he either cruelly slay or savagely drive forth.

Roger of Wendover has his own note of Ivar's plundering 'the isle of Ely and the monastery of women formerly so famous, in which the holy virgin and queen Etheldreda laudably discharged the office of abbess for many years'. Ely had been founded by Etheldreda on her divorce from Egfrith, king of Northumbria, in the early 670s and generously endowed with the lands which had earlier been her dowry.

The cult of the virgin queen Etheldreda had been widely promoted by Bede's *Historia* and had established Ely as the pre-eminent 'monastery of women' of Anglo-Saxon England. For Ivar it would have represented a lucrative slave-taking, which is clearly what John of Brompton means by his reference to 'holy maidens savagely driven forth'. The same motive would have lain behind the raid on the nunnery at Coldingham when Ivar's warband reached the Firth of Forth on their advance to Strathclyde. The church Bede called *Coludesbyrig* had been founded by the abbess Aebba, daughter of Aethelfrith of Northumbria and sister to the kings Oswald and Oswy, soon after Aidan's foundation of Lindisfarne, but it did not enjoy any impeccable reputation for monastic discipline. Bede disapproved of 'Christ's handmaids there weaving fine clothes, which they employ to the peril of their calling ... to attract attention from strange men'. The dubious reputation of the Coldingham nuns does seem to have entered into local folklore, while the fact that Roger of Wendover calls their abbess in 870 by the same name as the seventh-century founder must throw doubt on the historical authority of the grisly anecdote he associates with 'an innumerable multitude of Danes landing in Scotland under the command of Inguar and Hubba'.

> The rumour of their merciless cruelty having spread throughout every kingdom, Ebba the holy abbess of the monastery of Coldingham, fearing lest both herself and the virgins of whom she had the pastoral care and charge should lose their virgin chastity, assembled all the sisters and thus addressed them:
>
> 'There have come lately into these parts most wicked pagans, destitute of all humanity, who roam through every place, sparing neither the female sex nor infantine age, destroying churches and ecclesiastics, ravishing holy women, and wasting and consuming everything in their way. If, therefore, you will follow my counsels, I have hope that through divine mercy we shall escape the rage of the barbarians and preserve our chastity.'
>
> The whole assembly of virgins having promised implicit compliance with her maternal commands, the abbess, with an heroic spirit, affording to all the holy sisters an example of chastity profitable only to themselves, but to be embraced by all succeeding virgins forever, took a razor and with it cut off her nose, together with her upper lip unto the teeth, presenting herself an horrific spectacle to those who stood by. Filled with admiration at this admirable deed, the whole assembly followed her maternal example, and severally did the like to themselves. When this was done, together with the morrow's dawn came those most cruel tyrants to disgrace the holy women devoted to God, and to pillage and burn the monastery; but on beholding the abbess and all the sisters so outrageously mutilated, and stained with their own blood from the sole of their foot to their head, they retired in haste from the place, thinking it too long to tarry there a moment; but as they were retiring, their leaders before mentioned ordered their wicked followers to set fire and

burn the monastery, with all its buildings and holy inmates. Which being done by these workers of iniquity, the holy abbess and all the most holy virgins with her attained the glory of martyrdom.

However dubious its detail, Roger's horror story does serve as evidence for the attack on Coldingham when Ivar's host brought their longships to the furthest navigable reach of the Forth before carrying them overland to the Clyde.

The portability of the viking longship was a crucial factor in the navigation of the northmen, especially in Scotland where it enabled narrow overland crossings between sea lochs, and is commemorated in the Scottish place-names including the component *tarbert* from the Gaelic *tairm-bert*, an 'over-carrying'.

On the Clyde Ivar joined his old ally Olaf in the conquest of Alcluith of the Britons and in the following year of 871 their fleet brought its great slave-cargo into Dublin. Olaf returned to Norway in the same year, leaving Ivar as sole king of Dublin until his death entered by the annals at 873.

Imhar, king of the gaill of all Ireland and Britain, ended his life.

Eystein, Olaf's son by his Irish queen, inherited his father's former kingdom of Dublin, but Ivar's English conquests and kingdom passed to his brother Halfdan, last of the sons of Ragnar Lothbrok.

When Ivar had led his warband north to the Clyde, Halfdan had moved with the remaining great host from East Anglia into Wessex. There they overwintered at Reading where they prepared to face the onslaught of the West Saxon *fyrd* under Aethelred and Alfred. The *Anglo-Saxon Chronicle* records 'the host were put to flight and many thousands slain' at Ashdown in Berkshire in the first weeks of 871 and when the Danish king Baegseg fell in the blood-fray on the chalk ridge of 'the hill of the ash' Halfdan was left in command. The northmen retreated to their earthwork fortress at Reading where they regrouped to emerge and defeat the men of Wessex at nearby Basing and the unidentified *Merentun* in the early spring.

Aethelred, king of Wessex, died at the end of April and the kingdom passed to his brother, but the first years of Alfred's reign were less than auspicious for the king later called 'the Great'. Halfdan's great host had been reinforced by the arrival of 'the great summer host' and defeated the West Saxons at Wilton within a month of Alfred's succession. After nine more battle-victories the northmen were poised for the conquest of Wessex, effectively the conquest of all England, by the end of the year and the West Saxons could do no other than buy peace from the Danes.

The host overwintered in London, but the northern English had risen against the client king Egbert and with him Wulfhere, bishop of York, who also seems to have accommodated the Danish conquest. Both had been driven out and Halfdan began the raiding season of 872 with an advance into Northumbria to reclaim the north. There is no detailed account of the suppression of the northern revolt, but it must have been accomplished before the autumn when the host moved south to overwinter at Torksey on the Trent. By the autumn of 873 when they moved to a winter camp at Repton, Mercia had been crushed, its king driven from his kingdom to spend the rest of his life in Rome, a client ruler imposed on the Mercians and peace bought with the Danegeld.

In the following year the 'great heathen host', which had conquered two-thirds of Anglo-Saxon England in less than ten years, finally fell apart. It may have been that the treasuries of the English kingdoms, like the Irish monasteries a dozen years earlier, had been so drained of wealth as to bring diminishing returns on raiding. It may also have been that vikings who had been fighting between the Tyne and the Thames for almost a decade were growing weary of the warrior's way and, like the Norse who had descended on the western seaboard eighty years before, turning instead to land-seeking for settlement. There is also the possibility that the battle-wisdom of its leaders sensed the formidable prospect soon to be presented by the last surviving warlord of an English royal house in the person of Alfred of Wessex.

For whatever reason, the Scandinavian expansion in England passed through a great shape-changing in the year 874.

Guthrum and two other kings led their warbands to Cambridge in the autumn of that year, but the *Chronicle* records Halfdan's warfleet sailing up the east coast to Northumbria.

> Halfdan went with a part of the host into Northumbria, and took winter-quarters by the river Tyne; and the host subdued the land, and oft-times harried the Picts and the Strathclyde Britons.

152

Halfdan was a sea-raider son of Ragnar Lothbrok, a viking warlord born to the breed, and his ambitions ranged far beyond plunder-taking around Tyneside. The evidence of the English and Irish sources shows Halfdan Ragnarsson following his brother's warpath to reclaim the York–Dublin axis first forged by Ivar and enriching it, after the manner of Olaf, with the plunder of the dominions of Pict, Scot and Briton.

Halfdan's war began with the devastation of Northumbria north of the Tyne, the old sub-kingdom of Bernicia largely untouched by the earlier campaigning of the great host, and the *Historia de Sancto Cuthberto* confirms his first onslaught on the lands of Lindisfarne.

Halfdene, king of the Danes, entered the Tyne and sailed to Wyrcesforde, ravaging everything and sinning cruelly against Saint Cuthbert.

'Fire and sword', wrote Symeon of Durham, 'were carried from the eastern sea to the western'. Halfdan raided over Stainmoor to strike at Cuthbert's foundation at Carlisle, but before his warband arrived on Lindisfarne itself, the bishop had been warned of the danger in time to evacuate the island.

No such foreknowledge of disaster was to save the tiny monastery on the Isle of May in the Firth of Forth and its abbot Adrian from his red martyrdom. Adrian was an Irish holy man who had made his ocean hermitage among a small community of brethren, probably first founded from Hexham, on the remote island where the puffins call across the wide mouth of the Forth. The martyrdom of Adrian of May is entered in the calendars of saints at 4th March and has been convincingly aligned – by W. F. Skene, the eminent nineteenth-century historian of Celtic Scotland – with the passage of Halfdan's sea-raiders through the Forth early in the raiding season of 875.

Their further progress is marked by the entry in the *Annals of Ulster* at 875 of the fearsome massacre at Dollar in the Ochils around the head of the Forth.

An encounter of the Picts with the dubh-gaill, and a great slaughter of the Picts was committed.

Whatever treaties had existed between the Dublin kings and the lords of Alba were no longer recognised by Halfdan, but it is nowhere recorded that Constantine, king of Alba and Kenneth mac-

153

Alpin's son, fought at Dollar. It was to be another two years before he fell victim to Halfdan's warband at Inverdovat when, in the words of the *Cogadh*, 'the earth opened under the men of Alba'. The 'great slaughter' of 875 was a collateral blood-letting, as was also the raiding of the Strathclyde Britons entered in the *Anglo-Saxon Chronicle*, on the way to the real objective across the Irish Sea.

Halfdan's ambition lay in the *Ath-Cliath of Dubh linn* and he would seem to have achieved it by treachery rather than frontal assault when Eystein – called *Oistin* by the *Annals of Ulster* at 875 – who had succeeded Ivar in Dublin fell victim to Ivar's brother.

> Oistin, son of Amlaibh, king of the lochlann, was deceitfully slain by Alband [Halfdan].

The struggle for control of the Dublin kingdom of the *gaill* is more accurately presented as a contest between two dynasties of Scandinavian Ireland rather than between Norse and Dane as national enemies. Ragnar Lothbrok and his sons were Danish kings cast in a very different mould from that of the national overlords of the tenth and eleventh centuries. Ragnar is best characterised by Smyth's description of him as 'a sea-king' and his sons as 'a viking dynasty'. While his wives and concubines are best known from saga tradition, some of them can be shown to have been kindred to the Norse royal house of Vestfold and there is no reason why the Irish source claiming Ivar and Olaf as 'brothers' need have been so very wide of the historical mark.

Eystein Olafsson who followed Ivar as king of Dublin was the son of a Norse king and an Irish princess, and thus the grandson of the Irish high-king Aedh. His death at the hands of Halfdan must have prompted the *ard ri* to seek the vengeance indicated by the *Cogadh* reference to 'the gaill slaughtered by Aedh, son of Niall, at the banquet that was made for Ragnall's son at Ath Cliath'. It would have been this attempt at vengeance for the 'deceitful' slaying of Eystein which drove Halfdan out of Dublin and his reappearance in Northumbria is entered in the *Anglo-Saxon Chronicle* for 876.

> And in this year Halfdene apportioned the lands of the Northumbrians, and from that time they [the Danes] continued ploughing and tilling them.

A warrior at the age of thirty when he landed with the great host in

154

East Anglia would have been over forty if he had survived to return with Halfdan from Ireland in 876 and an elderly man by early medieval standards. Halfdan, in the old way of the warrior king as 'giver of rings', would have paid off such senior fighting men with farmsteads in the coastal plain of Northumberland and the dales of Yorkshire in return for services rendered. He himself, by contrast, was a man more inclined to the sword than the ploughshare and in the following year made his second bid to reclaim his brother's former kingdom of Dublin. The *Annals of Ulster* at 877 record how when he led his longships against the Norse on Strangford Lough – called *Loch-Cuan* by the annalist – Halfdan Ragnarsson had come at last to the end of his warrior's way.

> A battle at Loch-Cuan between the finn-gaill and the dubh-gaill, in which Albann, king of the dubh-gaill, was slain.

Those of his warband who survived the sea-fight to the death on Strangford Lough made their way back to Northumbria through southern Scotland and there expended the last of their battle-fury on Constantine and his men of Alba at Inverdovat in Fife. Thus the prophet Berchan had foretold.

> The cow-herd of the byre of the cattle of the Picts, the fair and tall one, lavish giver of wine ... will fall on a Thursday in pools of blood on the shore of Inber-Dub-roda.

The *Chronicle of the Kings* confirms Berchan's prophecy fulfilled.

> Constantine mac-Cinaed reigned for fifteen years; and he was slain by the northmen in the battle of Inverdovat, and was buried on the isle of Iona.

It is not known how many of Halfdan's host found their way back to Northumbria or how long they took to do so, but the *Chronicle of the Kings* records that 'the northmen passed a year in Pictland'. Their further ravages in the course of that year are also unrecorded, but it must have been the threat of such a warband at large in Scotland which lay behind the entry in the *Annals of Ulster* at 878.

> The shrine of Columcille and all his relics arrived in Ireland to escape the gaill.

155

The annalist confirms that the fury of the northmen had finally driven Columcille out of his long exile in 'Alba of the ravens' and home to Ireland where medieval tradition claims he was laid with Brigid and with Patrick in the earth of Ulster.

> In Down three saints one grave do fill,
> Patrick, Brigid and Columcille.

So also on the continent, the shrines of the saints had been taken up by their communities fleeing the escalating onslaught of the northmen. F. Donald Logan describes how clergy 'from cloisters unprepared for hostile attacks fled from such holy places as Saint Maixent, Charvoux, Saint Maur-sur-Loire, Saint Wandrille, Jumièges, and Saint Martin of Tours, and sought refuge in areas isolated from viking raiders. For two generations these fleeing monks were to be seen on the roads leading to Burgundy, the Auvergne and Flanders.'

Noirmoutier off the mouth of the Loire had been an early target of the sea-raiders. They seized it as their first winter camp in France and in 836 the monks of its island monastery took up the shrine of their founder Philibert – a contemporary of Cuthbert and highly regarded by Alcuin – to carry it across France for forty years before coming to its final resting place at Tournus. The monks of Saint Martin had fled their monastery with his shrine in 853, returned three years later and fled again in 862, 869 and 877 before they were able to bring it back at last to Tours.

The shrine of Cuthbert had already been taken from Lindisfarne to Norham on the Tweed at some point in the episcopacy of Egred and returned to Lindisfarne when the threat of the sea-raiders had passed. In the year of 875, when the monks of Noirmoutier found their last sanctuary for Philibert's shrine, Halfdan was on the Tyne and striking towards Lindisfarne. The uncorrupt body of the great saint of the northern English was no longer safe in his own country and his community took it up from the earth of his holy island to start out on the long road which was to lead to Durham.

The account of events preserved in Lindisfarne tradition is set down by Symeon in his *History of the Church of Durham.*

> Entering the Tyne with a considerable fleet, Halfdan landed at Tynemouth, where he meant to spend the winter; purposing in the spring to pillage the whole district lying towards the north of that river, which hitherto had enjoyed peace.

156

Having heard of his arrival, bishop Eardwulf, apprehensive that the entire destruction of the church of Lindisfarne and of the whole diocese was at hand, deliberated as to the means of escaping with his followers; but he was uncertain what he should do with respect to the most holy body of father Cuthbert. For it went against his heart that he should ever be parted from that treasure, whether he were residing in the church or driven from it. Having summoned Eadred [abbot at Carlisle], they deliberated what course it would be most expedient for them to pursue; and ... they thought on the last words bequeathed to them by the father Cuthbert as he was departing this life, and so resolved to abandon the place rather than to yield themselves up as a sacrifice to the barbarians. For amongst his other admonitions, he had in his paternal solicitude given them this advice:

'It would be much more pleasing to me that you should take up my bones from the tomb, and remove them from this place, and should continue to reside wherever God shall provide an abode for you, rather than that you should tamely submit to evil and bow your necks to the yoke of schismatics.' These words when they read them seemed to be prophetically uttered by father Cuthbert in anticipation of their present circumstances; and they saw in them a command which applied to themselves.

Raising, then, the holy and uncorrupt body of the father, they placed beside it in the same shrine the relics of the saints; that is to say, the head of Oswald the king and martyr, beloved of God, which had formerly been buried in the cemetery of the same church, and a part of the bones of Saint Aidan – for Colman, on his return to Scotland, had taken with him the other portion of them – together with the venerable bones of those revered bishops, the successors of the same father Cuthbert, that is to say of Eadbert, Eadfrid, and Aethelwold. Having collected these relics, they fled before the barbarians and abandoned that noble pile, the mother church of Bernicia, which had been the residence of so many saints.

This occurred in the year of our Lord's incarnation eight hundred and seventy-five, being two hundred and forty-one years since the time when king Oswald and bishop Aidan had founded that church, and had placed therein a bishop's see and a congregation of monks; and one hundred and eighty-nine years after the death of father Cuthbert, and in the twenty-second year of the episcopate of Eardwulf.

This was the eighty-third year since this church had been devastated under bishop Higbald, as we have already mentioned, by the pirates, and all the monks had been put to death, some in one way, some in another, with the exception of the few who had contrived to escape.

Symeon's account is a document of incomparable significance in the history of the community of Cuthbert. It records the uplifting of relics which can only be considered the *Hallows of Northanhymbre*, the mortal remains of saints and martyrs – foremost amongst them 'the holy and uncorrupt body' of Cuthbert himself – which enshrined the authority of the royal church of the Northumbrian kingdom. It was a decision of the greatest moment and was entered in all the medieval Durham sources, but Symeon's evidence is of especial importance, not only because he was the official guardian of Lindisfarne tradition but because he was one of the nine monks who had actually handled the body of Cuthbert on its translation into the new shrine in the Norman cathedral at Durham.

The coffin from which the remains were lifted in 1104 was the same casket of carved oak – still preserved today in the cathedral treasury – which had been carried from Lindisfarne two hundred and thirty years before. The history of the posthumous miracles of Cuthbert set down by Reginald of Durham in the third quarter of the twelfth century describes the parting of the great waters to allow the passage of Cuthbert's coffin and community to the mainland.

At the end of the year of our Lord 875, it befell that the land of England was laid waste with widespread destruction ... The people of the island of Lindisfarne, terrified by these outrages, took counsel with the bishop and clergy; and they deliberated long and anxiously as to what plan they should make. For they did not dare to leave his sacred body behind them on the island, in case it should fall prey to the enemy, and the fierce and cruel pirate should take away the precious treasure on which all their hopes depended; nor did they dare to conceal it in some secret place, for fear of stirring up the wrath of God to rage against them, or to take it with them from the island, in case they should incur the angry reproach and indignant censure of Saint Cuthbert ...

At last, therefore, recalling the words of Saint Cuthbert and seeing that, as he had foretold, they were faced with the need to choose between two evils, they decided, according to his command, to take up his bones from the tomb and bear them with them into exile ... For they knew ... that as long as they had Cuthbert in their company, they could never fall prey to the sword of their enemy, or suffer any loss or want.

Guided by these plans, they took the wooden coffin of Saint Cuthbert, in which till then he had lain at rest, and bore it with them, along with the church's other treasures, and so arrived at the seashore. It happened, at that moment, that the sea had filled its bed to an unusual height, and flooded beyond its customary bounds; and so the bearers of the sacred body, on arriving at the shore's edge, were too frightened to advance further, and resolved to stop there for a while and await the ebbing of the sea's winding waves.

158

Suddenly the sea, now swollen to its fullness, by a miraculous effort turned back its great waves upon itself, and opened up a path across the dry sand for all to cross by. For the waters were a wall for them on the right and on the left, and like a side-wall extended through the air in a straight line. And as the bearers of the sacred body were proposing to advance, always before their feet there appeared a dry flow of sand and a level path for their journey. And strangely, when all the men and women, boys and girls, herds of cattle and flocks of sheep had advanced so as to be enclosed by the surrounding sea, at once the waves of the sea followed their steps and flooded back; and immediately behind their backs the water reached to its full height. And in this way the sea always exposed a dry path in front of them, while behind their advancing steps it turned back into the bed of its former stream.

So at last, treading safely, they reached the further shore, and on turning back their eyes to the island they saw the whole ambit of the sea flooded with its full volume of water.

Reginald goes on to describe how the northmen arrived on Lindisfarne in the wake of the evacuation of its clergy and laity.

When they fled they left behind a cleric to guard the church, from whom they trusted to receive an accurate account of what befell the property of the church after the arrival of the barbarous thieves; and they intended to learn from his lips when they might hope to return.

It happened, therefore, that when the invaders reached the island and approached the threshold of the church, that priest, driven by fear, took refuge at Saint Cuthbert's tomb and begged for the right to live under his protection. Brandishing the gleaming blades of their drawn swords, they went round the church and searched most carefully ... but incredibly, the priest remained watchful and unharmed before Saint Cuthbert's tomb, and took most careful note of all their movements, their actions, and their clamour and threats. While they were unable to hear or see him, he could see them and accompanied them on their rampage, yet they were quite unable to distinguish or perceive him; for Saint Cuthbert spread over them a mist to prevent them seeing and discerning, such as is called in the Greek *aorosia*, and he did not permit them to behold what it was not expedient for them to see.

Reginald's anecdote is corroborated nowhere else in the sources and can only be attributed to an infusion of monastic folklore and his own creative writing. The grey blanket of the 'sea-haar' is familiar to everyone who knows the north-east coast, but Cuthbert's miraculous defensive mist does seem to have found its way into the later

159

tradition surrounding the saint. A bombing raid on Durham during the Second World War found the great cathedral obscured by dense fog and consequently left it undamaged. Reginald would have enthusiastically subscribed to the popular belief of wartime Durham that the impenetrable visibility had been sent by Cuthbert to shield his church and shrine from the bomb-aimers of the *Luftwaffe*.

When Cuthbert's community, guarded and guided by its saint, crossed the pilgrim's causeway in 875 it entered an English mainland which had been entirely transformed by the Scandinavian expansion.

The once-mighty kingdom of Anglo-Saxon Northumbria had shrivelled to an earldom – the tital of 'earl' deriving from the Old Norse *jarl* – in the shadow of the new Scandinavian kingdom bounded by Humber and Tyne and centred on Jorvik. To the north the kingdom of the Scots was the new power in the land beyond the Forth. To the south the frontier of what was to be recognised by treaty in 878 as the Danelaw spread across Mercia to the West Saxon frontier on the Thames. Wedged between them was the dominion of the 'earls of Bamburgh', the dynasty of English thanes who were able to assert shifting measures of independence for a territory approximating to the sub-kingdom of Bernicia for two hundred years after the northmen seized York.

The 'widespread destruction' which drove the community of Cuthbert out of Lindisfarne in 875 serves also to mark Northumbria's passage out of its viking age. The Scandinavian settlement north of the Humber which had begun with the seizure of York was confirmed by Halfdan's distribution of Northumbrian farmland to his warband. Symeon's sources can have known little of Halfdan's fate on his last expedition to Ireland in 877, but the terms in which they describe his departure from the Tyne clearly indicate that his host had grown more concerned with settling than raiding the land.

> God's justice determined that the wicked king Halfdene should at last suffer the punishment for his cruelty towards the church of the saint and other holy places. He was attacked at the same time by mental insanity and most severe bodily suffering; the intolerable stench exhaling from him made him an object of abomination for the whole host.
>
> Thus despised and rejected by all persons, he fled away in three ships from the Tyne, and shortly afterwards he and all his followers perished.

Symeon's bizarre account of events might be most realistically interpreted as describing a berserker warlord so out of step with the new mood of the northmen in England as to be able to recruit no more than three ship-crews of fighting men for his war-voyage to Strangford Lough.

For all their viking style, the greater waves of Scandinavian onslaught which swept over England through the tenth and eleventh centuries were invasions by national armies out of the Scandinavian homelands and their aim was conquest of the kingdom. The last such onslaught was that of the William, variously called 'the Bastard' and 'the Conqueror', who brought down the last English king Harold Godwinson in 1066. William's dukedom of Normandy had its origins in the tenth-century Scandinavian settlement around Rouen and its name of *Normandie* derived from the same *normanni* by which the continental chroniclers had called the sea-raiding vikings.

Each new direction taken by the community of Cuthbert throughout all the years of their wandering was prompted by some new development in the onslaught of the northmen, be they invading Norse and Dane or conquering Norman. Just as Halfdan's ravages drove them off Lindisfarne to wander the north country for seven years until they settled at Chester-le-Street, so the invasion by the Norse king Olaf Tryggvasson in the mid-990s drove them to seek temporary refuge at Ripon. It was after the departure of the Norsemen that they set out on the return journey from Ripon, a journey which reached its sudden end at Durham on the Wear. Symeon's *History* records how Cuthbert made known his decision that they had come to his last resting-place in 995.

But after three or four months, peace being restored, as they were returning with the venerable body to its former resting-place, and had now reached a spot near Durham called Wurdelau on the eastern side of the city, the vehicle on which the shrine containing the holy body was placed could not be induced to advance any further. Those who attempted to move it were assisted by others, but their efforts, though vigorous, were equally ineffective; nor did the additional attempts of the crowd which now came up produce any result in moving it; for the shrine containing the uncorrupted body continued where it was, as firmly fixed as if it were a mountain. This circumstance clearly intimated to all that he refused to be brought back to his former place of residence; but at the same time they did not know where they should deposit him, for the place on which they were now standing in the middle of a plain, was then uninhabitable. Hereupon the bishop addressed the people; and gave

161

directions that they should seek an explanation of this sign from heaven by a fast of three days' duration, which should be spent in watching and prayer, in order that they might discover where they should take up their abode along with the holy body of the father. This having been done, a revelation was made to a certain religious person named Eadmer, to the purport that they were required to remove the body to Durham and there to prepare a resting-place for it. When this revelation was publicly announced, all were comforted thereby ... and a very few of their number were now able to raise the saint's shrine, whereas the whole multitude had previously been unable to move it.

And thus with joy and thanksgiving they translated the holy body to Durham, the spot which had been pointed out to them from heaven.

Symeon goes on to tell how the shrine of Cuthbert had lain in its final resting place at Durham for three-quarters of a century when it was taken up once again in 1069 and brought briefly to Lindisfarne to escape the Norman harrying of the north country.

In the same year King William came to York with an army and devastated all the surrounding districts; whereupon bishop Egelwin [of Lindisfarne at Durham, 1056–1071] and the elders, having deliberated among themselves, took up the uncorrupted body of the most holy father Cuthbert, and commenced a retreat to the church of Lindisfarne. This was in the seventy-fifth year after it had been conveyed to Durham by Aldhun [bishop of Lindisfarne at Chester-le-Street and Durham, 990–1018].

... But when Lent was nigh at hand, and tranquillity had been restored, they carried the holy body back to Durham; and the church having been solemnly reconciled they entered it with lauds upon the eighth of the kalends of April [25th March, 1070] and restored the body to its own proper resting-place.

The first departure from Lindisfarne in 875 seems to have been conceived as a similarly temporary evacuation, although the intended sanctuary lay much further afield. It would appear, however remarkably, that Ireland was considered to offer the only sanctuary for the shrines of the saints in the last quarter of the ninth century. The relics of Columcille were brought to the Irish mainland 'to escape the *gaill*' in 878 and it was to Ireland that the community of Cuthbert first intended to flee in 875. Symeon's *History of the Church of Durham* tells how they were rerouted by the miraculous intervention of the saint himself.

Whence it was that the bishop and they who with him accompanied the holy body, nowhere found any place of repose, but going forwards and backwards, hither and thither, they fled from the face of those cruel barbarians.

Bishop Eardwulf and abbot Eadred, after having wandered over nearly the whole of the kingdom ... began to discuss the expediency of providing a safe refuge for the holy body by transporting it to Ireland, the more especially as now there appeared scarce the shadow of a hope that they would be able to continue in this country. Summoning, therefore, all those persons who were of approved wisdom and mature age, they opened to them their secret intentions. The project met with their approbation, and they said:

'We are clearly admonished to seek for a place of rest in a foreign land; for unless this were the will of God and his saint, doubtless there would long since have been provided for his holy one a place worthy of abode and convenient for our residence.'

So then they all of them, bishop, abbot and people, assembled at the mouth of the river which is called Derwent [at Workington, Cumbria]. A ship was there prepared for their transit, in which was placed the venerable body of the father; the bishop and the abbot, and the few to whom their resolution had been made known, embarked, while all the others were kept in ignorance of their intentions. They bade farewell to their friends who were standing on the shore, hoisted their sails so as to catch the prosperous gale, and the ship sped on her course towards Ireland. How can I describe the grief of those who were left behind at that time? 'Miserable men that we are,' said they, 'why have we fallen upon such days of sorrow? Thou, our father and patron, art like one carried away captive into exile: we, like miserable and imprisoned sheep, are consigned to the teeth of ravening wolves.' They had no time to say more; for the winds changed, and the angry waves rose up; the sea which till then had been calm, became tempestuous; and the vessel, now unmanageable, was tossed hither and thither by the stormy billows. They who were on board became like dead men. Three waves of astounding size struck the vessel, and filled it nearly half full with water; and by a terrible miracle, unknown even amongst the plagues of Egypt, the water was changed to blood. During this tempest the ship heeled over on one side, and the copy of the gospels, adorned with gold figures, fell overboard, and sank to the bottom of the sea.

After they had somewhat recovered their senses, and remembered who they were, they fell upon their knees and, prostrating themselves at the feet of the holy body, asked pardon for their foolish enterprise. They put the helm about, and steered the vessel back to the shore and their companions, whom they reached without difficulty, speedily carried thither by the wind which had now become propitious.

163

If Cuthbert refused to cross the Irish Sea, the guardians of his shrine could only seek out such sanctuary as might be found on the mainland. Bishop Eardwulf led his community to the monastery at Whithorn, founded by Saint Ninian in the fifth century and a Northumbrian see since the time of Bede, which had somehow escaped devastation by Halfdan and it was there on the northern shore of the Solway Firth that Cuthbert saw fit to restore his great gospel book to their care. Symeon tells how the Lindisfarne Gospels were brought intact and unharmed from the sea.

[Cuthbert] appeared in a vision to one of them named Hunred, and commanded them to search for the book which had fallen from the vessel into the depths of the sea; telling him that it was possible that by God's mercy, they might recover that which they thought had gone beyond recovery. The loss of this volume had indeed plunged them in the deepest distress. And he proceeded yet further, adding these words:- 'Rise up quickly, and let the horse which you will notice at no great distance from this place, see a bridle which you will find hanging upon a tree; he will then immediately come to you; do you put the bridle upon him, and yoke him to the carriage upon which my body is placed, and thus you will lighten your own labour.'

Having heard thus much he awoke, and forthwith he recounted the vision which he had seen, and he lost no time in despatching some of his companions to the sea, which was close at hand, that they might search for the lost book. At this time they were in the neighbourhood of Candida Casa, more commonly known by the name of Hwitern [Whithorn]. When these men reached the shore, the sea had receded much further back than usual, and going out three miles or more they discovered the volume of the holy gospels, which had lost none of the external brilliance of its gems and gold, nor any of the internal beauty of its illuminations, and the fairness of its leaves, but appeared just as if it had never come into any contact whatever with the water.

Even with their great gospel book restored to them, the community of Cuthbert had been greatly diminished by the hardship endured through two years of fruitless wandering. Symeon provides his own harrowing portrait of their odyssey approaching its lowest ebb.

At this time the people, exhausted by the long continuance of the labour and constrained by hunger and the want of every necessity, gradually ceased their attendance upon the holy body, and scattered themselves over these deserted localities in order that, by some means or other, they might preserve their lives. Indeed, they all went away, with the exception

164

of the bishop, the abbot and a very few others, other than those seven who were privileged to bestow more close and constant attendance upon the holy body. These persons had been reared and educated by those of the monks who had conveyed the body of the holy confessor from the island of Lindisfarne, and had resolved that as long as they lived they would never abandon it. Four of them, named Hunred, Stitheard, Edmund, and Franco, were of greater repute than the other three; and it is the boast of many persons in Northumbria, clergy as well as laymen, that they are descended from one of those families; for they pride themselves upon the faithful service which their ancestors rendered to Saint Cuthbert. So when the others fell away, these persons alone continued with this great treasure.

Whether or not Symeon was exaggerating the hardships of their wandering, as some modern authorities have suggested, it is clear that their route led them around the various estates of the Lindisfarne landholdings. They would have naturally, even necessarily, directed their steps to these *vills* where they would be assured of accommodation, some measure of security, and the benefit of whatever produce or sustenance was available. There were certainly lands around Carlisle endowed on Lindisfarne which would have supplied their needs before and after the unsuccessful attempt to cross the Irish Sea, unless they had been utterly devastated by Halfdan's raiding.

Symeon indicates an improvement in the situation in the years after Halfdan's final departure from Northumbria.

> On this occurrence the venerable body was removed to the monastery of Crayke, which was built within a vill which had formerly been the saint's own property; and having been most kindly received there by the abbot named Geve, they spent four months in that place, as if it had been their own.

Crayke in north Yorkshire had been endowed upon Cuthbert when he accepted the see of Lindisfarne at the personal insistence of King Egfrith in 684 and intended as an episcopal residence on the road to and from York. Cuthbert's posthumous return to his *vill* at Crayke at the end of 882 was the prelude to the extraordinary landmark in the history of Lindisfarne's relations with the northmen in the following year.

The *Historia de Sancto Cuthberto* contains the earliest account of how a Danish king of Jorvik came to be granted his kingdom on the coffin of Cuthbert of Lindisfarne.

At that time Saint Cuthbert appeared by night to the holy abbot of Carlisle, named Eadred, with the following strict instructions: 'Go to the army of the Danes on the Tyne, and tell them, if they wish to be obedient to me, to show you a youth named Guthred, son of Hardacnut, who was sold to a widow, and early in the morning do you and the whole army pay the widow the price for him. And let the price be paid at the third hour; and at the sixth hour bring him before the whole multitude, that they may elect him king. And at the ninth hour bring him with the whole army on to the hill called Oswigesdune, and there place on his right arm the golden bracelet, and so let them all appoint him king. Tell him also, after he becomes king, to give me all the land between the Tyne and the Wear, and that anyone who takes refuge with me, whether for homicide or any other need, shall have protection for thirty-seven days and nights.'

Assured by this vision and strengthened by the just command of the blessed confessor, the holy abbot hurried boldly to the foreign army; and he was received with respect, and carried out his instructions faithfully, in due order. For he found the youth and redeemed him, and appointed him king with the full support of the whole army, and was given the land and the right of sanctuary. Then Bishop Eardwulf brought to the army and to that hill the body of Saint Cuthbert, on which the king himself and the whole army swore peace and good faith as long as they lived; and they kept this oath well.

Something quite extraordinary had transformed the dealings of the northmen of Jorvik with the community of Lindisfarne between the devastation of 875 and the royal succession of 883. Some plausible explanation begins to emerge when the evidence of the *Historia* is supplemented with additional points of detail from other Durham sources.

Symeon prefaces his account in the *History of the Church of Durham* with the note that 'during this time the army being without a king, such of the inhabitants [of Northumbria] as survived were insecure'. There is no evidence for any king of the northmen at Jorvik between the departure of Halfdan in 877 and the succession of Guthred in 883. It would have taken some time, certainly a year and probably longer, for the news of Halfdan's death to reach Northumbria. There was apparently no Ragnarsson successor to Halfdan and independent warbands at large in Northumbria would have produced an unstable, potentially anarchic situation. Some numbers of northmen had been settled on the farmland of Yorkshire, even since the late 860s, and amongst them – just as in Ireland and the Hebrides – the first conversions to Christianity in Danish

Northumbria would have begun by 880. The succession of a legitimate overlord at Jorvik can only have been a welcome reassurance for the Danish settlers, by now effectively Yorkshire farmers, and the appointment of a Christian king of the northmen was certainly in the best interest of the itinerant Lindisfarne community.

Such a man was Guthred Hardacnutsson and Symeon associates his succession with the move of the community of Cuthbert from Crayke to a new episcopal seat within its newly-endowed land-holdings.

> The troublesome storms which had arisen were lulled, and tranquillity was restored; and upon this the episcopal see which had hitherto been established in the island of Lindisfarne was transferred to Cuncacestre [Chester-le-Street].

There is another and especially useful point of detail added to the evidence by the *Historia Regum*, which identifies Guthred as 'the son of Hardacnut, whom the Danes had sold as a slave to a certain widow at Whittingham'.

Whittingham is a village on the Aln which has been convincingly identified as the site of a Northumbrian royal *vill* where the synod of *Ad Tuifyrdi* appointed Cuthbert to his bishopric in 684 and local tradition links the succession of Guthred with a clash between English and Dane at Battle Bridge on the Edlingham Burn. It would have been more than unlikely for Danes to sell one of their own kind, even less one of evidently noble stock, as a 'slave', but it would have been quite characteristic for them to surrender a young noble as a hostage for truce after battle. Such might well have been the case when an independent Danish raiding party ventured up the Aln, perhaps intending to plunder the *vill* at Whittingham, and there encountered the local *fyrd*. Tradition tells of the burn running red with blood in a hard-won Danish victory, but the possibility of a young aristocratic warrior taken captive and held as guarantee of armistice cannot be discounted. It would also have been typical of the later ninth century for such a hostage to have agreed to Christian baptism, just as the Danish warlord Guthrum was baptised as a condition of the treaty with Alfred after the battle of Ethandune.

Such a situation at Whittingham would have placed the clergy of Cuthbert in a favourable negotiating position. They would have easily secured the release of the hostage and offered him in exchange for endowments of land and sanctuary from the Jorvik Danes. Such an agreement might well have been underwritten by the acceptance of the freed Guthred as king at York and sealed by his consecration on the shrine of the saint.

However it came about, the establishment of the episcopal see of Lindisfarne at Chester-le-Street is a matter of historical record and must reflect a newly sympathetic accommodation of English church and Danish state in the Northumbria of 883. The succession of a Guthred, or *Guthfrith*, as king of Jorvik, is borne out by coin evidence and, while the king-list of Danish York is an uncertain authority, Symeon was able to enter the obituary of Guthred in his *History of the Church of Durham* with remarkable confidence.

> In the year eight hundred and ninety-four from our Lord's incarnation king Guthred died, after having reigned for no short time in prosperity, leaving behind for the protection of others the inviolable privileges of the church of father Cuthbert.

At least as remarkable as the strange tale of Guthred's accession on the coffin of Cuthbert is the extent to which the hermit-bishop of Lindisfarne, so celebrated a self-denying ascetic in life, had been transformed in death into an eminence described by the modern Durham historian David Rollason as that of 'a lord of land'.

Cuthbert's mortal disregard for possessions had been displaced in the Durham sources by his posthumous acquisition of vast and valuable estates. Rollason well sums up the status of the incorrupt body of the saint in his oaken shrine for generations of ninth-century and later priests and pilgrims.

> The fundamental belief was that the saint was not only in heaven with God but was also present simultaneously in his earthly remains and could therefore respond to prayers made close to those remains by interceding for the supplicant in heaven.

Rollason goes on to emphasise how 'the saint's dual presence in his body and in heaven made him not only a suitable recipient of lands and other gifts but also an effective defender of them'. Just such is vividly illustrated by Symeon's anecdote from the less happy times which befell the church of Cuthbert in the second decade of the tenth century.

The harmonious relationship between Chester-le-Street and Jorvik survived the death of Guthred by some fifteen years until the rise of the Wessex kings and their military success against the Danes in the south of England eventually spelled the end of the Danish dynasty at York. It was Edward, son and successor of Alfred of Wessex, who first moved against the Northumbrian Danes in a five-week campaign north of the Humber in 909, but when a retaliatory strike was launched to the south in the following year the Danish host fell foul of the allied *fyrds* of Wessex and Mercia at Tettenhall in Staffordshire. The *Anglo-Saxon Chronicle* records 'many thousands slain' in a battle which represented the final destruction of the Danish warlords of Jorvik and left the way open for the Dublin Norse – under the command of Ragnall, grandson of Ivar the Boneless – to move into the resulting Northumbrian power vacuum.

Some three years after Tettenhall, Ragnall invaded northern England by way of the Solway Firth and advanced south over the old Roman Wall to defeat an alliance of Scots with the warband of Ealdred, earl of Bamburgh, at Corbridge in 914. Ragnall's movements over the next few years are unclear, but he was back in Northumbria and reinforced by a warfleet of Waterford Norse to win the second battle of Corbridge in 918. It was a victory won at some great cost, but Ragnall regrouped his forces over the winter to seize York in the following year as the first of a line of Norse kings at Jorvik which ended only with the death of Erik Haraldsson called 'bloodaxe' in 954.

For all the bloodletting at Corbridge, the greatest casualty of Ragnall's Northumbrian conquest from the viewpoint of Symeon of Durham seems to have been the loss of estates suffered by the community of Cuthbert. Ragnall was an enthusiastic land-seeker who confirmed the Norse settlement of Cumbria and appropriated Cuthbert's land to pay off his allied warlords, and most infamous among them one Olaf called *ballr*, 'the stubborn'.

In the same year in which king Alfred died [899], bishop Eardwulf departed from this life in a good old age ... in his stead Cutheard received the government of the episcopal see. Provident for the future security of those who should hereafter serve God in the presence of the uncorrupt body of the saint, he made ample provision for their wants, and the charter book of the church [the *Historia de Sancto Cuthberto*] manifestly declares how many were the vills which he purchased by the money of the saint.

While the episcopate of the Bernicians was under the rule of

Cutheard, a certain pagan king called Ragnall landed on the North-umbrian shores with a large fleet. Without any delay he broke in upon York and ... he next seized the whole land of Saint Cuthbert, and divided its vills between two of his leaders, one of whom was named Scula, the other Olaf Ball. The former of them, Scula, obtained possession of the district from Eden as far as Billingham [County Durham], and distressed the miserable inhabitants with heavy and intolerable tributes.

Olaf Ball took possession of another part of the vills, and showed that he was even more savage and cruel than his companion; but this he did to his own destruction, as was clearly proved to all. After he had inflicted many injuries on the bishop, the congregation and the people of Saint Cuthbert, and had laid violent hands upon the farms which of right belonged to the bishop, the latter, anxious to win the man over to God, said to him: 'Let me entreat you to lay aside your pertinacious harshness of disposition, and to restrain your hands from thus lawlessly laying hold of ecclesiastical property; for you may be well assured that the confessor will not be slack in punishing you severely for the injuries which you are inflicting on him and his.'

The other, filled with the spirit of the evil one, replied: 'What is the use of threatening me with this dead man? Of what worth is any help which this person in whom you trust can give you against me? I vow by the power of my gods that from this time forth I shall be a determined enemy to this dead man, and to all of you.'

The bishop and all the brethren fell down upon the ground and prayed that God and Saint Cuthbert would be pleased to bring to nothing these proud threats. The unfortunate being had at this time reached the door; one foot was even within the threshold and one had crossed over it, and there he stood fixed as if a nail had been driven through each foot; unable to advance, unable to retreat, unable to move in any direction. After having suffered many tortures, he was compelled to make public confession of the sanctity of the most blessed confessor, and then he gave up his wicked spirit in that same place.

Terrified by this example, none of the others dared, upon any pretext whatever, from that time forward to seize any of the lands or other property which lawfully belonged to the church.

For all the power of the saint in his shrine as defender of the land, the community of Cuthbert at Chester-le-Street in 919 found itself more vulnerable than at any time in a generation. The English earls of Bamburgh were never to recover from their defeats at Corbridge and the last English Christian bastion against both the ominous

170

presence of the Jorvik Norse and the hostile ambition of the new Scots nation lay far to the south in the kingdom of Wessex. After 919 the community of Cuthbert could look nowhere else for its defence but to the West Saxon kings of all the English.

Modern historians propose this new political context as the origin of the adoption of Cuthbert as the patron saint of the royal house of Wessex, but Symeon and his sources trace it four decades further back to the dark days of 878 when Alfred the king was in the Glastonbury marshes and – on the admission of his own words* – most harassed by the heathen host.

* 'It came about that we were all harassed by the heathen host', *King Alfred's Will*, c. 888.

epilogue

Ethandune, AD 878

In the year of our Lord's incarnation eight hundred and ninety-nine, died that most pious king of the English, Alfred, after having filled the throne for twenty-eight years and a half, and he was succeeded by his son Edward.

This latter sovereign was earnestly admonished by his father that he should always hold Saint Cuthbert and his church in the highest reverence and affection, bearing in mind how great were the perils and calamities from which he had delivered Alfred.

Symeon's *History of the Church of Durham*

I N THE *first months of 878, while the depleted community of Cuthbert was somewhere on its journey across the Pennines from Whithorn on the Solway to Crayke in Swaledale, Alfred of Wessex was suffering the most dangerous passage of his warrior's way.*

Those warbands of the great host which had remained in Mercia when Halfdan returned to Northumbria in 874 had been reinforced and were poised under the command of Guthrum for the conquest of Wessex.

AD 878 In this year, at midwinter,
after Twelfth Night, the host stole away to Chippenham [Wiltshire]
and overran the land of the West Saxons and occupied it.
And many of the people they drove beyond the sea
and the greater part of those who remained they harried
and the people submitted to them,
except the king Alfred.
And he with a small band, retreated through the woodlands
and into the fastnesses of the marshes.

The Anglo-Saxon Chronicle

At the same time the aforementioned king Alfred, with a few of his nobles and vassals led a troubled life among the woods and marshlands of Somerset; for he had none of the necessities of life, except what he could forage either openly or stealthily, by raiding from the pagans, or even from the Christians who had submitted to the rule of the pagans.

Life of Alfred by Asser, bishop of Sherborne, *c.* 893

One day, when Alfred had sent his whole household to catch fish, except for his wife and one personal attendant, a pilgrim appeared and came in to him, and asked for food. With kind condescension Alfred gave orders that he be generously provided for and on learning from his attendant that there was no food there for the whole day but one loaf and a little wine, he gave thanks to God and ordered half of each to be given to the pilgrim as his share. After the attendant had faithfully carried out this command and brought back the pilgrim's thanks to his master, he quickly returned there and found the bread and wine intact; but he did not find the pilgrim, nor could he discover how he had come or gone back through those marshes, especially as there was no boat there. While Alfred wondered greatly and pondered upon this, behold, at the ninth hour of the day his servants returned from fishing with three boats filled with fish, declaring that they had caught more that day than during the three [months] they had lived in the marshes.

Gladdened, therefore, and also disturbed by this occurrence, he passed that day more happily and more fortunately than usual. And when night came he went to bed with his wife.

While she was asleep Alfred lay awake disturbed by the day's events and, behold, a great light shone out like the sun, and in this light there appeared an old priest with black hair, wearing episcopal regalia and holding in his right hand a text of the Gospel decked with gold and jewels; and as Alfred lay awake he blessed him with these words:

'Do not be alarmed by the sudden splendour of my appearance, and let not fear of the heathens' fury trouble you any longer; for God, who does not despise the tears of his poor people, will presently put an end to your troubles. And henceforth I shall be a most ready ally to you'.*

And when asked by Alfred who he was and what was his name, he said, 'I am he to whom you generously offered food today, and my name is Cuthbert, a soldier of Christ. Be strong, and attend carefully and with a glad heart to what I tell you; for henceforth I shall be your shield, and your friend, and the defender of your sons. And now I shall tell you what you must do hereafter. Rise up at daybreak and sound three loud blasts on the horn, that your enemies may hear and tremble, and about the ninth hour you shall have five hundred men in arms: and by this sign you may believe that after seven days, by God's gift and my help, you will have the whole army of this land ready to support you, at the hill of Ethandune [Edington, Wiltshire]. And thus you will fight against your enemies and without doubt will overcome them.

'After this, be joyful, and strong, and without fear, because God has delivered your enemies into your hands, and all this land and the kingdom to be a legacy for you and your sons and your son's sons. Be faithful to me and my people, for the whole of Albion is given to you and your sons. Be just, for you are elected king of the whole of Britain. May God be merciful to you, and I shall be

* Cuthbert's opening words are inexplicably omitted from the *Historia de Sancto Cuthberto* and are represented here by the corresponding paragraph from the twelfth-century *Miracles and Translations of Saint Cuthbert*.

your friend, so that no adversary may be able to prevail against you.'

And so when morning came Alfred arose, went by boat to land, and gave the signal three times on his horn; and at the sound all his friends exulted, while his enemies were downcast. And in accordance with God's word, about the ninth hour of the day when five hundred of his best and dearest friends had come together, he made public his vision of the previous night, telling them what the holy confessor had said and how he had comforted him. He also declared to them that by the gift of God and the help of Saint Cuthbert, whom thenceforth they should duly obey, they would conquer their enemies and take possession of the land by right of inheritance.

Historia de Sancto Cuthberto

After this at Easter, Alfred with a small band,
raised a fortress at Athelney, and from it warred on the host,
with the men of that part of Somerset which was nearest to it.
Then, in the seventh week after Easter,
he rode to Egbryht's stone on the east of Selwood.
And there came to meet him all the men of Somerset
and the men of Wiltshire, and the men of that part of Hampshire
which was on this side of the sea; and they rejoiced on seeing him.
And on the following day he went from that camp to Iley,
and one night after that to Ethandune.
And there he fought against all the host and put it to flight,
and rode after it as far as the fortress [at Chippenham]
and laid siege to it for fourteen nights.
And the host gave him hostages with great oaths,
that they would depart from his kingdom;
and also promised him that their king would receive baptism;
and that they so fulfilled.
And three weeks after, king Guthrum came to him,
with thirty of the most noble men of the host,
at Aller, which is opposite to Athelney,
and the king was godfather at his baptism.

The Anglo-Saxon Chronicle for 878

AD 920 In this year king Edward [of Wessex, Alfred's son]
was chosen for father and for lord
by the king of Scots and all the people of the Scots;
and by the king Ragnall [of Jorvik],
and by all the Northumbrians;
and also by the king of the Strathclyde Britons
and by all the people of the Strathclyde Britons.

The Anglo-Saxon Chronicle

AD 927 In this year fiery beacons of light
appeared in the northern sky.
And Sitric [Ragnall's brother, king of Jorvik] died,
and king Athelstan [of Wessex, Alfred's grandson]
assumed the kingdom of the Northumbrians.
And he brought into submission all the kings who were in the island;
First Hywel, king of the West Welsh,
and Constantine, king of the Scots,
and Owen, king of Gwent,
and Ealdred, son of Eadulf, of Bamburgh:
and with pledges and with oaths they confirmed peace,
in the place which is called Eamot [Eamont Bridge, Cumbria],
on the sixth of the ides of July [12th July],
and renounced every kind of idolatry,
and after that departed in peace.

The Anglo-Saxon Chronicle

'Man comes not to I', says the proverb, 'but he comes times three.' I can't recall which of my journeys to Iona was the proverbial third pilgrimage, but as this book had first suggested itself to me on Lindisfarne, I planned to go once more to I-Columcille before I actually began to write it.

In the event it was not to be. I got no further than the Ross of Mull when a westerly gale blew up in the night. By the following morning it was storm force 10 gusting to force 11 and there were to be no more ferry crossings to Iona on that day or the few days following. I could do no better than watch the great wind from the Atlantic whipping white crests on the waves across the Sound.

It was that prospect of the western sea which brought to mind some lines set down in the margin of a manuscript grammar by an Irish monk in the first decades of the ninth century. Whether the author of the marginal note was the same man who brought the book to the monastery of St Gall beside Lake Constanz in Switzerland is unknown, but his quatrain has earned him his own measure of celebrity among the early sources.

They are lines set down in a monastery at the edge of the sea under the shadow of the fury of the northmen and they speak of that world and time with an immediacy such as I have read nowhere else. By reason of that special quality, they are placed here as a coda.

> **Bitter is the wind tonight;**
> **it tosses the white locks of the ocean;**
> **I fear not the coursing of a clear sea**
> **by the fierce warriors of the lochlann.**

chronology

521	Hygelac's raid on Frisia. Birth of Columcille.
c.525	Death of Brigid.
545	Foundation of Clonmacnois by Ciaran. Death of Ciaran.
c.550	Foundation of Moville by Finnian.
555	Foundation of Bangor by Comgall.
558	Foundation of Clonfert by Brendan.
c.560–80	North Atlantic voyages of Brendan and Cormac.
561	Battle of Culdrevny.
565	Foundation of Iona by Columcille.
577	Death of Brendan of Clonfert.
579	Death of Finnian of Moville.
591	Voyage of Columbanus from Bangor to the continent.
597	Death of Columcille. Arrival of Augustine's mission in Kent.
601	Death of Comgall of Bangor.
618	Martyrdom of Donnan on Eigg.
	Death of Coemgen of Glendalough.
635	Foundation of Lindisfarne by Aidan.
	Foundation of Rathlin by Segine.
639	Death of Laisren (Molaise).
651	Death of Aidan. Cuthbert enters Melrose.
657	Foundation of Whitby by Hild.
664	Synod of Whitby.
668	Foundation of Inishbofin by Colman.
672	Foundation of Applecross by Maelrubai.
673	Foundation of Ely by Etheldreda.
674	Foundation of Wearmouth by Benedict Biscop.
679–704	Adamnan, abbot of Iona.
679	Death of Etheldreda of Ely.
680	Death of Hild of Whitby. Bede enters Wearmouth.
682	Foundation of Jarrow.
684–87	Cuthbert, bishop of Lindisfarne.
685	Battle of Nechtansmere.
686–88	Adamnan's visits to Northumbria.
687	Death of Cuthbert.
697	Law of Adamnan.
698	Lindisfarne Gospels.

704	Death of Adamnan.
711	Islamic invasion of Spain.
716	Expulsion of Iona monks from Pictland.
722	Death of Maelrubai.
729	Islamic breakthrough on Frankish frontier.
732	Bede's *Historia Ecclesiastica*.
735	Death of Bede.
767	Alcuin's first journey to Rome.
771–801	Bresal, abbot of Iona.
774–79	First reign of Aethelred Moll in Northumbria.
780–802	Higbald, bishop of Lindisfarne.
782	Alcuin joins Charlemagne's court.
790–96	Second reign of Aethelred Moll in Northumbria.
793	First viking raid on Lindisfarne.
794	First viking raids in Hebrides. Raid on Wearmouth/Jarrow.
795	Raids on Iona, Inishbofin, Inishmurray, Skye and Rathlin.
796	Death of Offa, king of Mercia.
796–804	Alcuin, abbot of Tours.
798	Raid on Inis Patraic.
799	Danish raiding on Frankish coast.
800	Raids on Tynemouth and Hertenes.
	Coronation of Charlemagne as Holy Roman Emperor.
801–2	Connachtach, abbot of Iona. Book of Kells.
802–14	Cellach, abbot of Iona.
802	Burning of Iona.
804	Grant of Kells to community of Iona. Death of Alcuin.
806	Raid on Iona, massacre of sixty-eight monks.
807	Transfer of Iona community to Kells.
814	Death of Cellach on Iona. Death of Charlemagne.
*c.*820	Foundation of Dunkeld.
823	First raid on Bangor.
824	Second raid on Bangor. Raid on Skellig Michael.
825	Raids on Moville and Down. Martyrdom of Blathmac on Iona.
	Dicuil's *Libera de Mensura Orbis Terrae*.
832	Raids on Armagh, 'thrice in one month'.
834	Sack of Dorestad.
	Raids on Glendalough and Clonmacnois.
835	Burning of Clonmacnois.
	Danish raid on Sheppey.
836	Raid on Kildare.
	Evacuation of Noirmoutier.
837	Seizure of Dublin.
839	Massacre of Picts at Forteviot.

840	Kenneth mac-Alpin, king of Dalriada.
	Burning of Armagh.
843	Sack of Nantes.
845	Burning of Clonmacnois, Clonfert, Terryglass and Lothra.
	Drowning of Turgeis. Sack of Paris.
847–58	Kenneth mac-Alpin, king of Alba.
849	Division of the relics of Columcille between Kells and Dunkeld.
850	Danes overwintering on Thanet. Raid on Kells.
851	Attack on Dublin and Anagassan by Danes.
852	Battle of Carlingford Lough.
c.852–70	Sigurd the Mighty, first *jarl* of Orkney.
853	Arrival of Olaf in Dublin.
854–99	Eardwulf, bishop of Lindisfarne.
855	Danes overwintering on Sheppey.
857	Defeat of Ketil Flatnose by Olaf and Ivar.
858	Death of Kenneth mac-Alpin.
859–61	Sons of Ragnar raiding Spain and North Africa.
863	Plundering of the tombs of the Boyne by Olaf and Ivar.
865	Invasion of England by Ivar's 'great host'.
	Overwintering in East Anglia.
866	Invasion of Northumbria and seizure of York by the great host.
866–69	Olaf raiding Pictland.
867	Raiding of Whitby and other Northumbrian monasteries.
	Battle of York. Deaths of Aella and Osberht.
869	Olaf's return to Ireland. Raid on Armagh.
870	Martyrdom of Edmund, king of East Angles.
	Raids on Peterborough, Ely and Coldingham.
870–71	Siege and sack of Dumbarton by Olaf and Ivar.
871–99	Alfred, king of Wessex.
872	Death of Artgal, king of Strathclyde Britons.
873	Death of Ivar, 'king of all the *gaill* of Ireland and Britain'.
874	Division of the great host at Repton.
874–75	Halfdan overwintering on the Tyne.
	Devastation of Northumbria.
875	Evacuation of Lindisfarne. Martyrdom of Adrian on Isle of May.
	Halfdan's war on Picts and Strathclyde Britons.
	Massacre of Picts at Dollar. Death of Eystein of Dublin.
c.875	Death of Thorstein the Red.
	Migration of Aud and Hebridean Norse to Iceland.
876	Halfdan's 'apportioning' of Northumbria.
877	Death of Halfdan in battle of Strangford Lough.
877–78	Halfdan's warband in Scotland.
	Death of Constantine at Inverdovat.

878	Transfer of shrine and relics of Columcille to Ireland.
	Battle of Ethandune. Baptism of Guthrum.
883	Community of Cuthbert at Crayke.
883–94	Guthred, king of York.
883–995	Community of Cuthbert at Chester-le-Street.
891	First MS of *Anglo-Saxon Chronicle.*
895	Torf-Einar, *jarl* of Orkney.
899	Death of Alfred.
899–924	Edward, son of Alfred, king of Wessex.
900	Annexation of Strathclyde by Scots.
903–4	Raid on Dunkeld by the 'grandsons of Ivar'.
904	Death of Ivar, grandson of Ivar, in battle at Strathearn.
910	Battle of Tettenhall.
913	Invasion of northern England by Ragnall.
913–20	Norse settlement of Cumbria.
914	First battle of Corbridge.
918	Second battle of Corbridge.
919–20	Ragnall, king of York.
920	Submission of northern kings to Edward.
920–27	Sitric, king of York.
924–29	Athelstan, son of Edward, king of Wessex.
927	Submission of northern kings to Athelstan.
947–48	First reign of Erik Bloodaxe as king of York.
952–54	Second reign of Erik Bloodaxe as king of York.
954	Death of Erik Bloodaxe at battle of Stainmore.
981	Death of Olaf Cuaran on Iona.
986	Raid on Iona by Danes of Dublin.
	Erik the Red's voyage to Greenland.
990–1018	Aldhun, bishop of Lindisfarne at Chester-le-Street and Durham.
993–95	Olaf Tryggvasson and Swein Forkbeard raiding England.
995	Settlement of community of Cuthbert at Durham.
*c.*995	Baptism of Olaf Tryggvasson. Conversion of *jarl* of Orkney.
1014	Death of Swein Forkbeard at Gainsborough.
	Death of Brian Boru in battle at Clontarf.
1066	Battles of Stamford Bridge and Hastings.
	Norman conquest of England.
1069	Norman ravaging of Northumbria. Temporary return of Cuthbert's shrine to Lindisfarne from Durham.
1098	Magnus Olafsson's 'royal cruise' through the Hebrides.
1104	Translation of Cuthbert to Norman cathedral at Durham.

bibliography

ed. edited by   rev. revised edition
trs. translated and edited by   rep. reprint

Allan, M. & Calder, D. *Sources and Analogues of Old English Poetry*, Cambridge, 1976

Almgren, Bertil *The Viking* (trs. E. Cagner), Gothenburg, 1966

Anderson, Alan Orr (trs.) *Scottish Annals from English Chroniclers AD 500–1286*, Edinburgh, 1908; rev. Stamford, 1991
(trs.) *Early Sources of Scottish History AD 500–1286*, Edinburgh, 1922; rev. Stamford, 1990

Arbman, E. H. *The Vikings* (trs. A. Binns), London, 1961

Arnold, T. (ed.) *Symeonis Monachi Opera Omnia*, Rolls Series, 1882–85

Ashmore, Patrick *Maes Howe*, HMSO Edinburgh, 1990

Backhouse, Janet *The Lindisfarne Gospels*, London, 1981

Bamford, C. & Marsh, W. P. (eds.) *Celtic Christianity*, Edinburgh, 1982

Baring-Gould, S. *Lives of the English Saints*, 1907–13; rep. Felinfach, 1990
Lives of the Northumbrian Saints, 1907–13; rep. Felinfach, 1990

Battiscombe, C.F. (ed.) *The Relics of St Cuthbert*, Durham, 1956

Beavitt, Paul et al. *Archaeology on Lindisfarne: Fieldwork & Research 1983–88*, Leicester, 1988

Binns, Alan *Navigation of Viking Ships round the British Isles*, Fifth Viking Congress, Torshavn, 1965
Viking Voyagers, Then & Now, London, 1980

Blair, Peter Hunter *The World of Bede*, Cambridge, 1970
Northumbria in the days of Bede, London, 1976
An Introduction to Anglo-Saxon England, rev. Cambridge, 1977

Bonner, Gerald et al. *St Cuthbert, His Cult and Community to AD 1200*, Woodbridge, 1989

Brøgger, Anton W. *Ancient Emigrants*, Oxford, 1929

Brønsted, Johannes *The Vikings*, London, 1960

Browne, George F. *Alcuin of York*, London, 1908

Cambridge, Eric *Lindisfarne Priory and Holy Island*, London, 1988

Campbell, Alistair (trs.) *The Chronicle of Aethelweard*, London, 1962

Campbell, James (ed.) *The Anglo-Saxons*, Oxford, 1982

Clark, Wallace *Rathlin – Its Island History*, Limavady, 1988

Colgrave, Bertram (trs.) *Two Lives of Saint Cuthbert*, Cambridge, 1940

Collingwood, W.G. *Northumbrian Crosses of the pre-Norman Age*, London, 1927; rep. Felinfach, 1989

Cramp, Rosemary *Anglian and Viking York*, York, 1967
'Excavations at the Saxon Monastic Sites of Wearmouth/Jarrow', *Medieval Archaeology* vol. 13, 1969

Crawford, Barbara *Scandinavian Scotland*, Leicester, 1987

Davidson, H. R. Ellis *Gods and Myths of Northern Europe*, Harmondsworth, 1964

Donaldson, Gordon *A Northern Commonwealth: Scotland and Norway*, Edinburgh, 1990

Eldjárn, Krístjan 'The Viking Myth', *The Vikings*, ed. Farrell, 1982

Ellis, Peter Berresford *Celtic Inheritance*, London, 1985

Farrell, R. T. (ed.) *The Vikings*, Chichester, 1982

Faulkes, Anthony (trs.) *Snorri Sturluson: Edda*, London, 1987

Fletcher, Eric *Benedict Biscop*, Jarrow, 1981

Foote, P. G. & Wilson, D. M. *The Viking Achievement*, London, 1970

Gantz, Jeffrey (trs.) *Early Irish Myths and Sagas*, London, 1981

Giles, J. A. (trs.) *Roger of Wendover: Flowers of History*, London, 1849
(trs.) *Harmony of the Chroniclers during the Life of King Alfred*, 1863; rep. Felinfach, 1990

Godden, M. & Lapidge, M. (eds.) *Cambridge Companion to Old English Literature*, Cambridge, 1991

Graham-Campbell, James *The Viking World*, London, 1980
'Pagans and Christians', *History Today*, October 1986

Graham-Campbell, J. & Kidd, D. *The Vikings*, British Museum, 1980

Gransden, Antonia *Historical Writing in England c.550–c.1307*, London, 1974

Hall, Richard 'The Vikings as Town Dwellers', *History Today*, November 1986
Viking Age Archaeology in Britain and Ireland, Aylesbury, 1990

Hardy, T. D. & Martin, C. T. (trs.) *L'Estorie des Engles of Geoffroi Gaimar*, Rolls Series, 1888–89

Heath, Ian *Armies of the Dark Ages AD 600–1066*, London, 1980
The Vikings, London, 1985

Henderson, George *From Durrow to Kells: The Insular Gospel Books 650–800*, London, 1987

Hennessy, W. M. (ed.) *Chronicon Scotorum*, London, 1866

Hennessy, W. M. & MacCarthy, B. (trs.) *The Annals of Ulster*, Dublin, 1887–91

Henry, Françoise *Irish Art during the Viking Invasions – AD 800–1020*, London, 1967

Herbert, Máire *Iona, Kells & Derry*, Oxford, 1988

Higham, Nick *The Northern Counties to AD 1000*, Harlow, 1986

Hopkin, Alannah *The Living Legend of St Patrick*, London, 1989

Hughes, Kathleen *Early Christian Ireland: Introduction to the Sources*, London, 1972

Jones, Gwyn *The Norse Atlantic Saga*, Oxford, 1964
  A History of the Vikings, rev. Oxford, 1984

Keary, Charles F. *The Vikings in Western Christendom*, London, 1891

Kenney, J. F. *Sources for the Early History of Ireland*, New York, 1929

Kinsella, Thomas (trs.) *The Tain*, Oxford, 1970

Kruta, Venceslas *The Celts of the West*, London, 1985

Laing, Samuel (trs.) *Snorri Sturluson: Heimskringla*, London, 1889

Lavelle, Des *Skellig: Island Outpost of Europe*, Dublin, 1976

Leirfall, Jon *West Over Sea* (trs. K. Young), Sandwick, 1979

Logan, F. Donald *The Vikings in History*, rev. London, 1991

Lomax, Frank (trs.) *William of Malmesbury: The Antiquities of Glastonbury*, 1908; rep. Felinfach, 1992

Loyn, H. R. *The Vikings in Britain*, London, 1977

Lund, Niels (ed.) *Two Voyagers at the Court of King Alfred*, York, 1984

Mac Airt, Sean (trs.) *The Annals of Inisfallen*, Dublin, 1951

Macdonald, Aidan 'Two Major Early Monasteries of Dalriata: Lismore & Eigg', *Scottish Archaeological Forum* 5, 1973

Macquarrie, Alan *Iona through the ages*, Coll, 1983

Mac Niocaill, Gearóid *Ireland before the Vikings*, Dublin, 1972

Magnusson, Magnus *Hammer of the North*, London, 1976
  Lindisfarne, The Cradle Island, Stocksfield, 1984

Marsden, J. & Gregory, J. *The Illustrated Bede*, London, 1989
  The Illustrated Columcille, London, 1991

Marshall, D. W. Hunter *The Sudreys in Early Viking Times*, Glasgow, 1929

Mayr-Harting, Henry *The Coming of Christianity to Anglo-Saxon England*, rev. London, 1991

McGinn, B. *Visions of the End*, New York, 1979

McGrail, Sean *Ancient Boats*, Aylesbury, 1983

McNeill, F. Marian (ed.) *An Iona Anthology*, 1952; rep. Iona, 1990

Montalembert, C. F. R. de *The Monks of the West*, London, 1896

Moore, Arthur W. *A History of the Isle of Man*, London, 1900

Morris, Christopher D. *Church and Monastery in the Far North*, Jarrow, 1989

Mould, Daphne D. C. P. *Ireland of the Saints*, Dublin, 1953
  The Irish Saints, London & Dublin, 1964

Oakeshott, Ronald Ewart *Dark Age Warrior*, London, 1974

O'Corrain, Donncha *Ireland before the Normans*, Dublin, 1972

O'Donovan, John (trs.) *Annals of the Kingdom of Ireland by the Four Masters*, Dublin, 1848–51
  (trs.) *Duald MacFirbis: Fragmentary Annals of Ireland*, Dublin, 1860

Page, R. I. *Runes*, London, 1987

Pálsson, H. & Edwards, P. (trs.) *Orkneyinga Saga*, London, 1978
  Eyrbyggja Saga, London, 1989

187

Peers, Sir Charles & Radford, C. A. Ralegh 'The Saxon Monastery at Whitby', *Archaeologia* vol. LXXIX, 1943
Platt, Colin *Whitby Abbey*, HMSO, 1985
Raine, James *History and Antiquities of North Durham*, London, 1852
Reeves, William (trs.) *Adamnan: Life of Saint Columba*, 1874; rep. Felinfach, 1988
Ritchie, A. & Breeze, D. *Invaders of Scotland*, Edinburgh, 1991
Rollason, D. W. (ed.) *Cuthbert, Saint & Patron*, Durham, 1987
Sawyer, Peter H. *The Age of the Vikings*, London, 1962; rev. 1971
    'Some Sources for the history of Viking Northumbria', *Viking Age York & the North*, CBA Research Report No. 27, 1978
    Kings and Vikings, London, 1982
    'The Causes of the Viking Age', *The Vikings*, ed. Farrell, 1982
Severin, Tim *The Brendan Voyage*, London, 1978
Sharp, William (as 'Fiona Macleod') *Iona*, 1910; rep. Edinburgh, 1982
Skene, William F. *Celtic Scotland*, Edinburgh, 1886–90
Smith, A. H. 'The Sons of Ragnar Lothbrok', *Saga Book* 2, 1935
Smurthwaite, David *Ordnance Survey Guide to the Battlefields of Britain*, Exeter, 1984
Smyth, Alfred P. 'The Black Foreigners of York and the White Foreigners of Dublin', *Saga Book* 19, 1975–76
    Scandinavian Kings in the British Isles: 850–880, Oxford, 1977
    Scandinavian York and Dublin, Dublin & New Jersey, 1975–79
    Warlords and Holy Men: Scotland AD 80–1000, London, 1984
Stenton, Sir Frank *Anglo-Saxon England*, Oxford, 1971
Stevenson, Joseph (trs.) *Florence of Worcester: History of the Kings of England*, 1853–58; rep. Felinfach, 1988
    (trs.) *Symeon of Durham: History of the Kings of England*, 1853–58; rep. Felinfach, 1987
    (trs.) *Symeon of Durham: History of the Church of Durham*, 1853–58; rep. Felinfach, 1988
Stokes, Whitley (ed.) *Thesaurus Palaeohibernicus*, Cambridge, 1903
    The Martyrology of Oengus the Culdee, London, 1905
Sullivan, Sir Edward *The Book of Kells*, 1920; rep. London, 1986
Thompson, A. Hamilton (ed.) *Bede: His Life, Times & Writings*, Oxford, 1935
    Lindisfarne Priory, HMSO, 1949
Thorpe, B. (ed.) *The Anglo-Saxon Chronicle*, Rolls Series, 1861
Todd, James H. (trs.) *The War of the Gaedhil with the Gaill*, Rolls Series, 1867
Twohig, Elizabeth S. *Irish Megalithic Tombs*, Aylesbury, 1990
Vigfussen, Gudbrand (ed.) *Icelandic Sagas relating to the Northmen in Britain*, Rolls Series, 1887–94
Vigfussen, G. & Powell, F. Y. (ed./trs.) *Corpus Poeticum Boreale*, 1883; rep. New York, 1965
Wainwright, F. T. *The Northern Isles*, London & Edinburgh, 1962

Scandinavian England, London, 1975

Wallace-Hadrill, J. M. *Bede's Europe,* Jarrow, 1962

'The Vikings in Francia', *Early Medieval History,* Oxford, 1975

Walsh, Annie *Scandinavian Relations with Ireland,* London, 1922

Ward, Sister Benedicta *The Venerable Bede,* London, 1990

Whitelock, Dorothy (ed.) *English Historical Documents: Vol. 1,* London, 1955

After Bede, Jarrow, 1960

Whone, Herbert *Church, Monastery, Cathedral,* Shaftesbury, 1990

Williams, A., Smyth, A. P. & Kirby, D. P. *A Biographical Dictionary of Dark Age Britain,* London, 1991

Wilson, David M. 'Archaeological Evidence for Viking Settlement and Raids in England', *Frühmittelalterliche Studien* No. 2, 1968

The Vikings & their Origins, London, 1970

(ed.) *The Northern World,* London, 1980

Winterbottom, M. (ed.) *Three Lives of English Saints,* Toronto, 1972

Wormald, Patrick 'Viking Studies: Whence and Whither?' *The Vikings,* ed. Farrell, 1982

index

ab.   abbot/abbess of
bp.   bishop of
k.   king of